AF787300

Central and Eastern Europe as a Double Periphery?

Central and Eastern European Forum for Legal, Political, and Social Theory Yearbook

Edited by Jürgen Busch / Péter Cserne / Michael Hein / Miklós Könczöl / Miodrag Jovanović / Marta Soniewicka

Volume 9

PETER LANG

Tomáš Gábriš / Ján Sombati (eds.)

Central and Eastern Europe as a Double Periphery?

Volume of proceedings from the 11th CEE Forum Conference in Bratislava, Slovakia 25-26 April 2019

PETER LANG

Bibliographic Information published by the Deutsche Nationalbibliothek
The Deutsche Nationalbibliothek lists this publication in the Deutsche Nationalbibliografie; detailed bibliographic data is available in the internet at http://dnb.d-nb.de.

Library of Congress Cataloging-in-Publication Data
A CIP catalog record for this book has been applied for at the Library of Congress.

The volume is the outcome of two grant projects: The VEGA 1/0638/18 grant project Economic Legal History – Economy and Entrepreneurship in Legal History, and the VEGA 1/0138/18 grant project "Marxism Still Alive? To reconsider K. Marx's teachings in contemporary legal and economic thinking".

ISSN 2191-8317
ISBN 978-3-631-83061-1 (Print)
E-ISBN 978-3-631-83967-6 (E-PDF)
E-ISBN 978-3-631-83968-3 (EPUB)
E-ISBN 978-3-631-83969-0 (MOBI)
DOI 10.3726/b17760

© Peter Lang GmbH
Internationaler Verlag der Wissenschaften
Berlin 2020
All rights reserved.

Peter Lang – Berlin · Bern · Bruxelles · New York · Oxford · Warszawa · Wien

All parts of this publication are protected by copyright. Any utilisation outside the strict limits of the copyright law, without the permission of the publisher, is forbidden and liable to prosecution. This applies in particular to reproductions, translations, microfilming, and storage and processing in electronic retrieval systems.

This publication has been peer reviewed.

www.peterlang.com

Table of Contents

List of Contributors

Enrico Arona
University of Genoa (Italy), Faculty of Law

Marin Keršić
University of Split (Croatia), Faculty of Law

Andrea Kluknavská
Matej Bel University in Banská Bystrica (Slovakia), Faculty of Law

Miriam Laclavíková
Trnava University in Trnava (Slovakia), Faculty of Law

Rafał Mańko
University of Amsterdam (the Netherlands), Faculty of Law, Amsterdam Centre for Transformative Private Law (ACT)

Marica Mišić
University of Niš (Serbia), Faculty of Law

Ladislav Mrklas
CEVRO Institute, Prague (Czech Republic), Department of Political Science and International Relations

Rado Pezdir
University of Primorska (Slovenia); International School for Social and Business Studies; RE-FORMA, Research and Development, Ltd.

Josef Šíma
CEVRO Institute, Prague (Czech Republic), Department of Economics

Janez Šušteršič
RE-FORMA, Research and Development, Ltd. (Slovenia)

Adriana Švecová
Trnava University in Trnava (Slovakia), Faculty of Law

Boldizsár Szentgáli-Tóth
Hungarian Academy of Sciences (Hungary), Institute of Legal Studies; Eötvös Loránd University (Hungary), Constitutional Law Department

Foreword

The 2019 Central and Eastern European (CEE) Forum conference was hosted by the Comenius University in Bratislava, Faculty of Law, Department of Theory of Law and Social Sciences. The University, founded in 1919, is one of the leading research centres in Slovakia, with a broad array of international contacts and cooperation both in the field of natural sciences as well as in social sciences and humanities. The host institution thus offered an ideal venue for an interdisciplinary event of young legal, political and social theorists.

In the most general terms, the agenda of the 11th CEE Forum Conference in Bratislava, Slovakia, held on 25–26 April 2019 was focused on the reassessment of the CEE position in Europe and in the world, seeking for the specificities of this region, being often perceived as a double periphery – of the West and of the East. Since thirty years have passed since the disintegration of the bipolar world, the time has come for a critical reconsideration of the earlier scholarly findings or commonplaces and the formulation of more nuanced and refined conclusions.

Special emphasis was to be put on the following sub-topics, while expecting a thorough theoretical analysis of these:

(1) Colonialism, postcolonialism and neocolonialism – that is positioning and reconsidering the CEE in terms of province/periphery versus centre, dominance/hegemony versus subordination/subaltern status, power versus weakness, globalisation, Europeanisation and Americanisation.
(2) CEE on the Map of Europe – focusing on the continuities and discontinuities in constitutional terms and constitutional, political and economic transitions.
(3) States versus Nations/People – reassessing the Rule of Law, role of the Constitutions, sovereignty of the People and legal and political problems with nations and nationalism in the CEE region.
(4) CEE Legal Culture – attempting at identification of common features of legal systems in the CEE region, with emphasis on the role of

migrating legal concepts – legal transplants, legal imports and exports and legal multiculturalism.
(5) A Bridge or a Battlefield between the Worlds? – reconsidering the situation of civil society and free media in the CEE region and the position of the 'Other' in the CEE region.

Of course, not all the topics were indeed discussed in detail and even in case of those discussed, the final word has definitely not yet been spoken. Nevertheless, the topics offered a food for thought and incited long-lasting debates both during the conference as well as within the unofficial parts of the program.

As in the previous CEE Forum meetings, the target audience was the community of young theorists either working in CEE or studying topics with CEE dimensions, including young academics affiliated to the universities or research institutes outside the CEE region, with Central or Eastern European research interests. The selection of chapters offered by the organizers in this volume thus provides an up-to-date view of the CEE region and issues and problems shared by the CEE countries, 30 years after the 1989 changes. The views and perspectives offered thereby include both those of insiders as well as those from outside the CEE region – whereby even those from the outside clearly have an important message to convey for the current situation in CEE.

About the contributions

Our starting point in this book is what Rafał Mańko in his contribution calls a peripheral status of the CEE countries. He claims this region is marked by relatively short traditions of a national legal system and national legal culture, and the dominance of legal transfers – being two factors common for all CEE countries. And one may certainly add the authoritarian and bureaucratic traditions on top of that. Only the period of actually existing socialism might be considered as a period of advancement of some original ideas, with numerous attempts at modernising the region of CEE through free education and healthcare, and of the economy through planned industrialisation However, what was left from this period in legal terms was generally rejected and considered inferior in comparison with the West, the socialist heritage being aligned with the well-known phenomenon of ultraformalism or hyperpositivism in law. Nevertheless, the author claims that currently, after the failed attempts at imitating the Western world in the past decades, the older traditions are being revived once again – the CEE region is now witnessing a start of its another transformation, leaving behind the unfulfilled ideals of liberal democracy.

A number of arguments suggested by Rafał Mańko are echoed in other chapters within this volume, his chapter hence providing uniting leitmotivs for the whole volume. For example, concerning legal transfers, Boldizsár Szentgáli-Tóth's chapter proves that the CEE region is strongly influenced by legal borrowings – he shows this on the example of 'qualified laws', being close to Western organic laws and to 'laws with constitutional force'. The author thereby reconsiders the role and importance of this type of legislation during the transition period after 1989, claiming to having identified their task in guaranteeing the protection of fundamental rights in this region. Still, he also points to the fact that the evolution in individual CEE countries was not uniform, and each country has undergone specific development with regard to this type of legislation.

Similarly, Marin Keršić in his chapter explains the 'migration' of the idea of proportionality and balancing of principles as suggested by Robert Alexy, from Germany into the case law of Croatian Constitutional Court. The author is doing that on the analysis on selected cases where the Constitutional Court of Croatia explained the ideas of proportionality and balancing, based also on Article 16 of the Croatian Constitution, being a so-called balancing regulating norm.

The following section of the book dwells on an underlying idea of relationship between freedom and unfreedom in the CEE region. First of all, Enrico Arona reconsiders the idea of political freedom in analytical terms of freedom, unfreedom and not-freedom, claiming that there is a middle category, *tertium datur*, between the two extremes, himself being thus a representative of a trivalent theory of freedom – maybe reflecting the experience of the CEE region in political terms of yesterday and of tomorrow.

Building on the previous chapter, Josef Šíma and Ladislav Mrklas reassess the importance of freedom and unfreedom specifically in the Visegrad countries, whereby they explain that different historical experience is often the reason for current differences among the CEE countries in terms of their approach to liberal democracy and to liberalism and libertarianism in broader terms.

Finally, in his second piece in this volume, Enrico Arona moves to the relationship between religious freedom and freedom of expression, which certainly plays a role in the current discourse in the CEE region, where religion resurfaced in political debates after the 1989 transition. The author thereby observes that political liberalism generates restraint on the public use of religious reasons. Instead of religious arguments, the same goals are namely claimed to be easily reached by using other types of arguments, widely accepted in liberal democracies.

The following two parts of the volume are both looking back at the past of the CEE region. Despite Rafał Mańko in his introductory paper considering the CEE Forum conferences rather theoretical and sociological, and less historical, the present volume might mean a slight shift towards including legal historians as well. The next two chapters of this volume namely attempt at proving historically that the period of actually existing socialism indeed introduced an advancement mostly in terms of social status of the broader population – building on the arguments of the keynote speaker Rafał Mańko. This is clearly shown first in the chapter by Miriam Laclavíková and Adriana Švecová, who introduce the social status of children in Czechoslovakia prior to the changes introduced by the Communist Party after World War II. Then, Andrea Kluknavská in the following chapter introduces the radical changes in social security introduced under the rule of the Communist Party in Czechoslovakia, drawing thereby both from Western (Beveridge) as well as Eastern (Soviet) models.

Still, one should not forget even in the times of reconsidering the role of liberal democracy in CEE that the trends of moving away from liberal democracy often hide some darker aspects. These can be again clearly identified in the history of the CEE region, especially in the period of Communist rule, as shown by the two chapters in the last section of this volume. First, Rado Pezdir and Janez Šušteršič in their chapter made an interesting analysis of archival documents proving the existence of a parallel economy in socialist countries. This is on one hand a mark of the economic instability of the socialist systems, but on the other hand it also clearly shows that at the moment of transition from socialism, there were people with rich experience in the (black) market economy who could exploit the situation during the transition.

Finally, the last chapter by Marica Mišić is focused on both historical as well as on theoretical problems of the phenomenon of show trials. There is no doubt that the CEE countries share rich experience with show trials in the 20th century, but instead of a historical analysis of the individual cases, the author in her chapter rather points to the philosophical issues hidden behind the problem: the role of ideology in law, failures of law and problems with compensating the mistakes of the past.

All the selected chapters thus indeed touch upon the experiences and problems common to all of the CEE countries, currently longing for their own paths (and even mistakes), hoping to escape from their double peripherality witnessed throughout the greater part of the 20th century.

Ján Sombati – Tomáš Gábriš (editors)

I. Central and Eastern Europe and double peripherality: Key notions

Rafał Mańko

University of Amsterdam (the Netherlands), Faculty of Law, Amsterdam Centre for Transformative Private Law (ACT)

Being Central European, or some reflections on law, double peripherality and the political in times of transformation[1]

Abstract: To be peripheral means to be subject to the economic, political and – indeed – cultural hegemony of a certain Centre. Being peripheral means to suffer from symbolic violence, permanently running after the fetish of 'modernisation', permanently desiring to escape the curse of 'backwardness', permanently behind, permanently learning, and permanently emulating. How can a legal community, burdened by such symbolic oppression (self-oppression?), ascertain its pride, its prestige, its self-esteem? How can a society, and especially its elites, endure such long-term humiliation? Recent developments have shown that it can no longer. The apprentice of the demoliberal sorcerer has announced that he is quitting school and going his own way. Joining the crowd of cynically naïve liberals, mourning the 'rule of law' without much understanding of the reality (or refusing to understand it) is a road leading nowhere.

Keywords: Central Europe, double periphery, transformation, demoliberalism

1 The present chapter draws on my keynote lecture 'Central Europe as a Double Periphery,' delivered at the 11th CEE Forum in Bratislava (25–26 April 2019). I am grateful to all those who attended the plenary session and took part in the highly stimulating discussion which helped me clarify my ideas and arguments, and especially to Professor Tomáš Gábriš for the invitation. I would also like to thank Dr Przemysław Tacik (Jagiellonian University) and Anna Piekarska (Adam Mickiewicz University) for reading and commenting on an earlier version of this chapter, and thereby helping me in developing the argument in its current form. All views presented here are purely personal and expressed in my academic capacity; they do not purport to represent the position of any institution or organisation.

1. What do we have in common? Central Europe as a juridical space

At first sight, there might not be anything homogenous about the countries of Central and Eastern Europe (CEE), save for being a 'no man's land between West and East' (Sowa 2011, 15). Each has its own language, its own legal tradition and its own sovereign statehood. Some legal systems have been inspired by the French legal tradition, as the Romanian one, others by the Austrian legal tradition, as the Czech or Croatian one, yet others draw on the German legal tradition and its refined 19th-century *Pandektistik*, which has inspired lawyers in Hungary or Latvia. And yet, all these countries do have a lot in common in terms of legal culture, in line with the fact that '[t]he identification of Central-Eastern Europe has a deep civilisational-culture sense' (Sowa 2011, 16). First of all, their independent statehood has a much shorter history than in the case of most Western European countries. True, the Polish statehood created in 1918 can boast pre-1795 traditions, and Hungary's independence from the Habsburgs was preceded by the existence of a dependent and earlier independent Kingdom of Hungary in the past. Perhaps the longest uninterrupted form of statehood can be identified in the case of Romania, which, created as a state in 1881, was the result of a merger of two pre-existing principalities, Valachia and Moldavia, which had existed as state units in an uninterrupted manner for centuries. But Romania or Hungary are rather the exception than the rule. Latvia or Estonia, Slovakia or Slovenia are all countries which have emerged as nation states for the first time in the 20th century. This rather short and limited traditions of statehood are of no minor importance for legal culture. Even if state and law are not bound in their essence (law can exist without the state, and a state can be lawless), nonetheless for all practical purposes during the last two centuries the signifier 'law' has referred mainly to the law of a state or, more recently, of a supranational organisation of states (yet that law is still enforced by state courts, which should not be forgotten). Therefore, the fact that in the West of Europe states have existed for a much longer period (sometimes they were unified, as in the case of Italy or Germany, in the late 19th century) has a bearing on legal culture. Perhaps the most characteristic examples are the United Kingdom and France, on one hand, and the newly created Central European states, such as Slovakia, Slovenia or Estonia, on the other hand. The contrast between the 'ongoingness' of legal culture (Zimmermann 1995, 84) and the continuous presence of a 'living' legal tradition, in the case of the West, and the incessant ruptures and changes, in the East, could not be more pronounced. This brings me to the second element which unifies all CEE countries: the massiveness of legal borrowing. Of course, it is true as Alan Watson has stated that legal borrowing (legal transplants) is a vehicle of legal development and that it is ubiquitous (Watson 1993[1974]). But whereas in Western Europe we can speak of borrowing from the past (Roman law) and the circulation of legal models, in CEE one can speak almost only about the *influx* of legal transplants (Mańko 2019a, 69–70).

The relatively short traditions of a national legal system and national legal culture, and the dominance of legal transfers are two factors common to all CEE countries. The transformation from state socialism to capitalism around 1989–1990 and the membership in Western European supranational forms of legal integration from 2004 onwards not only did not weaken these tendencies, but only led to their strengthening (Mańko 2017; Tacik 2019, 35).

2. The Curse of Formalism

There are of course other characteristic features of legal culture that could be identified. One of them is ultraformalism (Kühn 2011) or hyperpositivism (Mańko 2013), a phenomenon characteristic of judicial culture and methods of legal interpretation which places an excessive emphasis on formal law (rather than on its goals and broader context), and within formal law – on the letter of the statute, rather than on more sophisticated aspects such as general principles, systemic aspects, constitutional axiology, proportionality or balancing. Of course, to give a definitive answer about CEE formalism and comparing it to Western Europe (especially to such 'suspects' of formalism as France) (cf. Cserne 2015; Mercescu 2020, 15) would require a large-scale international research project which would dig through tens of thousands of judicial decisions from many European countries. Before such a project (which is, for that matter, a very desirable idea) is accomplished, we can rely only on anecdotal evidence, personal experience (as lawyers and as *justiciables*), as well as reflections of experienced judges and lawyers, such as Professor Zdenek Kühn from the Czech Supreme Administrative Court (Kühn 2004, 2011), Professor Ewa Łętowska, former judge at the Polish Supreme Administrative Court and former justice at the Constitutional Court (Łętowska 1997, 2002) or Professor Alan Uzelac, an experienced Croat practising lawyer and distinguished legal academic (Uzelac 2010). Their accounts, based on their own first-hand experience as judges or lawyers, and their own knowledge of domestic and foreign legal practice, concur in pointing out that Central Europe *is formalist*. In our countries, judges prefer to dismiss cases on formal grounds, avoid taking courageous interpretive decisions and have a tendency to hide behind institutions, preserving their own anonymity as cogs in a bureaucratic machine of the judiciary.[2] Therefore, to the two features identified above, we can safely also add hyperpositivism (ultraformalism) as a specific trace of *being Central European* in the juridical field.

I will stop with these three features, which characterise the juridical in its inner dimension, without going to broader sociological considerations, such as the role of law and courts in society, social trust in the judiciary or its prestige in society. These are important issues, but they are not crucial for addressing the key question of the present chapter, namely the status of *double peripherality*.

3. Peripherality as status

Studies of peripherality (e.g. Wallerstein 2004; Zarycki 2016a) are characterised by introducing an important binary dimension: core (centre) – periphery, which is enriched by adding a 'semi-periphery' in between them (Zarycki 2016b, 105). As regards double peripherality, the concept used by sociologists is that of an *interface periphery*, that is a certain territory (with its society, economy and culture) which is exposed, at the same time, to two centres, being precisely a double periphery (Zarycki 2016b). We should note that for most of the time Central Europe was not an interface periphery, but a simple periphery, that is it was peripheral

2 The same seems to be true for Russian legal culture too (Antonov 2018, 486; Rudt 2019, 176).

vis-à-vis one single centre (or 'core'). Referring only to the modern period (from the beginning of the 19th century), we can safely claim that the Central European territories of the Austro-Hungarian Empire, such as the Polish-Ukrainian Galicia-Lodomeria, the Czech Bohemia and Moravia, the Hungarian, Slovak, Croat and Romanian lands of the Crown of St Stephen – were all peripheral *vis-à-vis* Vienna, or German-speaking Austria, as the centre of the Empire. The lands of the Russian Empire inhabited by Poles, Lithuanians, Latvians and Estonians – its westernmost provinces – were peripheral *vis-à-vis* Saint-Petersburg, and so forth. Two important notes arise in this context. First, some of the areas mentioned here, such as the Kingdom of Bohemia in the Habsburg Empire, or the Kingdom of Poland in the Russian Empire, or the Baltic provinces, were actually quite well-developed economically and socially, and their peripherality was, therefore, limited to the political dimension. Second, the centres (cores) themselves – Vienna or Saint-Petersburg – did not enjoy the status of the global core, rather a semi-periphery (German-speaking parts of Austria or Russia [Turkowski 2016, 150]). This brings us to the question of double peripherality or 'interface peripherality' (Zarycki 2016b, 107) which would be identified already in that period, namely through the (semi-)peripherality of the relative 'core' towards which Central Europe itself was peripheral.

In terms of legal culture, the questions are even more complicated. Let us take the example of the Kingdom of Poland, initially a sovereign, later autonomous, and later not even an autonomous entity within the Russian Empire (or, as the Russians nicely call it, *в составе Российской Империи*). It stretched over land corresponding roughly to today's central and eastern Poland, with such cities as Warsaw, Łódź, Kielce and Lublin. The origins of this entity date back to 1807, when Napoleon created the Duchy of Warsaw and introduced French law, including the famous *code civil*. Subsequently, the Duchy (transformed into Kingdom in 1815) could maintain its French legal system, although certain areas, such as family law, were recodified (1825) and later replaced by Russian law (1836). The same applied to procedural law, which was replaced by Russian-prepared codes in 1864, when the Kingdom had been stripped of its autonomy as a reaction to anti-Russian uprisings waged by short-sighted local radicals. In terms of peripherality, the Kingdom of Poland, with a French-Polish-Russian legal system, was indeed a *peripheria duplex*, following the case law of the French *Cour de cassation* (reported in Polish legal press) and, as from the 1870s, the Saint-Petersburg *Правующий Сенат* (the Governing Senate) to which appeals in civil, criminal and administrative cases would be launched after the Kingdom had lost most of its judicial autonomy.

The creation of independent Central European countries in 1918 – Poland, Czechoslovakia, Hungary, Yugoslavia, Latvia, Lithuania and Estonia – only superficially concluded the region's peripherality. True, first moves towards becoming a core for oneself were established: The Polish-Czechoslovak and Polish-Yugoslav attempts at joint codification are remarkable in this respect. Judicial decisions would no longer be subject to appeals to Vienna, Saint-Petersburg or Berlin.

But then, following World War II, the fate of Central Europe was sealed at Yalta – 'the periphery of western capitalism became a periphery of the Soviet Empire' (Giaro 2013, 45). The Baltic states became (in 1940, and then again in 1944) directly part of the USSR, whereas other countries of the region were part of the Soviet sphere of influence, just like Greece, Italy, West Germany or France became part of the American sphere of influence. This had an immense impact not only upon politics and the economy, but also on legal culture. In a sense, the creation of the East-West divide in Europe led to the consolidation of Central European legal identity, putting all the former peripheries of Vienna, Berlin and Saint-Petersburg once again in a peripheral position, but this time towards state-socialist Moscow. Legal models originating in the USSR, some of them with pre-revolutionary traditions, started flowing steadily from the East to the West. Legal institutions like the *nadzornaia instantsiya*, the omnipotence of a centralised prosecution service, authorised to intervene even in civil and administrative proceedings (Mańko 2007), Soviet civil law institutions, such as stratified property, planned contracts or special legal capacity (Mańko 2015a), but also institutions of public law, such as the uniform character of state power, the system of democratic centralism, the superiority of the Party and its decisions over the *lex scripta* (Antonov 2018) – all this became part of the legal heritage of Central Europe for over four decades. Of course, differences existed. Czechoslovakia and East Germany were most advanced in terms of creating socialist civil codes (Giaro 2013, 47–48), while such countries as Poland, Hungary and

Romania preserved more traditional forms of private law. But the common elements prevailed, giving rise to what Western observers described as the 'Socialist Legal Family' (David and Brierley 1968; Zweigert and Kötz 1987, cf. Uzelac 2010; Mańko 2013).

Then came the demise of actually existing socialism, either negotiated and civilised, as in Poland with its Round Table Agreement (Tacik 2020, 161), followed by an accelerated implementation of the 'shock therapy', or brutal and bloody, as in the Romanian case. One of the countries of the region, Yugoslavia, plunged in a bloody bath of ethnonationalist fratricide that took down the whole country leaving a deeply damaged society, now divided into small nation states, which, with the exception of Serbia and Montenegro, had none or rather distant and limited traditions (Croatia) of independent statehood.

4. Of blackouts and pycnolepsy, or on the subtle art of forgetting

Today, the legacy of the Socialist Legal Family is deliberately forgotten if not downright repressed in what Tomasz Giaro described with the metaphor of a 'blackout' (Giaro 2013, 45–48), that is a state when the subject not only loses consciousness, but even does not recall any memories, following an excessive consumption of alcohol. Cosmin Cercel, in turn, put forward the more philosophically grounded metaphor of *pycnolepsy* (Cercel 2016), drawing on the erudite scholarship of Paulo Virilio. Pycnolepsy is a state in which the subject also loses memory and cannot recall any past events, but at least this is not linked to excessive alcohol consumption. After all, the period of actually existing socialism was not one big binge-drinking party, contrary to what Giaro's metaphor might suggest. In terms of civilisation, it was probably the greatest attempt at modernising the region of Central Europe, characterised by an unprecedented advancement of society through free education and healthcare, and of the economy through planned industrialisation (Żółtkowski 2012; Leszczyński 2013; cf. Leder 2019). To cite just the Polish example, one can safely say that a backward rural society, as Poland was between 1918 and 1939, was transformed in the 1950s and 1960s into a modern industrial economy, analphabetism was eradicated, famine – a plague of the

1930s – disappeared and a massive housing programme enabled millions of Poles to move from dilapidated wooden cottages into modern blocks of flats, not worse than the social estates in the UK or France.

In legal terms, the period of actually existing socialism had its peculiarities and cannot be said to be a mere continuation of the pre-1939 situation. The legal transfers from the USSR, mentioned above, tell only part of the story. More importantly, the place of both public and private law was quite different in comparison to the capitalist period. Once the state took over key sectors of the economy, such as medium and large industry, banking and retail, the role of private law instruments – such as contract law or company law – greatly diminished, giving way to public economic law. This was reflected on the procedural side, too. Civil courts would now focus on family disputes or small property disputes between individuals, whereas the bulk of important economic cases was taken over by the State Economic Arbitration (the *arbitrazh* as, using the Russian term, legal Sovietologists would say).

The restoration of capitalism at the turn of the 1980s and 1990s undoubtedly took the legal community by surprise. However, one cannot say that it was completely unprepared in intellectual terms. To take the Polish example, one can point to the fact that the Commercial Code of 1934 was still partly in force, and with the transformation it was fully restored. The Civil Code of 1964, although heavily influenced by socialist legal institutions, still contained a capitalist private law core, preserved by the Polish private law dogmaticians who prepared its draft. All in all, the Civil Code was not that different from the Western capitalist laws it was modelled on, such as the German BGB and the Swiss ZGB. At the same time, it was rather different from the Czech Civil Code or Economic Code or the East German ZGB. In a sense, therefore, the bourgeois private law had survived 45 years of actually existing socialism and could be taken back into the light without much effort. Public law was a more complex issue. If administrative law is concerned, Poland had a very high quality Code of Administrative Procedure, enacted in 1960, which ensured the protection of private interest; and since 1980 Poland already had judicial review of administrative acts, with the Chief Administrative Court entitled to quash administrative decisions if they were illegal. Therefore, in the sphere of general administrative law, the legal system was quite prepared for the transformation. In the sphere of constitutional law, one can point to the creation of the Constitutional Court in 1986 (Sulikowski 2016, 20), and the Ombudsman in 1987. However, key elements of the *Rechtsstaat* would be introduced only in 1990, and for want of domestic traditions (Poland did not have a democracy nor 'rule of law' before 1939, save for a very short period), German models would be imported. The Polish Constitutional Court after 1990 drew very strong inspiration from the case law of the German *Bundesverfassungsgericht* and from German constitutional doctrine. Many concepts, like those concerning 'fundamental rights' and their limitation, were literally copied from German models (cf. Tacik 2020, 162). The 'rule of law' ideology[3] was a novelty, but the Constitutional Court became a 'sacred cow' (Sulikowski 2016, 21) and enjoyed a special status (Sulikowski and Wojtanowski 2019, 186–187).

The period between 1990 and 2004 could have been a period of relatively independent development of legal culture in Central Europe, but it was not. Reception dominated over domestic legal developments, and the prospects of integration with Western European supranational structures only strengthened those tendencies (Örücü 2007, 176; Tacik 2019, 35). However, there was a consensus in place, which did not allow to question this direction of development. The judiciary's role was to rubber-stamp neoliberalism (Sulikowski 2016, 28). In the words of Cosmin Cercel:

> It is indeed this unholy alliance between the intellectual elite and the markets that is perhaps at the core of the vagaries of the post-communist transformation (…). With the consensus that markets are the depositary of an ultimate social meaning and the position of the free individuals responsible for their actions, constitutional theory and what was left of the jurisprudential enterprise, were bound to turn into a search for ways of limiting state discretion as to offer a constant predictability and freedom of action for economic actors. (Cercel 2019, 25–26)

Adam Sulikowski, in turn, notes that:

3 A topic which remains to be researched is the role of the "rule of law" ideology in the subjection and conquest of Central Europe by Western capital and its imperial structures of domination. Indeed, as Ugo Mattei and Laura Nader point out: "The transformation of the rule of law ideal into an imperial ideology has accompanied the move from a need of social justice and solidarity towards the capitalist requirements of efficiency and competition" (2008, 3).

> After 1989 the Polish elite had become part of the neoliberal Western world and accepted the imported economic system as universally true. (...) A critique of law was regarded as something useless or even dangerous, something that only impedes the correct development of the country, something that might provoke those people who are irrational and do not understand the *raison d'etat*. (...) The [Constitutional Court] had become not only a voice of the pro-Western political elites but also the guardian of Catholic influence. (...) This system was strongly supported by the constitutionalists and other scholars. (...) The Polish mainstream "knowledge-power complex" was formed around the belief that "universal Western liberal modernity" was all we needed in Poland. (Sulikowski 2016, 25–27)

This was the state of ideological hegemony prior to the arrival of populism.

5. 'A great escape from the West': Central Europe's third transformation and the withering away of liberal legality

It was only with the arrival of right-wing populism that the consensus started to break down. In Poland, the leadership of Jarosław Kaczyński opened the perspective of a critique of legal transfers, especially in the sphere of public law. Populism has led to what Medushevsky describes as the 'retraditionalisation' of constitutional law in the region (Medushevsky 2018a; 2019b); however, we have to keep in mind that the traditions in the region are neither liberal nor democratic. As I have mentioned already above, when World War II broke out, Poland was an authoritarian country, ruled by a clique of military politicians (Garlicki 2008). The 1935 Constitution[4] did not even provide for the division of powers, effectively sanctioning a monocentric and autocratic political regime, where the 'uniform and indivisible state power' was concentrated in the hands of the President (Article 2(4)). Candidates for elections could not be put forward by citizens,[5] effectively eliminating pluralism. After World War II, these authoritarian traditions were simply continued, although initially

4 Ustawa Konstytucyjna z dnia 23 kwietnia 1935 r. [Constitutional Act of 23 April 1935], Dz.U. no. 30, item 227.

5 See Articles 34–50 of the Ustawa z dnia 8 lipca 1935 r. - Ordynacja wyborcza do Sejmu [Act of 8 July 1935 – Electoral Law of the Sejm], Dz.U. no. 47, item 319. The rules were even less democratic in the case of the Senate – see Articles 14–39 of the Ustawa z dnia 8 lipca 1935 r. - Ordynacja wyborcza do Senatu [Act of 8 July 1935 – Electoral Law of the Senate], Dz.U. no. 47, item 320.

through a doublespeak rhetoric (formally there was pluralism, but de facto it was excluded), but in the 1980s the letter of the law and practice once again coincided (the electoral laws specified which organisation may put forward candidates to parliament and local councils) (Mażewski 2011, 68–78). Even the hegemonic role of the communist party and the eternal alliance with the USSR were codified in constitutional rules. Therefore, if we speak of constitutional traditions, they are authoritarian, not liberal, democratic. The 'rule of law' is not a concept invented in Poland, Czech Republic or Hungary, but it is a legal transfer, which came to the region from the West, or, more precisely, which was imposed. After all, as Mattei and Nader point out:

> Western countries have developed a strong identity as being governed by the rule of law, no matter what the actual history or the present situation might be. Such identity is obtained – as is the usual pattern – by comparison with "the other," almost invariably portrayed as "lacking" the rule of law. (2008, 16)

If Central Europe wanted to become part of the mythical 'West', as it did three or two decades ago, it had no choice but to succumb to its ideological narratives, including the 'rule of law' and 'good governance' (cf. Mattei and Nader 2008, 15). Today, with the neoauthoritarian tendencies, these legal transfers are in the process of being rejected. The legal culture treats them as foreign bodies.

Ziemowit Szczerek, one of the most inspiring Polish writers of the young generation, in his novel *Międzymorze* ('Intermarium') has recently recalled the two ways of perceiving Central Europe in the eyes of the West – Ruritania and Borduria (Szczerek 2017, 337–343). Ruritania (a term invented by Anthony Hope) stands for a mythical, rustic and backward Central Europe, which is docile towards Western influence, but at the same time sheepishly naive. Borduria (a term invented by Hergé), in contrast, stands for Central Europe which rejected 'Western values', and went down the track of nationalism and authoritarianism. 'Regardless of what it was, Ruritania did not want to be Ruritania', writes Szczerek, adding that: 'It is understandable, who would want to be it' (2007, 339). As a result, 'Borduria returned', and in the *Intermarium* region 'a great escape from the West is taking place' (Szczerek 2007, 343). When back in 2002 Radoslav Procházka entitled his book on constitutional courts in Central Europe resorting to the characteristic idiom *Mission Accomplished*

(Procházka 2012), he seemed to suggest that the well-behaved Ruritania was addressing, in a neocolonial gesture of homage, the Western big Other (cf. Reid 2019, 113). At that time, early on in the post-socialist transformation, nobody expected that the idyllic picture of Westernized Ruritanian neophytes, where legal transfers from Western Europe – constitutional courts, judicial independence and the 'rule of law' functioned ideally – would soon be disrupted by the return of old Bordurian demons. Today, the West's *mission civilisatrice* seems to have been unsuccessful, at least with regard to some Central European nations. The liberal vision of the 'rule of law' as something essentially apolitical shattered into pieces before our eyes. The myths have fallen, and the political – as an inescapable dimension of social antagonism – has been laid bare (Sulikowski and Wojtanowski 2019). The role of the judge, initially understood according to the classical formalist paradigm as a faithful interpreter and 'applicator' of statutes, first gave way to a liberal 'functional formalism' of the Constitutional Court. Now, following the constitutional crisis of 2015–2016 in Poland, neither myth holds. As Przemysław Tacik observes:

> The Constitutional Court, previously hailed by the liberal doctrine as a stronghold of impartiality, independence and loyalty to the Constitution (…) was now denounced — in a vulgar version of the typical critical approach to law — as elitist, postcommunist and politicised. (2020, 168).

Following the so-called takeover of the Constitutional Court, its role changed. It became 'loyal' to the coalition, endorsing its key decisions and effectively desisting from protecting the constitutional order against unconstitutional measures (Tacik 2020, 167).

There can be no doubt that Central Europe is currently going through its third transformation, if we take the transformation from capitalism to state socialism as the first one (effected in the later 1940s) and the transformation from state socialism to liberal-democratic capitalism (effected in the early 1990s) as the second one. This third transformation is leading from liberal democratic 'rule of law' capitalism to capitalism 'with Central European values', to paraphrase the notion of 'capitalism with Asian values' (Žižek 2018). These 'Central European values' are, of course, 'conservative-clerical' and 'authoritarian', including especially a 'revision of the principle of division of powers and the concentration of competences in the hands of the executive' (Medushevsky 2018, 131). Of course, at this point we do not know where this transformation will lead,[6] but if the current direction is upheld, we can safely speak of a rejection of Western legal transfers in the field of public law, especially constitutional review and liberal 'rule of law' more in general. The 'Central European values' are Bordurian *par excellence* and are the embodiment of anti-liberalism in all spheres. They include an 'illiberal democracy' (Sadowski 2020, 176–177) but also a very illiberal approach to social life and culture, especially in the sphere of human sexuality and reproductive rights, what Medushevsky describes as 'conservative-clerical values' (2018a, 131). At the same time, however, the tenets of capitalism are not being questioned (Tacik 2019, 35–36).

6. A look into the future

The current situation in CEE is characterised by the withering away of liberal legality (Medushevsky 2018a, 114; Cercel 2019, 21; Tacik 2019, 41), that is the breaking down of a given Symbolic order (in the Lacanian[7] sense). As Cosmin Cercel openly characterises the situation:

> Authoritarianism is here and most likely here to stay, and legality does not have any necessary connection to democracy and liberalism as our colleagues acting in the populism and constitutionalism and democracy cottage industry would have it. (2020)

This opens up new possibilities. One of them is the simple 'retraditionalisation' of our constitutionalism (Medushevsky 2018b), that is a simple transition towards authoritarianism, effected in a subtractive manner (*status quo* minus liberal 'rule of law'). However, the breakdown of liberal legality opens up also new possibilities which, I think, could

6 As Medushevsky correctly affirms, the point of no return is the moment when the principle of political pluralism is rejected or can no longer be fulfilled (Medushevsky 2018a, 132–133).

7 Lacan identifies three orders: the Symbolic, the Imaginary and the Real. The Imaginary concerns the illusory surface of phenomena which conceals their inner structure, and is linked to our self-image. The Symbolic order, in contrast, is the big Other, that is the expectations of society towards the subject. The Real is what escapes symbolisation, that is cannot be verbalised, described in the available language (ideology).

be used to build something new. I have two specific ideas in mind. The first one is the construction of a Central European school of critical legal thinking. The 'masks have fallen', as Sulikowski and Wojtanowski (2019) write, and the smokescreen of liberal legal mythology no longer covers the political. Our reaction to right-wing populism should not be the defence of the 'trenches of the Holy Trinity' of liberalism, but rather the embracement of a left-wing populism, as advocated by Mouffe (2018). The weakness of the liberal intellectual set-up has never been greater since 1989, and such an occasion may not repeat itself in the foreseeable future.

Indeed, the development of Central European critical legal theory has recently accelerated. As the founding moment of a certain movement one can indicate the 1st International Workshop on Law and Ideology (the first and only truly critical workshop of this series) which ultimately led to the publication of a collective volume of a highly programmatic nature: *Law and Critique in Central Europe: Questioning the Past, Resisting the Present* (Mańko, Cercel and Sulikowski 2016). It is precisely there that we formulated the idea that Central Europe is a *peripheria duplex* (ibid., 3). In 2015, the University of Wrocław hosted the Critical Legal Conference (CLC) – the main annual gathering of English-speaking critical legal scholars. This was the first time that the CLC was held in Central Europe and the importance of this event cannot be overestimated. A selection of papers from the CLC 2015 came out last year (Bieś-Srokosz, Mańko and Srokosz 2019). The most recent expression of Central European critical legal theory is a special issue of the *Folia Iuridica* journal (Mańko 2019a).

7. The idea of Central European legal identity and the importance of research networks

The second idea I have in mind is a deepened reflection upon Central (and Eastern) European legal identity. We are, after all, 'a post-colonial space which should reclaim the right to do things for oneself' (Mercescu 2020, 16). In the current atmosphere of an upheaval, we could take a step back and think more deeply on what we have in common as Central Europeans, following the 'logic of *distinctiveness*' (Mercescu 2019, 52). I have tried to indicate some areas of a common past and common legal culture in the first section of this chapter. I think we ought to make them a subject of in-depth research, involving transnational teams.[8] Even if we agree with Alexandra Mercescu that 'Central and Eastern Europe remains too heterogenous for one to be able to speak of a common culture' (2019, 57), the same probably obtains for Europe as a whole. Nonetheless, in her view 'it is possible to work with *Central and Eastern European cultural resources*' (ibid.) The same applies to the notion of a legal family: Even if we do not accept the plea for recognising a fully fledged 'Central European Legal Family' (Mańko, Škop and Štěpáníková 2016), we can nonetheless speak of a Central Europe as a 'legal union' (Mańko 2019, 74–75; cf. Nazmutdinov 2019, 90–91) or perhaps of a 'legal space' (Mańko 2019, 75–76). Balázs Fekete highlights the importance of Central European legal mentality (2011, 47–49), and together with Katalin Kelemen puts forward the idea of Central Europe being an 'autonomous group' within the Civil Law Tradition (Fekete and Kelemen 2014, 222). These vexed questions are open to debate and cannot be resolved in national isolation; rather, they should be subject to transnational, pan-Central European research fora. The idea of a Central (and Eastern) European legal identity, or shortly 'CEE legal identity', can be conceived as an antidote against the narrow nationalism that is currently waking up.[9] Too different from the West to identify with Western Europe, we are still similar enough among ourselves to overcome ethnic divides in the broader space between the Baltic, Black and Adriatic seas that we have shared for centuries, despite differences and even conflicts.

---

8 A first step in this direction could be the project "European Constitutional Imaginaries: Utopias, Ideologies and the Other" led by Professor Jan Komárek, a Czech scholar now based at the University of Copenhagen, who intends to research Central European "constitutional imaginaries." See the website of the project: [https://jura.ku.dk/icourts/research/imagine/, accessed 29 March 2020].

9 Cf. Cercel 2020: 'What becomes apparent is the resilient ideological trope of the nation as a distinct organic unity grounded in both blood and soil, constructed and rooted in the long-standing effects of the revolutionary defeats and derails of the past centuries. This opiate with its particular strength, surviving as an undead, as precisely the shadowy double of the globalized capital and never actually challenged as such, is not some extraneous alien by-product of crises befalling otherwise rule-of-law centred democracies, let alone some trick employed by power-thirsty demagogues. Rather it has always been at the core of our constitutional arrangements, beyond pledges, safeguards and supranational, regional or international scrutiny.'

In this respect, the importance of Central European *research networks* cannot be underestimated (Mercescu 2019, 55). Currently, there are three such networks, which I mention here in chronological order of their creation: the Central and Eastern European Network of Jurisprudence ('CEENJ'), established in 2005 in Pécs, Hungary; the Central and Eastern European Forum of Young Legal, Political and Social Theorists ('CEE Forum'), established in 2009 in Katowice, Poland, and the newest one, and at the same time most inclusive and versatile, that is the CEE Network of Legal Scholars ('CEENELS'), established in 2015 in Brno, Czech Republic. Each of these three networks has different characteristics, appeals to different *milieus* of legal researchers and has different goals. The narrowest focus of appeal is that of CEENJ, a network clearly limited to legal theorists (Mańko 2018, 97). The focus of the CEE Forum is broader in terms of subject matter (not only legal theorists, but also social theorists and political theorists), but at the same time it is addressed mainly to young scholars, which – 10 years later – also includes young full professors, but still it is a rather narrow area of appeal. Its subject-matter limitation is also due to its focus on theory, thereby excluding legal historians, empirical sociologists of law, comparatists and dogmaticians. Finally, the CEENELS is a network that is addressed to *all* legal scholars, and indeed the only CEE legal network open not only to legal theorists, but also legal historians and representatives of the legal dogmatics – specialists in private law, administrative law, criminal law and constitutional law. As a result, it has chances to establish itself as the broadest network.

Whereas the 12th CEENJ conference in Riga in 2017 gathered 62 participants (Mańko 2018, 97), the subsequent ones have been reduced to only 32 participants,[10] effectively transforming the CEENJ into a small specialised workshop limited to legal philosophers. In contrast, the CEE Forum has grown from only 34 participants at the 1st conference in Katowice to as many as 72 at the 10th edition in Timişoara (Fekete 2020, 29), which shows a clear tendency towards inclusiveness and openness. The CEENELS conference initially hosted some 40 participants at its 1st and 2nd editions (Zomerski 2017), but the number later grew considerably,

10 See the call for papers for the 13th edition held in Zagreb: https://ivronlineblog.files.wordpress.com/2018/02/ceenj_cfp.pdf.

exceeding 60 participants at the 3rd edition in Riga (Szymaniec 2018), and reaching 71 participants at its latest, 4th edition that took place at the Higher School of Economics in Moscow (Poldnikov 2019b). The 5th edition was to take place in Debrecen in June 2020, but has been postponed to 2021.

More interesting than the sheer number of participants is the intellectual journey each of these conferences has made. In this respect, CEENJ is a static one: Each year's topic is simply defined as 'Jurisprudence in Central and Eastern Europe: Work in Progress' meaning that no *leitmotiv* is selected. However, given the topics of the 12th edition, which I have attended, it is visible that there is no attempt to focus on typically Central European questions; rather, a general analytical jurisprudence approach, emulating the Western mainstream, dominates (cf. Mańko 2018, 101). The CEE Forum, in turn, initially focused on rather abstract topics, such as 'separation of powers' (5th edition), 'important features of law' (6th edition) or even 'global governance' (7th edition), before making a turn towards more CEE-focused topics – 'Central and Eastern European Socio-Political and Legal Transition Revisited – Theoretical Perspectives' (8th edition), 'Constitutional Memory and Social Identities in Central and Eastern Europe' (10th edition) and 'Central and Eastern Europe as a Double Periphery?' (11th edition in Bratislava). A characteristic feature of the CEE Forum, which unfortunately has not been followed by CEENJ or CEENELS, is the habit of publishing conference proceedings in book form. A special series, called the 'Central and Eastern European Forum ... Yearbook', has been established for this purpose at the German publisher Peter Lang (Fekete 2020, 30–31), thereby ensuring a global distribution and a high-end quality of publication.[11]

As far as the CEENELS network is concerned, the focus of its annual conferences presents an interesting pattern of development. The first and inaugural conference of this informal network, hosted by the Masaryk

---

11 Until now eight volumes have been published, and especially the last two ones have provided an important insight into Central European legal identity – the seventh volume on *Central and Eastern European Socio-Political and Legal Transition* (Fekete and Gárdos-Orosz 2016) and the most recent one on *Constitutional Identities in Central and Eastern Europe* (Mercescu 2020b).

University in Brno, the capital of Moravia, in April 2015, was devoted to *25 Years After the Transformation: Law and Legal Culture in Central and Eastern Europe Between Continuity and Discontinuity* (Zomerski 2016). With distinguished keynote speakers – Professors Czarnota, Koczanowicz and Sulikowski – the network kicked off by taking a deep dive into Central Europe's most vexed legal conundrum: the transition from state socialism to capitalism and Western-style liberal democratic 'rule of law' state. The second edition, held in freezing (-20 °C!) and smog-covered Kraków, former capital of the Kingdom of Poland, was devoted to the topic of *An Uneasy Legacy: Remnants of Socialist Legal and Political Thinking in Central and Eastern Europe*. Acknowledging the importance of the 1989 transformation as a kind of watershed, we nonetheless recognised the importance of what had been before, the 'remnants' and 'legal survivals' (Mańko 2015; 2016) of our common state-socialist past (cf. Kuźmicka-Sulikowska 2019, 148). We discovered that this experience, perhaps problematic from some points of view, is nonetheless a great force of unifying character for our region. Having made an 'examination of conscience' with our past, we could move towards the present. In Riga, at the 3rd CEENELS conference, we focused on *Legal Identities and Legal Traditions in Central and Eastern Europe* (Szymaniec 2018). Although, for obvious reasons, the discussion was dominated by the evolution in Poland and Hungary (ibid., 151), nonetheless I think that we did make some progress in attempting to answer the question regarding our common elements, on one hand, and the differences, on the other. I have tried to articulate them in a paper, written about that time[12] jointly with Professor Martin Škop and Dr Markéta Štěpáníková from Masaryk University in which we claim that we, Central Europeans

> ...need to define ourselves in terms of neighbouring legal families, with their distinct legal identities. On the one hand, we cannot agree to being amalgamated in an unqualified manner with the Romanic and/or Germanic legal family – Central Europe is certainly distinct from Western Europe and its legal families, even if it was (and is again) subjected to the taking in of legal transfers originating from that region. Of course, the gesture of (re-)establishing Central Europe as a legal

12 The issues of the *Wroclaw Review of Law, Administration and Economics* are ante-dated by two years.

> family is a counter-hegemonic one, and therefore not easy or straightforward to take. (2016, 22)

We acknowledged that the division of Europe into legal families is a dynamic one, something that can change over time, and something which is linked to the political:

> Legal taxonomy is political. This is a fact which we cannot deny, and proposing Central Europe as a *sedes* of a legal family we are making a conscious move. A move intended to underscore the similarities and common heritage, whilst concealing the differences. And, at the same time, a move distinguishing us from the West and the East, but not closing down channels of juridico-cultural communication. To the contrary, if the last three decades were marked by an unprecedented reception of juridico-cultural transfers from the West, and the previous decades (of Actually Existing Socialism) were marked by the infiltration of Soviet legal ideas, we hope that the self-identification and self-determination of our legal communities qua Central Europe will be instrumental in promoting a greater equilibrium in the flow of legal ideas within geographical macrospaces. (2016, 22)

If the above quote describes the idea and atmosphere[13] of our 3rd conference in Riga, at our next meeting we decided to ask if we have something constructive to offer to the world. Hence, the convenors of our 4th conference, Professor Poldnikov and Dr Starżeniecki, opted for the topic of *Legal Innovativeness in Central and Eastern Europe*.[14] However, it seems that the original legal solutions, which were to be discussed in the conference,

> ...were limited to marginal examples (...) and often met with a negative evaluation. Moreover, the sessions revealed that the very concept of originality is inadequate with regard to law and legal scholarship. (Poldnikov 2019b).

These findings are, as such, important. They indicate that originality and innovativeness is something *yet to be accomplished* by Central Europe, it is something to be sought after, rather than something to be uncovered in our common legal heritage. Furthermore, these findings do not really come as a surprise to us: given the fact that our common legal history has been dominated by incoming legal transfers (Mańko 2019, 69–70), and so is

---

13 A 4.5-hour video recording of the plenary session of the 3rd CEENELS conference is available on YouTube: https://www.youtube.com/watch?v=Z8k2AiNulN0, accessed 21 March 2020.

14 http://ceenels.org/events/cfp-ceenels-4/, accessed 21 March 2020.

our present predicament (Mańko 2017), originality and innovativeness are only to come, they belong to a Central Europe *à venir*. Importantly, these findings resonated with the findings of general cultural studies, which indicate that in CEE

> there are no "own" models, because cultures of this region have always been derivative (...). Practically in any sphere of culture (...) we cannot find serious achievements which would have impacted upon European culture, let alone world culture. (Sowa 2011, 19)

Having come to these painful conclusions, for our next, 5th conference, to be held in June 2020 in Debrecen, hosted by Professor Matyas Bencze and Dr Krisztina Ficsor, we were supposed to discuss the somewhat more humble topic of *Re-thinking Legal Institutions in Central and Eastern Europe.*[15] Hopefully, the 5th CEENELS Conference will take place in June 2021.

8. Conclusions: From the shame of (double) peripherality to the pride of populism

Peripherality, let alone double peripherality, is no reason to pride. It is, 'with all due respect to the scientific objectivity of the concept, a *humiliating condition*. To be peripheral means to be subject to the economic, political and – indeed – cultural hegemony of a certain Centre' (Mańko, Škop and Štěpáníková 2016, 21, emphasis added).[16] Being peripheral means to suffer from symbolic violence (Mańko 2019, 69–70). Permanently running after the fetish of 'modernisation' (cf. Gałędek 2020), permanently desiring to escape the curse of 'backwardness', permanently behind, permanently learning and permanently emulating. How can a legal community that is burdened by such symbolic oppression (self-oppression?) ascertain its pride, its prestige and its self-esteem? How can a *society*, and especially its elites, endure such long-term humiliation? Recent developments have shown that it can no longer. The former 'best pupil in class', the apprentice

15 http://ceenels.org/events/5ceenels2020debrecen/, accessed 21 March 2002.

16 Peripheral actors suffer from being deprived of agency, and they attempt to compensate this lack in the ideological narratives they create (Zarycki 2013).

of the demoliberal sorcerer, has announced that he is quitting school and going his own way. Where will his path lead him? Is Ruritania's transition into Borduria – Central Europe's *third* transformation in a century – a definitive or temporary one? Concluding this chapter today, when the outbreak of Covid-19 is spreading through my native Central Europe, I have no final answers to offer. What I can say, though, is that there is no return to pre-populist times. Liberal legality is 'dead and buried', at least on this side of the former Iron Curtain. The 'masks have fallen' (Sulikowski and Wojtanowski 2019, 193); and nobody will believe in the old liberal myths about an 'apolitical judiciary', 'rule of law not men' or other ideological fantasies from the worn-out imaginary of 'demoliberalism'. We are perhaps facing the same situation as the one described by our fellow Central European philosopher, Slavoj Žižek, in one of his first Western books, *Tarrying with the Negative* (Žižek 1993): the scene of Romanian workers, flying the Romanian flag but with the national emblem cut out – for Žižek this symbolised the 'intermediate phase when the former Master-Signifier, although it has already lost the hegemonical power, has not yet been replaced by the new one'. Today, when the decay of liberal legality is occurring before our eyes (Cercel 2019, 21; Tacik 2019, 41), the old Master Signifier of the 'rule of law' and other 'Western values' are exiting the historical scene, being replaced – in Central Europe – by authoritarian, right-wing populist regimes. Whereas in political terms the situation remains, at least in Poland and at least as of now, still open, in intellectual and ideological terms we have crossed a Rubicon. We, the legal community, can remain passive and, as in 1989, allow ourselves to be 'taken by surprise' (Mańko, Škop and Štěpáníková 2016, 21), but equally well we can try to take an active part in the shaping of our future. This does not necessarily mean joining the populist bandwagon, even if right-wing populists are using, in a distorted manner, some selected tools of critical legal thinking (Zomerski 2018, 101), but rather by taking carefully chosen ideological positions. On one hand, building our common, Central European legal identity can help us articulate regional interests, bringing into focus our regional 'self-determination' (Mercescu 2020, 16); on the other, insisting on a critical legal programme (Mańko 2019b, 11) can help rebuild the legitimacy of the judiciary, and more generally, of lawyers, in the future (Otręba 2020, 132). As Sulikowski and Wojtanowski argue with regard to the Polish Constitutional Court (the 'TK'):

> If the TK survives the storm (or, to be more precise, if it is resuscitated as a true constitutional court by some future political majority), it should undertake an attempt to regain social trust; it should present its decisions as an outcome of a deep reflection, also in a political sense, as a result not only of an analysis of norms, but also the possibility of political representation (in a substantive, not merely formal sense) of the interests of various social groups. Raising the sensitivity (towards social justice) and a partial giving up of legalistic camouflage are, in our view, desirable. A constitutional court more conscious of its political character should seek broad social support, not just support of the elites. (2019, 194)

I think this should be the minimum programme of our critical legal engagement in these times. Reviving legal hypocrisy and joining the crowd of cynically naïve liberals, mourning the 'rule of law' without much understanding of the reality (or refusing to understand it) is a road leading nowhere (cf. Tacik 2019, 38–41). The stakes are high, and the old Master-Signifier of demoliberalism is gone. Although the majority of Central European legal scholars will go with the tide, a minority of critical jurists has the duty to resist and to lead the way.

References

Antonov, Mikhail. 2018. Legal Realism in Soviet and Russian Jurisprudence. *Review of Central and East European Law* 43(4): 483–518.

Cercel, Cosmin. 2016. Law Out of Bounds: Legal Picnolepsy, Intellectual Austerity, and Romania's Legal Past. In *Law and Critique in Central Europe: Questioning the Past, Resisting the Present*, ed. R. Mańko et al., 44–65. Oxford: Counterpress.

Cercel, Cosmin. 2019. The Destruction of Legal Reason: Lessons from the Past. *Acta Universitatis Lodzienis. Folia Iuridica* 89: 15–30.

Cercel, Cosmin. 2020. The Reality of the Exception and the Task of the Critical Lawyer. *Exceptions* (28 March 2020). [http://exceptions.eu/2020/03/28/the-reality-of-the-exception-and-the-task-of-the-critical-lawyer/, accessed 28 March 2020].

Cserne, Peter. 2015. Formalism in Judicial Reasoning: Is Central and Eastern Europe a Special Case? In *Central European Judges under the*

European Influence: The Transformative Power of the EU Revisited, ed. Michal Bobek, 23–42. Oxford: Hart Publishing

David, Rene and John Brierley. 1968. *Major Legal Systems in the World Today*. New York: Simon and Schuster.

Fekete, Balázs. 2011. Cultural Comparative Law? In *Legal and Political Theory in the Post-National Age*, ed. Peter Cserne and Miklos Könczöl. Berlin: Peter Lang.

Fekete, Balazs. 2020. The (First) Ten Years of the CEE-Forum: Timeline, Data and Assessment. In *Constitutional Identities in Central and Eastern Europe*, ed. Alexandra Mercescu, 25–36. Berlin: Peter Lang.

Gałędek, Michał. 2020. Introduction: Modernisation, National Identity, and Legal Instrumentalism. In *Modernization, National Identity and Legal Instrumentalism: Studies in Comparative Legal History. Volume 1: Private Law*, ed. Michał Gałędek and Anna Klimaszewska. Leiden-Boston: Brill-Nijhoff.

Giaro, Tomasz. 2013. Some Prejudices About the Legal Tradition of Eastern Europe. In *Comparative Law in Eastern and Central Europe*, ed. Bronisław Sitek et al., 26–50. Newcastle-upon-Tyne: Cambridge Scholars Publishing.

Kelemen, Katalin and Balázs Fekete. 2014. How Should the Legal Systems of Eastern Europe Be Classified Today? In *International Conference for the 10th Anniversary of the Institute of Comparative Law*. Potsdam: Universitätsverlag Potsdam.

Kühn, Zdeněk. 2004. Worlds Apart: Western and Central European Judicial Culture at the Onset of the European Enlargement. *American Journal of Comparative Law* 52(3): 531–567.

Kühn, Zdeněk. 2011. *The Judiciary in Central and Eastern Europe: Mechanical Jurisprudence in Transformation?* Leiden-Boston: Martinus Nijhoff.

Kuźmicka-Sulikowska, Joanna. 2019. The Politics of Limitation of Claims in Poland: Post-Communist Ideology, Neoliberalism and the Plight of Uninformed Debtors. *Acta Universitatis Lodziensis. Folia Iuridica* 89: 131–160.

Leder, Andrzej. 2019. *Polen im Wachtraum. Die Revolution 1939–1956 und ihre Folgen*. Osnabrück: Fibre Verlag.

Leszczyński, Adam. 2013. *Skok w nowoczesność. Polityka wzrostu w krajach peryferyjnych 1943–1980*. Warszawa: Wydawnictwo Krytyki Politycznej.

Łętowska, Ewa. 1997. The Barriers of Polish Legal Thinking in the Perspective of European Integration. *Yearbook of Polish European Studies* 1: 55–72.

Łętowska, Ewa. 2002. Kilka uwag o praktyce wykładni. *Kwartalnik Prawa Prywatnego* 11(1): 27–64.

Mańko, Rafał. 2007. Is the Socialist Legal Tradition "Dead and Buried"? The Continuity of Certain Elements of Socialist Legal Culture in Polish Civil Procedure. In *Private Law and the Many Cultures of Europe*, ed. Thomas Wilhelmsson et al., 83–103. Alphen aan den Rijn: Kluwer Law International.

Mańko, Rafał. 2013. Survival of the Socialist Legal Tradition? A Polish Perspective. *Comparative Law Review* 4(2): 1–28.

Mańko, Rafał. 2015a. "We Do Not Recognise Anything 'Private' ": Public Interest and Private Law Under the Socialist Legal Tradition and Beyond. In *Private Interest and Public Interest in European Legal Tradition*, ed. Bronisław Sitek et al., 31–65. Olsztyn: WPiA UWM.

Mańko, Rafał. 2015b. Legal Survivals: A Conceptual Tool for Analysing Post-Transformation Continuity of Legal Culture. In *Tiesību efektivitāte postmodernāsabiedrībā*, ed. Jānis Rozenfelds, et al., 17–27. Rīga: LU Akadēmiskais apgāds. [https://www.academia.edu/13535801/, last accessed 21 March 2020].

Mańko, Rafał. 2016. "Demons of the Past"? Legal Survivals of the Socialist Legal Tradition in Contemporary Polish Private Law. In *Law and Critique in Central Europe: Questioning the Past, Resisting the Present*, ed. Rafał Mańko, Cosmin Cercel, Adam Sulikowski, 66–89. Oxford: Counterpress. [https://www.academia.edu/28087945/, last accessed 21 March 2020].

Mańko, Rafał. 2017. Legal Transfers in Europe Today: Still "Modernisation Through Transfer"? In *Mutual Interaction Between Contemporary Systems and Branches if Law in European Countries*, ed. Paulina Bieś-Srokosz, Jacek Srokosz and Ewelina Żelasko-Makowska, 139–156. Częstochowa: Podobiński Publishing House. [https://www.academia.edu/36953623/, accessed 21 March 2020].

Mańko, Rafał. 2019a. Delimiting Central Europe as a Juridical Space: A Preliminary Exercise in Critical Legal Geography. *Acta Universitatis Lodziensis. Folia Iuridica* 89: 63–80. [https://www.academia.edu/41582133, accessed 21 March 2020].

Mańko, Rafał. 2019b. Critical Legal Theory in Central and Eastern Europe: In Search of Method. *Acta Universitatis Lodziensis. Folia Iuridica* 89: 5–14. [https://www.academia.edu/42289160/, accessed 22 March 2020].

Mańko, Rafał, Martin Škop and Markéta Štěpáníková. 2016. Carving out Central Europe as a Space of Legal Culture: A Way out of Peripherality?' *Wroclaw Review of Law, Administration and Economics* 6(2): 4–28. [https://www.academia.edu/36121716/, accessed 21 March 2020].

Mażewski, Lech. 2011. *System rządów w PRL (1952–1989).* Warszawa-Biała Podlaska: Arte.

Medushevsky, Andrei Nikolaevich. 2018a. Популизм и конституционная трансформация: Восточная Европа, постсоветское пространство и Россия. *Полития* 90(3): 113–139.

Medushevsky, Andrei Nikolaevich. 2018b. Конституционная ретрадиционализация в Восточной Европе и России. *Сравнительное конституционное обозрение* 122(1): 13–32.

Mercescu, Alexandra. 2019. What Kind of Critique for Central and Eastern European Legal Studies? Comparison as One of the Answers. *Acta Universitatis Lodzienis. Folia Iuridica* 89: 45–61.

Mercescu, Alexandra. 2020. Introduction: From Country to Country, from Time to Time, Questions and Answers of Self and Other. In *Constitutional Identities in Central and Eastern* Europe, ed. Alexandra Mercescu, 13–24. Berlin: Peter Lang.

Örücü, Esin. 2007. A General View of "Legal Families" and of "Mixing Systems." In *Comparative Law: A Handbook*, ed. Esin Örücü and David Nelken. Oxford: Hart Publishing.

Otręba, Krzysztof. 2020. Book review: Rafał Mańko, *W stronę krytycznej filozofii orzekania. Polityczność, etyka, legitymizacja*, Łódź 2018, Wydawnictwo Uniwersytetu Łódzkiego, 296 s. *Państwo i Prawo* 1: 130–132.

Poldnikov, Dimitriy. 2019a. Европа и мы // Обзор конференции о праве Центральной и Восточной Европы (Часть первая) (13 September 2019). [https://www.hse.ru/ba/privlaw/news/307939836.html, accessed 21 March 2020].

Poldnikov, Dimitriy. 2019b. Европа и мы // Обзор конференции о праве Центральной и Восточной Европы (Часть вторая) (17 October 2019) [https://www.hse.ru/ba/law/news/312393718.html, accessed 21 March 2020].

Procházka, Radoslav. 2002. *Mission Accomplished: On Founding Constitutional Adjudication in Central Europe*. Budapest: CEU Press.

Reid, Julian. 2019. Pedagogies of the Poor: Resisting Resilience in Eastern Europe and Beyond. *Acta Universitatis Lodziensis. Folia Iuridica* 89: 111–129.

Rudt, Yulia. 2019. Ideology in Modern Constitutional Practice. *Acta Universitatis Lodziensis. Folia Iuridica* 89: 161–177.

Sadowski, Mirosław Michał. 2020. Central Europe in the Search of (Lost) Identity. The Illiberal Swerve. In *Constitutional Identities in Central and Eastern Europe*, ed. Alexandra Mercescu, 173–193. Berlin: Peter Lang.

Sowa, Jan. 2011. *Fantomowe ciało króla. Peryferyjne zmagania z nowoczesną formą*. Kraków: Universitas.

Sulikowski, Adam and Mateusz Wojtanowski. 2019. The Polish Constitutional Court Crisis: Some Remarks on the Political, Liberalism and Culture. In *The Gradual Emergence of the Juristocratic State*, ed. Béla Pokol, András Téglási. 181–199. Budapest: Dialóg Campus.

Szczerek, Ziemowit. 2017. *Międzymorze: Podróże przez prawdziwą i wyobrażoną Europę Środkową* [Intermarium: Journeys Through Real and Imagined Central Europe]. Warszawa: Agora and Wydawnictwo Czarne.

Szymaniec, Piotr. 2018. Discussion about the Legal Identity of Central and Eastern Europe. 3rd Annual CEENELS Conference "Legal Identities and Legal Traditions in CEE." *Acta Universitatis Lodziensis. Folia Iuridica* 85: 139–153 [http://yadda.icm.edu.pl/yadda/element/bwmeta1.element.ekon-element-000171541145, accessed 21 March 2020].

Tacik, Przemysław. 2020. Polish Constitutional Identity under the Illiberal Turn. In *Constitutional Identities in Central and Eastern Europe*, ed. Alexandra Mercescu, 157–172. Berlin: Peter Lang.

Tacik, Przemysław. 2019. A New Popular Front, or, on the Role of Critical Jurisprudence under Neo-Authoritarianism in Central Europe. *Acta Universitatis Lodzienis. Folia Iuridica* 89: 31–44

Uzelac, Alan. 2010. Survival of the Third Legal Tradition? *Supreme Court Law Review* 49: 377–396.

Wallerstein, Immanuel. 2004. *World-System Analysis: An Introduction.* Durham: Duke University Press.

Watson, Alan. 1993 [1974]. *Legal Transplants: An Approach to Comparative Law.* Atlanta: University of Virginia Press.

Zarycki, Tomasz. 2013. Podmiotowość na peryferiach: rola wewnętrznych i zewnętrznych aktorów w debatach nad upadkiem komunizmu i „transformacją" postkomunistyczną w Polsce. In *Sprawstwo: Teorie, metody, badania empiryczne w naukach społecznych*. ed. A. Mrozowicki et al., 285–296. Kraków: Nomos.

Zarycki, Tomasz. Ed. 2016a. *Polska jako peryferie.* Warszawa: Wydawnictwo Naukowe Scholar.

Zarycki, Tomasz. 2016b. Polska jako peryferie stykowe. In *Polska jako peryferie*, ed. Tomasz Zarycki, 105–147. Warszawa: Wydawnictwo Naukowe Scholar.

Zimmermann, Reinhard. 1995. Civil Code and Civil Law. The Europeanisation of Private Law within the European Community and the Re-emergence of a European Legal Science. *Columbia Journal of European Law* 1: 63–105.

Żółtkowski, Wiesław. Ed. 2012. *Zrozumieć PRL.* Warszawa: Muza SA.

Zomerski, Wojciech. 2008. Czy Europie Środkowej potrzebna jest krytyczna teoria prawa? (artykuł recenzyjny). *Państwo i Prawo* 9: 95–108.

Zomerski, Wojciech. 2016. Conference Report: 1st International Conference of the Central European Network of Legal Scholars (CENELS) on "25 Years After the Transformation: Law and Legal Culture in Central and Eastern Europe Between Continuity and Discontinuity," Masaryk University, Brno, Czech Republic, 16–17

April 2015. *Wroclaw Review of Law, Administration and Ecoonmics*. 4(2): 103–108.

Zomerski, Wojciech, 2017. 2nd CEENELS Annual Conference (2017, Kraków). [http://ceenels.org/news/ceenels-2017/, accessed 21 March 2020].

Zweigert, Konrad and Hein Kötz. 1987. *Introduction to Comparative Law*. Vol. I: *The Framework*. 2nd ed. Oxford: Clarendon Press.

II. Migrating legal concepts?

Boldizsár Szentgáli-Tóth

Junior research fellow of the Hungarian Academy of Sciences, Institute of Legal Studies, junior research fellow of the Constitutional Law Department of the Eötvös Loránd University

The regional migration of a constitutional idea: Qualified laws as instruments for the protection of fundamental rights in Central Europe

Abstract: In this study, qualified law is examined as a potentially effective instrument for the protection of fundamental rights in Central Europe. My argumentation is based on the comparative analysis of the Hungarian,[1] the Romanian,[2] and the Moldovan constitutional development. These are those three countries in Central Europe where qualified laws have been implemented during the democratic transition. The relevant elements of a fourth constitutional framework, the Austrian experience, will be also outlined, but this concept differs remarkably from the three aforementioned constitutional designs.

Keywords: Qualified laws, organic laws, legal migration, laws with constitutional force

Introduction

As a preliminary consideration, we shall define the term "qualified law." The relevant national legal systems outline the concept of qualified law differently; however, certain common points are identifiable between the various approaches. Qualified law is a constitutionally prescribed subcategory of laws, which covers at least theoretically the most crucial legislative subject matters, and which is subject to stricter procedural safeguards,

1 Art. *T.* (4) of the Fundamental Law of Hungary [25.04.2011].
2 Art. 73. (3) of the Constitution of Romania [08.12.1991].

than the requirements of the ordinary legislative process (Camby 1998, 1686–1698; Jakab and Szilágyi 2014; Avril and Gicquel 2014).

After having provided a brief international overview, and some further introductory considerations, I would focus on the comparison, which would be based on three aspects: the historical background, the procedural safeguards, and the scope of qualified law. The analysis will provide an overarching picture from the Central European development of qualified law, which demonstrates also an excellent example to assess, how could a constitutional idea spread within the region. My hypothesis would be the strong role of qualified legislation in Central Europe as an indirect tool for the protection of fundamental rights, but the scope of qualified law shall be determined narrowly, and most fundamental rights shall not fall explicitly within the enumeration of qualified subject matters.

The different national legal systems apply a wide range of expressions for the denomination of qualified laws. Despite the fact that the terminology is not a decisive factor for the substantial analysis, in this particular case, it is worth to assess this issue, since the terminology demonstrates well the different functions of this legal concept: The constitutional, the political, the historical, and the sovereignty-based approach shall be highlighted.

The term "organic law" is used by the Constitutions of France,[3] Spain,[4] Romania, and Moldova, and by several countries outside Europe. This terminology focuses on the approach of constitutional law. In Spain, organic laws fall within the broader constitutional design, the constitutional bloc, and in most relevant constitutional systems, organic laws may be invoked during the constitutional review of ordinary laws.[5]

The category of "laws with constitutional force" was introduced in Hungary during the democratic transition. These laws had the same legal force, as the articles of the Constitution (Kilenyi 1994). The form of "laws adopted by two-thirds majority" was also applied during two decades in Hungary between 1990 and 2011. This approach highlighted the political

3 Art. 46. of the Constitution of France [04.10.1958].
4 Art. 81. (1) of the Constitution of Spain [07.12.1978].
5 N° 66–28, DC du 8 juillet 1966 (Rec., p. 15)., cf. Troper and Chagnollaud (2012, 346).

relevance: Instead of simple majority, broad consent was necessary to adopt or amend qualified laws.

The Fundamental Law of Hungary established, or even reinstated, a new legal concept, the cardinal law,[6] which had almost the same logic, as the former "laws adopted by two-thirds majority." This symbolic step strengthened the historical rhetoric of the new Fundamental Law (Küpper 2014, 2–5).

Foreign models

France and Spain represent two main models for legislation with a qualified majority. However, the issue of qualified law concerns not only these two countries, but also several other constitutional systems of the world.

In spite of the fact that some elements of the English constitutional development were close to the logic of qualified law (Leyland 2012), the modern history of qualified law dates back to 1958, when the Constitution of the Fifth French Republic was adopted.[7] After the decolonization of Africa, numerous African countries have implemented organic law into their constitutional design (David 1964, 630). Currently, approximately 21 African Constitutions provide expressly for organic law, such as Algeria,[8] Senegal,[9] or Tunisia,[10] and further countries across the continent.[11]

6 Art. T. (4) of the Fundamental Law of Hungary [25.04.2011].
7 Art. 46. of the Constitution of France [04.10.1958].
8 Art. 123. of the Constitution of Algeria [15.05.1996].
9 Art. 78. of the Constitution of Senegal [07.01.2001].
10 Art. 65. of the Constitution of Tunisia [26.01.2014].
11 Art. 166. (2) b) and Art. 169. (2) of the Constitution of Angola [21.01.2010]; Art. 97. of the Constitution of Benin [02.12.1990]; Art. 155. of the Constitution of [02.06.1991]; Art. 127. of the Constitution of Chad [1996]; Art. 66. of the Constitution of Djibouti [1992]; Art. 104. of the Constitution of Equatorial Guinea [1991]; Art. 71. of the Constitution of Ivory Coast [08.11.2016]; Art. 60. of the Constitution of Gabon [1991]; Art. 83. of the Constitution of Guinea [07.05.2010]; Art. 124. of the Constitution of the Democratic Republic of Congo [18.02.2006]; Art. 125. of the Constitution of the Republic of Congo [2001]; Art. 52. 70. 73. 77. 80. 85. 87. 89. 92. 93. 99. 101. 102. 103. and 105. of the Constitution of the Central African Republic [27.12.2004]; Art. 88. and 89. of the Constitution of Madagascar [14.11.2010]; Art. 85. and 86. of the Constitution of Morocco [01.07.2011]; Art. 67. of the Constitution of Mauritania [12.07.1991]; Art. 131. of the Constitution of Niger [31.10.2010];

The second wave of the spread of qualified law were connected to the fall of nationalist dictatorships in Spain and Portugal:[12]Qualified laws were introduced in both constitutions (Conversi 2002), and later, this model was followed by a considerable number of Latin-American countries, such as Ecuador[13] or Venezuela,[14] and other countries.[15]

Finally, owing to the third wave of the spread of qualified law, after the failure of the communist regimes, this solution was also implemented in the Hungarian, in the Romanian,[16]and in the Moldovan[17]constitutional systems.

Apart from this, after the democratic transition, some former Soviet republics have also implemented organic law, but the relevant constitutional articles were soon repealed.

It is also worth contemplating that the qualified subject matters of organic laws are divided into two main categories: the fundamental rights and the basic institutional framework of the state.[18] Qualified laws cover often a wide range of fundamental rights, such as freedom of assembly, freedom of association, freedom of religion, or the fundamental political rights. In addition to this, the key rules on the main constitutional actors and institutions fall also within the scope of organic law. For instance, in Hungary, the act on the Parliament,[19] on the Constitutional

---

Art. 92. of the Constitution of Togo [14.10.1992]; Art. 73. (3) and Art. 86. (2) b) of the Constitution of Cape Verde Islands [1980].

12 Art. 81. (1) of the Constitution of Spain [07.12.1978], Art. 136 (3) of the Constitution of Portugal [02.04.1976].

13 Art. 133. of the Constitution of Ecuador [28.09.2008].

14 Art. 203. of the Constitution of Venezuela [20.12.1999].

15 Art. 63. of the Constitution of Chile [21.10.1980]; Art. 112. of the Constitution of the Dominican Republic [13.06.2015]; Art. 151. of the Constitution of Colombia [04.07.1991]; Art. 164. of the Constitution of Panama [1972]; Art. 106. of the Constitution of Peru [31.12.1993].

16 Art. 73. (3) of the Constitution of Romania [08.12.1991].

17 The Constitution of Moldova, Art. 61. (2), Art. 63. (1) and (3), Art. 70. (2), Art. 72. (3) and (4), Art. 74. (1), Art. 78. (2), Art. 80. (3), Art. 97, Art. 99. (2), Art. 108. (2), Art. 111. (1) and (2), Art. 115. (4), Art. 133. (5) [29.07.1994].

18 14/B/2002. ruling of the Hungarian Constitutional Court, ABH 2003, Pp. 1476, 4/1993. (II.12.) ruling of the Hungarian Constitutional Court, ABH 1993, Pp. 48.

19 Art. 4. (5), Art. 5. (8), and Art. 7. (3) of the Fundamental Law of Hungary [25.04.2011].

Court,[20] on the general accounting office,[21] on the National Bank,[22] and on the organization of the judiciary[23] shall be adopted by two-thirds majority of the deputies present.

The present study focuses on the fundamental rights protection aspect of qualified legislative majority; however, this could not be assessed in an isolated way. Consequently, the institutional side will be also concerned in certain respects, as an indirect tool for the protection of fundamental rights.

Scope of qualified legislation

After having elaborated a cursory glance on the organic laws of the world, now I turn to those circumstances, which entail general introduction to this legal concept. First, some very brief points would be provided from the French and the Spanish background, as these two countries are really influential worldwide in this regard. Then, the relevant Central European experience will be conceptualized, which gives us some insight, on why the function of qualified laws in the field of fundamental rights protection have been deemed as significant in Central Europe. Finally, certain statements will be provided from the Austrian constitutional framework, which contains elements that had a crucial impact on the development of Central European qualified laws. However, the Austrian development entails inherently different constitutional challenges, than the Hungarian, Romanian, and Moldovan context.

In France, organic laws were introduced by De Gaulle, who highlighted the institutional aspect, and almost neglected the role of organic laws as an instrument for rights protection (Acher 2012). Owing to this approach, the French organic laws cover mostly the basic institutional framework of the state (Troper 2008, 13). On the contrary, in Spain, certain balance is applied between the fundamental rights and the institutional approach.[24] Contrary to France, in Spain, a broad circle of fundamental rights are

20 Art. 24. (8) of the Fundamental Law of Hungary [25.04.2011].
21 Art. 43. (4) of the Fundamental Law of Hungary [25.04.2011].
22 Art. 41. (6) of the Fundamental Law of Hungary [25.04.2011].
23 Art. 25. (8) of the Fundamental Law of Hungary [25.04.2011].
24 SJCC 76/1983, of 5 August, LC 2; 160/1987, of 27 October LC 2.

regulated by organic laws.[25] The Spanish Constitutional Court has elaborated consequently a restrictive interpretation of the organic legislative domain to avoid the unnecessary limitation on the governmental margin of appreciation (Barceló y Serramalera 2004, 30–31).

In the following, I will focus on the comparison of the Hungarian, the Romanian, and the Moldovan experience.

During the democratic transition, the huge fear from the unlimited governmental power constituted a crucial factor, generated by the memories from the communist period.

This was a key consideration, which explains the introduction of organic laws in these countries (Bozóki 1999, 2478). Political transition may often lead to extended violence, or even armed conflicts; therefore, a further target was to exclude violent incidents, or at least take immediate control over aggressive tendencies (Elster 2012, 7–9, 21–37).

Despite certain similarities, the historical background differs remarkably in the three relevant Central European countries. In Romania, the drafters of the Constitution could not rely on national traditions – one could refer only to a document from the middle of the nineteenth century, which was called "organic law of Romania." However, this organic law had a constitutional status, rather than a distinguished form of legislation.[26] Nevertheless, the French, and in certain respects the German, the Italian and the Belgian constitutional systems were also influential during the drafting of the Romanian democratic framework (Deleanu 2006, 220). Apart from this, from the 1980s, the Romanian society had several direct and painful experiences from the overbroad power of the dictatorship, with systematic and serious breaches of fundamental rights. In Romania, instead of peaceful means, the transition was achieved by a revolution. This situation required serious carefulness from the drafters of the new Constitution: several legal instruments were considered, which could promote the stability of the constitutional system. Romania is thus the

25 JCC no. 236/2007.

26 On the basis of the interview with Prof. Simina Elena Tanasescu, and Prof. Stefan Deaconu, lecturers of the Constitutional Law Department at the University of Bucharest. [Bucharest, 23.01.2017].

only European country, where qualified laws were implemented to the Constitution shortly after an armed conflict.

In Moldova, local constitutional traditions were apparently irrelevant, since an independent Moldovan State just existed during the last period of World War I, and even then only for some months (Lengyel 2011, 55). As a consequence, the foreign models were highlighted: In reality, the structure and the logic of the Romanian Constitution dominated the Moldovan constitution-making process (Carnat 2005, 129–130). It is also worth noting that the Moldovan society was divided by a great number of conflicts during the process of the democratic transition: the tensions between the Romanian and the Russian population, the claim for independence from the Transnistrian Territory, as well as the autonomous status of Gagauzia were also controversial issues. In the light of these concerns, it may have been justifiable to require a higher level of parliamentary majority for the adoption of organic laws. However, it should be also noted that according to certain Moldovan experts, during the constitution-making process, the aforementioned conflicts and risk factors had not yet been identified; therefore, these considerations did not influence the introduction of organic laws. The representatives of this theory claim that Moldovan organic laws were introduced due to the strong Romanian and Russian impact, and several other legal arguments were also raised.[27]

The Hungarian case is more complex in this regard, as it originates from the era of the historical constitutional development (Marczali 1907, 110) from before 1945, when the so-called cardinal laws were the cornerstones of the Hungarian constitutional framework (Hajnóczy 1958, 236–240). Nevertheless, the scope of cardinal laws was not outlined precisely, and these laws were subject to the same legislative procedure, as ordinary acts (Ferdinándy 1902, 77). In 1989, the six laws that determined the character of the democratic transition were also often summarized as "cardinal laws" (Antal et al. 2011, 5). Almost simultaneously with this development, the category of laws with constitutional force was established to supplement the democratic constitution: Similar to the constitution, for

27 On the basis of the interview made with Prof. Violeta Cojocaru, the leader of the Constitutional Law Department of the University of Chisinau. [Chisinau, 14.09.2017].

the adoption or amendment of these laws, the two-third majority consent of all parliamentary members was required.[28] According to the contemporary approach, all legal rules, which concern fundamental rights, were to be covered by laws with constitutional force. However, the overbroad application of qualified majority requirement thereby undermined the governance of the country, since almost all legislative fields concern – at least indirectly – fundamental rights (Antal et al. 2011). The qualified majority requirement was thus stricter in 1989, than nowadays. A wider circle of laws fell within its scope, than currently, under the Fundamental Law of Hungary. The concept of laws with constitutional force was thereby created to decrease uncertainty: the participants of the political arena could not foresee the outcome of the forthcoming parliamentary elections, and the intentions of the future winners. As a consequence, almost every political actor had strong interest to establish an inclusive legislative process (Szalai 2011).

Since the distortive effect of the overbroad qualified majority requirement was recognized generally, after the first democratic elections, during the spring of 1990, the new government and the opposition concluded a compromise to reduce the domain of qualified laws. The "laws with constitutional force" were replaced by the terminology of "laws adopted with two-thirds majority," and the qualified legislative subject matters were more or less exhaustively enumerated by the Constitution.[29] Instead of the "large qualified majority," only the two-thirds majority consent of those deputies was prescribed, who participated in the particular vote. This solution was close to the Spanish logic, which is based on a proper balance between the rights protection and the institutional approach (Chofre Sirvent 1994, 59–61).

On January 1, 2012, the Fundamental Law of Hungary entered into effect, highlighting the historical traditions by reinstating the term of "cardinal law," albeit the current content of this expression is not equivalent to the historical meaning (Barna and Szentgáli-Tóth 2013). Currently, the cardinal subject matters are enumerated exhaustively by the Fundamental Law (Bodnár and Módos 2012, 33–34). The required majority is always

28 Art. 8. of Act XXXI. of 1989.
29 Act XL. of 1990.

the two-thirds majority consent of the parliamentarians present. However, the fundamental rights have almost disappeared from the list of cardinal fields under the new constitutional framework (Szentgáli-Tóth 2012). The current Hungarian interpretation is thus close to the French as well as to the Romanian/Moldovan approach, since the institutional side is dominant, and only a little number of fundamental rights, and a narrow circle of indirect safeguards for fundamental rights protection is regulated by cardinal laws (Jakab 2014).

Hungary is a special model of qualified legislation, because during less than 30 years, at least three different models of qualified law have been introduced. While in other countries, the established version of qualified law – with its advantages and weaknesses – determines the constitutional development during long decades, Hungary has experienced the regular reconsideration of the qualified law concept (Kukorelli 2006, 155).

The Hungarian, the Romanian, and the Moldovan systems differ remarkably as regards the relevant procedural rules. In Romania, following the French model, the absolute majority of both chambers is required instead of the two-thirds majority of the deputies present.[30] A further difference should also be taken into consideration: Any governmental decree could intervene in the organic domain only on the basis of parliamentary authorization. The urgent decrees might be approved by the Parliament a posteriori, but these legal instruments could not interfere with the organic domain (Vida 2006, 52–62).

Concerning the level of required majority, similar logic is applied in Moldova. However, the Moldovan Parliament is a unicameral legislative body. Apart from this, the parliamentary stage of the organic legislative process is subject to stricter rules than the ordinary legislation.[31]

The Hungarian Parliament is also unicameral, but only "small two-thirds consent" is prescribed for the adoption and the amendment of these laws.[32]

---

30 Art. 76. (1) of the Constitution of Romania [08.12.1991].
31 Art. 74. (1) of the Constitution of Moldova [29.07.1994].
32 Art. T. (4) of the Fundamental Law of Hungary [25.04.2011].

Specificities of qualified legislation

In reality, the organic legislative process is not a unitary concept in most of the relevant constitutional systems. In France, certain organic laws have a quasi-constitutional status (De Duy Braibant 1996), while in Spain, the organic laws from autonomous regions are subject to stricter legislative procedure, than other organic laws (mandatory a priori constitutional review is required) (Sosa Wagner 1979, 199–204). A similar tendency may be experienced in Moldova, where the autonomous status of Gagauzia is covered by an organic law, which shall be adopted or amended by three-fifths parliamentary majority instead of the mere absolute majority.[33] The Hungarian concept also applies procedural distinction between qualified laws. The "small two-thirds requirement" means the two-thirds majority of the deputies present, while the "large two-thirds majority" means the two-thirds majority consent of all parliamentarians.[34] In the light of the abovementioned examples, there is a widespread tendency to make procedural distinction between qualified laws; however, fundamental rights are not concerned by this issue. One cannot identify constitutional systems, where the special qualified laws would only cover fundamental rights.

As it was stated earlier, the two main branches of qualified legislation deal with the institutional and the fundamental rights aspect.[35] The institutional aspect is not analyzed here in depth; however, in almost all relevant legal systems, the extra-constitutional rules on the functioning, on the organization, and on the relationships of basic state institutions shall be covered by qualified laws. Among the qualified subject matters, one may find fundamental rights, and the regulation of those institutions, which play key role as to the protection of fundamental rights. In my view, this ambiguity may be interpreted as the two levels of rights protection by qualified laws. The direct level constitutes that certain fundamental rights shall be covered by qualified law, while the indirect aspect provides that the rules on the constitutional court, on the ombudsman, on the judicial

33 Art. 111. (7) of the Constitution of Moldova [29.07.1994].
34 Art. E. (4) of the Fundamental Law of Hungary [25.04.2011].
35 1/1999. (II. 24.) ruling of the Hungarian Constitutional Court, ABH 1999, 25.

system, and on the status of judges shall be adopted by qualified majority, as a safeguard of independence.

As the historical references demonstrate well, the scope of qualified law is reconsidered regularly in Hungary; however, at the moment, the Hungarian, the Romanian, and the Moldovan solutions are relatively close to each other: All three constitutional systems operate with qualified laws only in a very narrow scope as a tool for the direct protection of fundamental rights. Two examples may be mentioned here: the freedom of religion[36] and the right to citizenship.[37]

The qualified majority requirement concerns not only, and not primarily, the fundamental rights, but also such institutions, which guarantee the prevalence of human rights. In the Hungarian, Romanian, and Moldovan Constitutions, three such institutions are included within the qualified legislative domain: the constitutional court, the ombudsman, and the judicial system. In reality, qualified laws play even a more complex role as an indirect safeguard for the protection of fundamental rights: For instance, in Romania and Moldova, the system of public education is also considered as a field of qualified legislation.[38]

Despite the fact that these common points seemingly explain in which circle qualified laws influence the protection of fundamental rights in Central Europe, the effective functioning of the system could not be understood without analyzing such techniques, by which the bounds of the qualified legislative domain are identified.

The Hungarian Fundamental Law introduced a new system to make a more coherent distinction between qualified and ordinary provisions. The Fundamental Law provides that the detailed, or the fundamental, rules of certain subject matters shall be adopted by two-thirds majority (Schmidt 2013). Since according to the jurisprudence of the Constitutional Court,

36 Art. XIX. (3) of the Fundamental Law of Hungary [25.04.2011], Art. 73. (3) point S. of the Constitution of Romania [08.12.1991], Art. 72. (3) point K) of the Constitution of Moldova [29.07.1994].

37 Art. G) (4) of the Fundamental Law of Hungary [25.04.2011], Art. 5. (1) of the Constitution of Romania [08.12.1991], Art. 17. (1) of the Constitution of Moldova [29.07.1994].

38 Art. 73. (3) point N) of the Constitution of Romania [08.12.1991], Art. 72. (3) point K) of the Constitution of Moldova [29.07.1994].

the same law may contain qualified and ordinary provisions as well,[39] in such laws, which contain cardinal provisions, a cardinal clause shall be incorporated. The Constitutional Court has the competence to review the constitutionality of cardinal clauses: for instance, to verify whether the cardinal provisions of the act on citizenship are equivalent to the term of "detailed rules on citizenship."[40]

The Fundamental Law thereby does not provide a separate list of cardinal subject matters. Instead of this, several constitutional articles refer to the qualified majority requirement. The Fundamental Law does not constitute a legal hierarchy between cardinal and ordinary laws at all – this approach is discussed and contested regularly (Cserne and Jakab 2015, 40–47). The Constitutional Court has issued several rulings, which analyze the legal relationship between the two categories of law, and the boundary between the cardinal and the ordinary domain have been also under scrutiny.[41]

Art. 73. of the Constitution of Romania prescribes most of the qualified subject matters; however, several other legislative fields are also classified by the Constitution as "organic." The scope of organic law is remarkably broader in Romania, than in Hungary. Each act declares whether it is an organic or an ordinary law; however, both types of provisions may coexist within the same act. The Romanian Constitutional Court made several times a clear distinction between organic and ordinary provisions within the same legal text.[42]

---

39 55/2010. (V. 5.) ruling of the Hungarian Constitutional Court, ABH 2010, 366.

40 As an example for this logic, please see: 17/2013. (VI. 26.) rulings of the Hungarian Constitutional Court, ABH 2013, 583; 16/2015. (VI. 5.) ruling of the Hungarian Constitutional Court, ABK 09.06.2015, 741.

41 As examples, please see: 5/1990. (IV. 9.) ruling of the Hungarian Constitutional Court, ABH 1990, 32.; 26/1992. (IV. 30.) ruling of the Hungarian Constitutional Court, ABH 1992, 135.; 4/1993. (II. 12.) ruling of the Hungarian Constitutional Court, ABH 1993, 48.; 54/1996. (XI. 30.) ruling of the Hungarian Constitutional Court, ABH 1996, 173.; 66/1997. (XII. 29.) ruling of the Hungarian Constitutional Court, ABH 1997, 397.; 48/2001. (XI. 22.) ruling of the Hungarian Constitutional Court, ABH 2001, 330.; 27/2008. (III. 12.) ruling of the Hungarian Constitutional Court, ABH 2008, 289.

42 For the demonstration of the relevant Romanian jurisprudence please see: Decision of Constitutional Court no 88/2.06.1998, Official Gazette no 207/3.06.1998; Decision of Constitutional Court no 442/10.06.2015,

The scope of Romanian organic law is considerably wider, than its Hungarian counterpart, but the required level of majority is lower, so the legal consequences are less serious. In Romania and Moldova, the civil code, the criminal code, and further codes, which cover a wide range of social relationships, are also considered as organic laws. In Hungary, these laws are not classified as cardinal, because it is claimed that this categorization would exclude even the most necessary amendments of these codes.

As regards Moldova, it shall be noted that the real circle of organic laws may not be identified on the sole basis of the constitutional text (Carnat 2005, 114–115, 129–130). An enumeration of organic subject matters is provided by Art. 72(3) of the Constitution of Moldova, but other constitutional articles also declare further fields of organic legislation.[43] The Parliament has also the possibility to adopt organic laws on such matters, which are not listed by the Constitution as required fields of organic legislation. In such case, the organic character of the act shall be provided expressly.[44] This margin of decision of the Parliament is not only a theoretical issue: On the basis of this competence, the Parliament has adopted organic law on the general prosecutor, organization of armed forces, status of the judiciary, lawyers, and national security services.[45]

In practical terms, this means that the hierarchy of legal sources is based on the Constitution and on organic laws, and the organic character shall be considered as usual in Moldova rather than exceptional. The scope of Moldovan organic law may be described as overbroad – consequently, the number and significance of ordinary laws is lower than elsewhere. This background clarifies why the necessity of organic law has not been contested in Moldova. Similarly, the supreme legal effect of organic law over ordinary law is beyond doubts. For this reason, organic law is often considered a safeguard, as a prolongment of the Constitution, while the

Official Gazette no 526/15.07.2015; Decision of Constitutional Court no 568/15.09.2015, Official Gazette no 844/12.11.2015; Decision of Constitutional Court no 622/13.10.2016, Official Gazette no 60/20.01.2017.

43 Art. 72. (3) point P) of the Constitution of Moldova [29.07.1994].

44 Art. 72. (3) point R) of the Constitution of Moldova [29.07.1994].

45 On the basis of the interview made by Teodor Carnat, the member of the Judicial Council of Moldova and the professor of the Constitutional Law Department in the State University of Moldova [Chisinau, 14.09.2017].

unwanted or distortive consequences are almost neglected.[46] Under the Moldovan jurisprudence, only the substantial constitutionality of organic laws might be dubious, and the formal legal character of organic law is not assessed in depth.[47]

Austrian model

Some paragraphs of this contribution shall be also devoted to the Austrian experience, which constitutes a different model of implementation of qualified legislation. The Austrian system does not operate explicitly with any terminology of qualified law, but in practice, the internal structure of the Austrian Constitution implies certain components of qualified legislation. The Austrian constitutional framework is a multilayer and inherently fragmented concept, which makes a clear difference between ordinary legislative provisions and those statutory articles, which are vested with quasi-constitutional force. The Austrian Federal Constitution is composed of numerous federal acts, starting from the 1867 Grundgesetz[48] and the 1920 Federal Constitutional Act. The international conventions of constitutional rank (for instance, the European Convention on Human Rights) and the statutory provisions with constitutional force should be also mentioned: To demonstrate this distinction between the two categories of legal norms, the first paragraph of the act on data protection is a quasi-constitutional norm, while the second paragraph of the same act is an ordinary statutory provision. From our perspective, this ambiguity is a relevant point here (Jakab 2010, 142).

Moreover, in Austria, any amendment to the constitutional framework should not be passed always as constitutional amendments. Therefore, the constitutional concept does not provide for a transparent and coherent

46 On the basis of the interview made with Rodica Secrieru, the general secretary of the Constitutional Court of Moldova [Chisinau, 15.09.2017].

47 For example, please see: Decision no. 36. of 2013. of the Constitutional Court of Moldova [05.12.2013].

48 A Birodalmi Tanácsban képviselt királyságok és országok polgárai általános jogairól szóló Állami Alaptörvény 1867. December 21. (Staatsgrundgesetz vom 21.12.1867 über die allgemeinen Rechte der Staatsbürger für die im Reichsrathe vertretenen Königreiche und Länder).

system of norms of the whole legal system. During the coalitional periods, it was a generally accepted practice that the two-thirds parliamentary majority amended the constitutional framework unilaterally, by vesting certain statutory provisions with quasi-constitutional force, instead of amending the constitutional documents themselves. This tendency has not been relevant during the last years, though. These considerations explain why the Austrian literature operates with the concept of unconstitutional constitutional law, and why the Austrian Constitutional Court is entitled to review the constitutional amendments substantially.[49]

The Austrian constitutional development has a special historical background due to certain continuity with the constitutional design of the Austrian Empire. Furthermore, despite the geographical proximity, the country fell outside from the socialist sphere of interest. As a consequence, those elements of the Austrian constitutional framework, which are close to the concept of qualified law, have not been implemented to secure democratic transition by peaceful means, but rather to complement an inherently fragmented, historically entrenched constitutional surrounding. Due to these differences, the Austrian experience does not constitute a separate model of Central European qualified laws, but it should be assessed as a close point of reference for those lawyers and politicians, who argued for the introduction of qualified laws in Hungary, Romania, and Moldova.[50] Apart from this, the Austrian statutory provisions with quasi-constitutional force play a significant role in protecting certain fundamental rights, which in fact inspired the Hungarian and Romanian drafters to consider qualified majority as a potential safeguard for the protection of fundamental rights and human dignity.

Qualified legislation in Central Europe

On the basis of this brief comparison, one may argue that qualified law is a proper instrument to strengthen the protection of fundamental rights in the post-communist countries of Central Europe. In my view, at least two

49 VfSlg 11.756 (1988); VfSlg 11.829 (1988); VfSlg 11.916 (1988); VfGH 11.10.2001, G 12/00.

50 The oral statement of István Somogyvári, a former Hungarian secretary of state during a personal interview made with him on 27 October 2016.

historical situations should be distinguished clearly at this point. The qualified law requirement enforced the consensual legislation, meaning this was a crucial peaceful means to promote the democratic transition in Hungary, Romania, and in Moldova. This may have been a model to follow by other states of the region as well. Furthermore, during the democratic transition, the Central European states were not bound by a series of international agreements and memberships in organizations for the protection of fundamental rights, and the internal institutional framework of these states often failed to enforce effectively and predictably the fundamental rights. In contrast, now several international agreements provide standards and legal duties for Central European countries, and well-organized state and civil institutions monitor the reality of fundamental rights closely so that the relevant political parties would not undermine the democratic character of the constitutional framework, and would not establish an authoritarian regime.

However, the recent Hungarian and Romanian experience raises the following issue: In the hands of a strong parliamentary majority, qualified law could function easily as an instrument to fix governmental policies for long-term periods. It would be difficult, or almost impossible, to amend rules adopted with qualified majority. In the light of these considerations, during the democratic transition, the implementation of a broad qualified law concept was justifiable; however, among the current circumstances, the same logic would result in unjustifiably serious limitation of the margin of appreciation of the respective states and governments.

Strong arguments support the idea that qualified laws may be valuable parts of the Central European constitutional systems, especially with regard to protection of human rights, but the unnecessary distortion of the parliamentarism should thereby be avoided. When qualified law is introduced in any field of legislation, the particular law should not be able to be enacted without oppositional votes.

Finally, I will provide certain points on qualified law as a migrating constitutional idea within the Central European region.[51] In my view, we should clearly distinguish at this stage the external and the internal

51 Regarding the general tendencies of circulation of constitutional ideas, see Choudry (2006, 1–35).

direction of the constitutional migration. On the one hand, qualified law has been such a constitutional solution, which has been borrowed from foreign, mostly Western European models. But this implementation meant not a mere copy of external frameworks – it adapted a globally acknowledged legal concept to the local circumstances, which vary remarkably from country to country. Moreover, the introduction of the new constitutional idea is strongly attached to a particular historical situation, and it is also influenced considerably by the long-term historical tradition of each country.

The constitutional migration has also an internal aspect, which demonstrates how the path of qualified law advanced within the Central European region. The similar historical moment in the countries of the region explains why the almost parallel introduction of this constitutional concept took place. Nevertheless, it was also important that the three countries (Hungary, Romania, and Moldova) inspired each other as well. Qualified law spread from the West towards the East, but it might be an exaggeration to describe this as a conscientious or coherent process. Qualified law was introduced firstly in Hungary in the Autumn of 1989. The Hungarian decision relied on the West European (French and Spanish) and the Austrian model, while the historical predecessors from the medieval centuries were also relevant. It seems that, for the Romanian drafters, the Hungarian implementation of qualified legislation in 1989 was not an important point of reference. The Romanian constitution-making process had a special regard to the French development, which brought the idea of organic law into the Romanian constitutional discourse. Two years after the Romanian introduction of organic law, this legal category appeared also in the Constitution of Moldova. It is beyond doubt that this constituted an almost direct and automatic transfer from the Romanian practice; however, certain Moldovan experts relativized this explanation and highlighted other constitutional and political considerations, which motivated the implementation of organic law in Moldova.

Conclusions

To summarize, how this brief assessment could contribute to the discussion on Central European constitutional migration, it is deemed that this region mostly relies on West European theoretic concepts. However, the Central European countries do not copy West European solutions automatically. Moreover, in certain respects, the local traditions play down or at least amend remarkably the exported concepts. There are logical and historical similarities between the Central European constitutional frameworks, but their development is independent from each other, and their external influence is stronger than their interdependence.

After having considered each relevant argument, on the basis of the Hungarian, Romanian, and Moldovan models, my point is the following: Qualified law should play a crucial role as an indirect tool for the protection of fundamental rights. The relevant institutions (such as the constitutional court, the ombudsman, and the judicial system) should be covered by qualified laws. Nevertheless, for the fundamental rights themselves, the simple legislative majority would constitute sufficient safeguard – this solution would combine proper structural guarantees with a reasonable governmental margin of decision.

The present study provided an overview from the Central European experience of qualified legislation. In this region, the historical role of qualified majority requirement was to support the inherently peaceful character of the post-communist democratic transitions. Nevertheless, qualified law might be influential in the field of human rights protection, even nowadays: Among other institutional guarantees, qualified law would enhance the general level of rights protection. Still, bearing this in mind, it is recommended to outline and interpret the scope of qualified law in a restrictive way, to preserve the logic of parliamentarism.

This study forms part of the research project NKFIH no. 128796. "The Normative Content of the Principle of Democracy – in Practice and Theory from a Constitutional Law and European Union Law Perspective."

References

Acher, Philip. 2012. Le Parlement en France. [The Parliament in France]. *Etude (broché)*, (8) : 11–23.

Antal, Attila, Braun, István, Finta, László, Török, Zoltán. 2011. Sarkalatos kérdések. [Cardinal issues]. *Méltányosság Politikaelemző*

Központ, 24.11.2011. [www.meltanyossag.hu/files/meltany/imce/doc/kp_sarkalatos_kerdesek_111122.pdf; accessed on 13.11.2017].

Avril, Pierre, Gicquel, Jean. 2014. *Droit parlamentaire.* [Parliamentary law]. Paris: Dalloz.

Barceló i Serramalera, Merce. 2004. *La ley Organica ámbito material y posición en el systema de fuentes.* [Organic laws, and their status within the hierarchy of norms]. Barcelona: Atelier Libros Juridicos.

Barna, Dániel, Szentgáli-Tóth, Boldizsár. 2013. Stabilitás vagy Parlamentarizmus? A sarkalatos törvényekkel kapcsolatos egyes jogalkotási problémák. [Stability or parliamentarism? Certain constitutional issues concerning cardinal laws]. *Ars Boni Law Review,* 14.02.2013.

Bodnár, Eszter, Módos, Mátyás. 2012. A jogalkotás normatív kereteinek változásai az új jogalkotási törvény elfogadása óta. [The normative framework of law-making under the new act on legislation]. *Kodifikáció,* 2012(1).

Bozóki, András (ed.). 1999. *The Roundtable Talks of 1989: The Genesis of Hungarian Democracy.* Budapest: Central European University Press.

Camby, Jean-Pierre. 1998. Quarante ans de lois organiques. [Forty years of organic laws]. *Revue de droit publique,* 1998, 5(6) : 1686–1698.

Carnat, Teodor. 2005. *Constitutional Law.* Chisinau: State University of Chisinau.

Chofre Sirvent, José F. 1994. *Significado y función de las leyes orgánicas.* [The functions and significance of organic laws]. Madrid: Tecnos.

Choudhry, Sujit (ed.). 2006. *The Migration of Constitutional Ideas.* Cambridge: Cambridge University Press.

Conversi, Daniele. 2002. The smooth transition. *National Identities,* 4(3): 223–244.

Cserne, Péter, András, Jakab. 2015. A kétharmados törvények helye a magyar jogforrásihierarchiában [The place of laws with two-thirds majority within the hierarchy of norms]. *Fundamentum,* 2001(2): 40–47

David, René. 1964. *Les grands systemes de droit contemporains.* [The major legal systems of the world]. Paris: Dalloz.

Deleanu, Ioan. 2006. *Institutii si proceduri constitutionale.* [Constitutional procedures and institutions]. Bucuresti: C.H. Beck.

Elster, John. 2012. Constitution-making and violence. *Journal of Legal Analysis* 4: 7–39.

Ferdinándy, Géza. 1902. *Magyarország közjoga.* [The public law of Hungary]. Budapest: Politzer Zsigmond és Fia kiadása.

Genevois, Bruno. 1996. Normes de références du contrôle de constitutionnalité et respect de la hiérarchie en leur sein. [Reference norms for constitutional review, and the respect of hierarchy of norms]. In *L´Etat de droit Mélanges en l´honneur de Guy Braibant.* Paris: Dalloz.

Hajnóczy, József. 1958. [1791]. Magyarország Országgyűléséről. [From the parliament of Hungary]. In *Hajnóczy József közjogi-politikai munkái.* Budapest: Akadémiai Kiadó, 1958.

Jakab, András. 2010. Az európai alkotmányjogi gondolkodás két szembenálló paradigmája: Ausztria és Németország. In Chronowski, Nóra, Petrétei, József: *Tanulmányok Ádám Antal professor emeritus születésének 80. évfordulójára – emlékkönyv.* Pécs: PTE ÁJK.

Jakab, András, Szilágyi, Emese. 2014. Sarkalatos törvények a magyar jogrendszerben. [Cardinal laws in the Hungarian legal system.] *Új MagyarKözigazgatás,* 2014(3): 96–110.

Kilényi, Géza. 1994. Az alkotmányozási folyamat és a kétharmados törvények. [The constitution-making process and the qualified laws.] *Jogtudományi Szemle,* 1994(5): 201–209.

Kukorelli, István. 2006. *Tradíció és modernizáció a magyar alkotmányjogban.* [Tradition and modernization in the Hungarian constitutional law]. Budapest: Századvég Kiadó, 2006.

Küpper, Herbert. 2014. A kétharmados/sarkalatos törvények jelensége a magyar jogrendszerben. [Cardinal laws in the Hungarian legal system]. *MTA Law Working Papers,* 2014/46.

Lengyel, László. 2011. *A Moldáv Köztársaság.* [The Moldovan Republic]. Budapest: Magyar Moldáv Baráti Társaság.

Leyland, Peter. 2012. *The Constitution of the United Kingdom: A Contextual Analysis.* Portland, OR: Hart Publishing.

Marczali, Henrik. 1907. *Az 1790/1-diki országgyűlés.* [The Hungarian Parliament in 1790, and act I. of 1790]. Budapest: A Magyar Tudományos Akadémia Kiadása.

Schmidt, Péter. 2013. *A sarkalatos törvények dilemmája* [The issue of cardinal laws]. [szalaykor.blog.hu/2013/05/15/dr_schmidt_peter_a_sarkalatos_torvenyek_dilemmaja; accessed on 14.11.2017].

Sosa Wagner, Francisco. 1979. Aproximación al tema de las leyes orgánicas. [Introduction to the system of organic laws]. *Revista española de derecho administrativo,* No. 21: 199–204.

Szalai, András. 2011. *A kormányzati hatalom ellensúlyai Magyarországon.* [The counterbalances of the government in Hungary]. [www.propublicobono.hu/pdf/Szalai_2.pdf, accessed on 13.11.2017].

Szentgáli-Tóth, Boldizsár. 2012. Alapjogok új alapokon? (társszerzőkkel) [Fundamental rights on new basis?]. In *Változások a magyar alkotmányjogban. Tanulmányok az Alaptörvényről.* [The Hungarian constitutional reform: studies from the Fundamental Law of Hungary]. Budapest: FÁMA Zrt. - Nemzeti Közszolgálati és Tankönyv Kiadó, 2012: 53–79.

Troper, Michel. 2008. Constitutional Law. In *Introduction to French Law.* Alphen aan den Rijn: Kluwer Law International: 1–34.

Troper, Michel, Chagnollaud, Dominique. (ed.). 2012. *Traite international de droit constitutionnel.* (Az alkotmányjog nemzetközi alapjai) vol. 1. Paris: Dalloz.

Vida, Ioan. 2006. *Legistica formala.* [Formal legislation]. Bucharest: Lumina Lex.

List of relevant constitutional documents:The Constitution of Algeria [15.05.1996.]: www.constituteproject.org/constitution/Algeria_2016.pdf?lang=en

The Constitution of Angola [21.01.2010.]: www.wipo.int/edocs/lexdocs/laws/en/ao/ao001en.pdf

The Constitution of Benin [02.12.1990.]: www.constituteproject.org/constitution/Benin_1990.pdf?lang=en

The Constitution of Burkina Faso [02.06.1991.]: www.constituteproject.org/constitution/Burkina_Faso_2012.pdf?lang=en

The Constitution of Burundi [28.02.2005.]: www.constituteproject.org/constitution/Burundi_2005.pdf

The Constitution of Cape Verde Islands [1980]: www.constituteproject.org/constitution/Cape_Verde_1992.pdf?lang=en

The Constitution of the Central-African Republic [27.12.2004.]: www.constituteproject.org/constitution/Central_African_Republic_2010.pdf

The Constitution of Chad: [1996]: www.constituteproject.org/constitution/Chad_2005.pdf

The Constitution of Chile [21.10.1980.] www.constituteproject.org/constitution/Chile_2015.pdf?lang=en

The Constitution of Colombia [04.07.1991.] www.constituteproject.org/constitution/Colombia_2005.pdf

The Constitution of the Comoros Islands [23.12.2001.] www.constituteproject.org/constitution/Comoros_2009.pdf

The Constitution of the Democratic Republic of Congo [18.02.2006.]: www.constituteproject.org/constitution/Democratic_Republic_of_the_Congo_2011.pdf?lang=en

The Constitution of the Dominican Republic [13.06.2015.]: www.constituteproject.org/constitution/Dominican_Republic_2015.pdf?lang=en

The Constitution of Djibouti [1992.]: www.constituteproject.org/constitution/Djibouti_2010.pdf?lang=en

The Constitution of Ecuador [28.09.2008.] pdba.georgetown.edu/Constitutions/Ecuador/english08.html

The Constitution of Equatorial Guinea [1991]: www.constituteproject.org/constitution/Equatorial_Guinea_2012.pdf?lang=en

The Constitution of Ivory Coast [08.11.2016.] www.constituteproject.org/constitution/Cote_DIvoire_2016.pdf?lang=en

The Constitution of France [04.10.1958.] www.constituteproject.org/constitution/France_2008.pdf?lang=en

The Constitution of Gabon [1991.]: www.constituteproject.org/constitution/Gabon_2011.pdf?lang=en

The Constitution of Guinea [07.05.2010.] www.constituteproject.org/constitution/Guinea_2010.pdf?lang=en

The Fundamental Law of Hungary [25.04.2011.]: www.constituteproject.org/constitution/Hungary_2011.pdf

The Constitution of Italy [22.12.1947.]: www.constituteproject.org/constitution/Italy_2012.pdf?lang=en

The Constitution of Madagascar [14.11.2010.]: www.constituteproject.org/constitution/Madagascar_2010.pdf

The Constitution of Morocco [01.07.2011.]www.constituteproject.org/constitution/Morocco_2011.pdf

The Constitution of Mauritania [12.07.1991.] www.constituteproject.org/constitution/Mauritania_2012.pdf

The Constitution of Moldova [29.07.1994.]: www.constituteproject.org/constitution/Moldova_2006.pdf?lang=en

The Constitution of Niger[31.10.2010.]: www.constituteproject.org/constitution/Niger_2010.pdf

The Constitution of Panama [1972.]: www.constituteproject.org/constitution/Panama_2004.pdf?lang=en;

The Constitution of Peru [31.12.1993.]: www.constituteproject.org/constitution/Peru_2009.pdf?lang=en

The Constitution of Portugal [02.04.1976.] www.constituteproject.org/constitution/Portugal_2005.pdf

The Constitution of the Republic of Congo [2001.]: *constituteproject.org/constitution/Congo_2015.pdf?lang=en*

The Constitution of Romania [08.12.1991.]: www.constituteproject.org/constitution/Romania_2003.pdf?lang=en

The Constitution of Rwanda [30.05.1991.] www.constituteproject.org/constitution/Rwanda_2015.pdf?lang=en

The Constitution of Senegal [07.01.2001.] www.constituteproject.org/constitution/Senegal_2009.pdf?lang=en

The Constitution of Spain [07.01.1978] www.constituteproject.org/constitution/Spain_2011.pdf?lang=en

The Constitution of Togo [14.10.1992.] www.constituteproject.org/constitution/Togo_2007.pdf?lang=en

The Constitution of Tunisia [26.01.2014.] www.constituteproject.org/constitution/Tunisia_2014.pdf

The Constitution of Venezuela [20.12.1999.] www.constituteproject.org/constitution/Venezuela_2009.pdf?lang=en

Marin Keršić

University of Split

Proportionality and balancing in the practice of the Constitutional Court of Croatia from the theoretical framework of Robert Alexy

Abstract: Proportionality analysis plays a key role nowadays in the area of constitutional adjudication. The related notion of balancing, a method of solving conflicts between constitutional rights is of similar importance. Proportionality norms can be found in constitutions, and they play an important role in the practice of the constitutional courts of some legal systems. For example, Article 16 of the Croatian Constitution is an example of the so-called balancing regulating norm. The chapter deals with proportionality in the Croatian legal system through an analysis of two cases from its recent Constitutional Court practice. Besides being a descriptive endeavour, the main objective of the chapter is to compare the theory regarding proportionality and balancing by applying Alexy's theoretical framework on the constitutional court practice to determine the degree of the connection between them in the Croatian legal system.

Keywords: Proportionality, balancing, Robert Alexy, Croatia

Introduction

The topic of this chapter is proportionality and balancing, and it aims to analyse the degree to which they are applicable (as elaborated in Alexy's work) in the practice of the Constitutional Court of Croatia. The structure of the chapter is as follows: first, general remarks regarding normative conflicts between constitutional norms and their structure are presented; second, the principle of proportionality and balancing as a method of solving conflicts between constitutional norms will be presented; third, a reference to the Croatian legal system and its constitution and an analysis of two cases from its constitutional court practice regarding proportionality and balancing will be made. Finally, the chapter ends with conclusions, which aim to answer the main question posed: What is the relation between the principle of proportionality and balancing in theory understood in Alexy's way, and practice of the Constitutional Court in the Republic of Croatia?

1. Normative conflicts

Proportionality and balancing, generally defined, are methods for solving certain types of normative conflicts. The idea of a legal system entails the normative regulation of human behaviour. But since legal systems are in practice fraught with normative inconsistencies, normative conflicts necessarily appear. Resolving such inconsistencies is one of the central aspects of any legal system, in order to ensure legal certainty and provide predictability, at least to some extent (Alchourrón 1991, 413). While there are (many) normative conflicts which are solvable by the well-known rules (or meta-rules) on conflict resolution (*lex superior*, *lex posterior* and *lex specialis*, Kelsen 1991, 123–127; Ross 1958, 128–132), there are also conflicts which cannot be solved by using these methods. Often, these conflicts are even "stronger", that is more difficult to resolve, since judges are left with fundamentally the conflict between two values, principles or guiding ideas, however one calls them, with no clear method or guidance how to solve them. In these cases, *lex superior* is not applicable; neither is *lex posterior* (except in the cases when the constitution has been later amended); *lex specialis* is also not applicable since there is "no relation of general and specific" (Guastini 2011, 205). The conflicts referred to here are conflicts between constitutional provisions, which are usually understood as "legal principles". One can think of a conflict between freedom of speech and the right to privacy, the conflict between market freedom and state intervention or the right to equality and property rights, etc.

A normative conflict exists when two or more norms are applicable to the same situation with irreconcilable consequences (Duarte 2010, 51). Two conditions are necessary for a normative conflict: first, the incompatibility of legal consequences and second, similar conditions of applicability (ibid., 51). Such situations appear in the mentioned cases of conflicts between constitutional provisions. The "normative elements" in conflict here are "legal principles, as opposed to legal rules", also termed "constitutionally protected goods" or "constitutional values" or similar terms (Martínez-Zorilla 2011, 730). These conflicts are understood as conflicts *in concreto*, and not conflicts *in abstracto* (Guastini 2011, 205; Martínez-Zorilla 2011, 730). This means that:

> The conflicts between fundamental legal rights (or between principles, in general) are not, unlike antinomies between rules, determinable a priori or *in abstracto*, because the norms involved are not logically inconsistent. Instead, the norms are logically consistent or compatible and the conflict arises due to the specific (i.e. empirical) circumstances of the particular case. (Martínez-ibid., 730)

Such position is labelled by Martínez-Zorilla (2011, 730) as the "Standard conception" on conflicts between fundamental legal rights (it is contested by some author, for example, Zucca 2008, 21). In modern democratic constitutions, many provisions are either explicitly characterized in the constitutional text as principles or interpreted as such in the process of interpretation. If one looks at the Croatian Constitution, there are provisions which are explicitly referred to as principles, such as Art. 4 (principle of separation of powers) or Art. 51 (principles of equality and equity), while many other provisions are interpreted as expressing legal principles, such as Art. 5 (principle of legality), Art. 14 (equality before the law), Art. 38 (freedom of speech), Art. 40 (freedom of religion), Art. 49 (market freedom), Art. 50 (the right to property), Art. 70 (the right to a healthy life), etc. One constitutional provision, Art. 3, located in the section Basic provisions (Art. 1–13) of the Croatian Constitution states that:

> Freedom, equal rights, national and gender equality, peace-making, social justice, respect for human rights, inviolability of ownership, conservation of nature and the environment, the rule of law and a democratic multiparty system are the highest values of the constitutional order of the Republic of Croatia and the basis for interpreting the Constitution.

Even though Art. 3 mentions "highest values of the constitutional order" which form "the basis for interpreting the Constitution", it is obvious that conflicts between general normative statements (regardless of how we refer to them, as values, principles, etc.) are possible. The question is, what would be some of the possible ways of resolving such conflicts when they inevitably appear? The legal theory and practice in the decades after the Second World War widely accepted proportionality analysis and balancing as an answer to this question.

2. Legal rules and legal principles

It was mentioned that the standard conception of conflict between constitutional provisions treats them as "legal principles". The discussion regarding rules and principles as types of norms has been around for the last several decades, and the author with whom the beginning of the discussion is associated is Ronald Dworkin (Dworkin 1967, 22–29). The distinction between rules and principles put forward and elaborated by Ronald Dworkin was later expanded by Robert Alexy, who is considered as "the most prominent example" of the so-called standard conception of conflicts between constitutional rights (Martínez-Zorilla 2011, 730; for Alexy's position, see Alexy 2002, 44–56; Alexy 2003a, 131–140; Alexy 2003b, 433–449). This "standard conception" rests on a thesis that differentiates between rules and principles as two types of norms, which are structurally different. In the literature, three positions regarding the rule-principle distinction can be found: the first one, the *strong* or *qualitative* one, according to which there are structural differences between rules and principles; the second one, *weak* or *quantitative* one, according to which the difference between rules and principles is only a matter of degree of possessing certain characteristics; and the third one that "there are no solid grounds to make a distinction between the two" (Moniz Lopes 2017, 472; Pino 2012, 80–89). In the context of constitutional adjudication, the most influential supporter of the *strong* or *qualitative* distinction between rules and principles is Robert Alexy (2002, 44–48; Borowski 2011, 579). Even though many arguments have been put forward against the *strong* or *qualitative* distinction thesis (see, e.g. Brożek 2012, 221 – 225; Pino 2011, 81, 89–94; Poscher 2009, 449), that distinction forms the "basic pillar" of Alexy's theory of principles (Alexy 2002, 44), which, along with his theory of balancing, represents the most influential method of solving conflicts in constitutional adjudication. In Alexy's understanding, the difference between rules and principles is the following:

> ... principles are norms commanding that something be realized to the highest degree that is actually and legally possible. Principles are therefore optimization commands. They can be fulfilled in different degrees. The mandatory degree of fulfilment depends not only on actual facts but also on legal possibilities. The field of legal possibilities is determined by countervailing principles and rules. Contrariwise, rules are norms that can only be complied with or not. If a rule is

> valid, it requires that one do exactly what it demands, nothing more and nothing less. Rules therefore comprise a decision in the field of actual and legal possibilities. They are definitive commands. This means that the difference between rules and principles is a difference in quality and not only one of degree. Every norm is either a rule or a principle. (2003, 295)

The difference between rules and principles as two types of norms is most visible, according to Alexy, when one analyses the way of solving conflicts between them: a conflict between rules is solved either by introducing an exception to one of the rules or by declaring one of them invalid, while a conflict between principles must be solved by balancing or weighing (2000, 295; 2002, 49–56). This indicates the connection between Alexy's understanding of norms (with every norm being either rule or principle) and his notion of balancing or weighing, closely connected with the notion of proportionality.

3. Proportionality and balancing

3.1. Proportionality

The principle of proportionality (or proportionality analysis) became a key concept in the constitutional adjudication in the last several decades (Aleinikoff 1987, 943–945; Klatt, Meister 2012, 4; Stone Sweet, Matthews, 2008, 73–74), and the preferred method of solving constitutional conflicts in the practice of the many constitutional courts (Alexy 2005, 572; Borowski 2011, 579; Cianciardo 2010, 177–178; Webber 2010, 179–181). Originating in German administrative law at the end of 19th century and connected with the idea of *Rechtsstaat* (Cohen-Eliya and Porat 2010, 271–276), it spread throughout Europe, Commonwealth legal systems, Israel and Latin America (Möller 2007, 709; Pirker 2013, 6–7; Stone Sweet and Matthews 2008, 73–74). It has also been applied by the European Court of Justice and the European Court of Human Rights (Borowski 2011, 579). The basic idea behind the principle of proportionality is the idea that the limitations of constitutional rights "must not be excessive or go beyond what is necessary" (Bernal Pulido 2013, 489).

The principle of proportionality has several different conceptions, but many scholars and courts agree it consists of three sub-principles: suitability, necessity and proportionality in the narrow sense or balancing

(Alexy 2014, 52; Bernal Pulido 2013, 484; Sieckmann 2019, 5). However, there are scholars and judges, as Bernal Pulido indicates (2013, 484), who differentiate between four sub-principles of the proportionality principles and consider the first sub-principle to consist of two different sub-principles: the "legitimacy of the end" and the "factual appropriateness of the limitation to achieve the end". These two conceptions, however, are not mutually incompatible. Historically, the idea that the principle of proportionality consists of the three mentioned sub-principles was expressed after the enactment of the Basic Law of the Federal Republic of Germany by Rupprecht von Krauss in his dissertation (1955, 14), in which he treated proportionality as a constitutional principle of German constitutional law (Bernal Pulido 2013, 492). Each of these sub-principles represents a requirement that any limitations to constitutional rights must meet to be considered justified (ibid., 484).

The first sub-principle, suitability (sometimes referred to as "appropriateness" by Alexy 2000, 298), requires that the limitations to constitutional rights "contribute to the achievement of a legitimate end" (Bernal Pulido 2013, 484). This sub-principle, according to Alexy, has the status of "negative criterion", which cuts out "unsuitable means" (2002, 398). An example Alexy uses (2014, 53) is the decision of the German Federal Constitutional court BVerfGE 55, 159 ("Falconry Hunting Permit", 1980) regarding the law, which required that people who apply for falconry license must pass a shooting examination, same as the persons who apply for general hunting license. The Court concluded that the shooting examination for falconers presents the infringement of the general freedom of action of the falconers, guaranteed by the Art. 2(1) of the Basic Law. The Court declared that the requirement of shooting examination for falconers is not suitable in promoting the "proper exercise of these activities as intended by the legislator" (Alexy 2014, 53). The Court stated that there was no "substantially clear reason" for the infringement of the general freedom of action of the falconer guaranteed by the Art. 2(1) of the Basic Law (Alexy 2014, 53, quoting BVerfGE 55, 159 [166–167]). The regulation was declared unproportional and, therefore, unconstitutional by the Court.

The second sub-principle, necessity, requires that the limitations to the constitutional rights are made with the "least restrictive of all means that are equally suitable to achieve the pursued end" (Bernal Pulido, 2013, 484). A case example Alexy gives here is the decision of the German Federal Constitutional Court BVerfGE 53, 135 ("Chocolate Easter Bunny", 1980) regarding the labelling of sweets (2014, 53–54). A ban on puffed rice sweets was issued to protect the consumers from confusing puffed rice sweets with chocolate products. The Court found this ban to be a violation of the sub-principle of necessity, arguing that consumer protection could be achieved "in an equally effective but less incisive way by a duty of marking" (Alexy 2014, 54, quoting BVerfGE 53, 135 [146]). The Court declared the ban to be unconstitutional since equally effective consumer protection could be achieved by less intensive means of marking the products.

The third sub-principle, proportionality in the narrow sense, requires that the limitations on constitutional rights "achieve the pursued end to a degree that justifies the extent of the constraint on the constitutional right" (Bernal Pulido 2013, 484). The proportionality in the narrow sense is, in Alexy's theory, identical with the so-called Law of balancing, which states that "the greater the degree of non-satisfaction of, or detriment to, one principle, the greater must be the importance of satisfying the other" (2002, 102). It was previously mentioned that Alexy understands principles as optimization commands, claiming that they can be fulfilled in different degrees. Optimization relative to competing principles consists of, in Alexy's words, "nothing other than balancing" (2002, 401).

3.2. Balancing

Balancing is a method associated with the practice of the German Federal Constitutional Court and Robert Alexy. Balancing (also called "weighing") is a method used to solve normative conflicts between legal principles, which are supposedly different from legal rules. Alexy's "Law of Balancing" can be, according to the formulation of its author, broken down in three stages, which represent three stages of balancing (2002, 401). In the first stage, the degree of non-satisfaction or detriment to the first principle is established. In the second stage, the importance of satisfying the competing principle is established. In the third and final stage, it is established "whether the importance of satisfying the competing principle justifies the detriment to, or non-satisfaction of, the first" (2002, 401).

Alexy aims to prove, through the analysis of the judicial practice of the German Federal Constitutional Court, that judicial balancing is a rational method that ought to be used when solving conflicts between competing principles. For the application of his theory on the judgements of the German Federal Constitutional Court, see the decisions BVerfGE 95, 173 ("Tobacco Warning Label Case") and BVerfGE 86, 1, ("Titanic Magazine", Alexy 2003a, 136–140). Even though Alexy's theory of judicial balancing, articulated in his 1985 book *Theorie der Grundrechte* (*A Theory of Constitutional Rights*, translated into English in 2002 by Julian Rivers), comes from the analysis of a single legal system, that of Germany, his ideas were accepted and applied as a general theory of constitutional rights (Kumm 2007, 136; Sardo 2012, 85; Stone Sweet and Matthews 2008, 93). In the next paragraphs, the brief analysis of the Alexy's understanding of the principle proportionality and balancing will be applied to the Croatian legal system and its constitutional court adjudication, to determine the relationship between legal theory and judicial practice.

4. Croatian legal system

Besides being found in the judicial decisions of constitutional courts, the principle of proportionality is also formulated in the provisions of the constitutions. In the Croatian Constitution, a so-called balancing regulating norm (the norm which "somehow tells us how to balance", Sampaio 2018, 72) is expressed by the Art. 16(2):

> (1) Freedoms and rights may only be restricted by law in order to protect the freedoms and rights of others, the legal order, and public morals and health.
> (2) Any restriction of freedoms or rights shall be proportionate to the nature of the need for such restrictions in each individual case.

Croatian Constitution was enacted in December 1990 (Official Gazette 56/1990), while Art. 16(2) was introduced later, in constitutional changes in November 2000 (Official Gazette 113/2000; see Croatia National Report 2017, 5; Goldner Lang et al. 2019, 1141). The principle of proportionality in the Croatian legal system first appeared in the decision of the Constitutional Court of Croatia (U-I-673/1996, Official Gazette 39/1999,

Rodin 2000, 45–46; Rodin 2008, 2). In this decision, which was an abstract review of the provisions of the Law on Compensation for Property Taken during the Time of the Yugoslav Communist Rule, the Court stated that:

> The Constitution provides for the possibility of restricting the freedoms and rights of man and citizen (e.g. Art. 16(2), Art. 43, Art. 50(3), Art. 59(2), Art. 60). However, any restriction (even when necessary and based on the Constitution) is a state of emergency because it deviates from the general rules on constitutional freedoms and rights. Therefore, restrictions should not only be based on the Constitution, but in proportion to the goal and purpose that the law seeks to achieve, that is, that goal or purpose must be achieved with as little encroachment on the constitutional rights of citizens (of course, if restrictions can be determined gradually). This rule on the proportionality of restrictions on the goal and the purpose which the law seeks to achieve is a general constitutional principle that is immanent to all constitutional provisions on the freedoms and rights of man and citizen (translation by the author).

The principle of proportionality was further elaborated in the decision U-I-1156/1999, Official Gazette 14/2000 (Bačić 419–420; Barić 2016, 15–17). The decision in question was an abstract review of the provisions of the Act on the Restrictions of the Use of Tobacco Products of 1999 (Croatian National Report 2017, 13–14):

> Although the Constitution of the Republic of Croatia does not provide for any direct norms to regulate the principle of proportionality, its ubiquitous significance cannot be denied. This Court starts from the position that the fundamental freedoms and rights of citizen, as regulated by the Constitution, are limitless in principle. Any restriction of these freedoms and rights must be prescribed by law, and restrictions must be proportionate to the legitimate goal to be achieved thereby. This stems indirectly from the provisions of Article 17 of the Constitution, which provide for the possibility to restrict the fundamental freedoms and rights under the so-called extraordinary circumstances in the state. Namely, Article 17, paragraph 2 of the Constitution expressly stipulates that the extent of such restrictions shall be proportionate to the nature of the danger, and at the same time it shall preclude any impermissible consequences, i.e. those which must not be allowed to occur as a result of the implementation of such restrictions.

The Court concluded that “in a situation where the Constitution expressly compels the implementation of the principle of proportionality (the proportionality test) under extraordinary circumstances”, the principle “should be even more valid under ‘ordinary circumstances’ in the country” (Croatian National Report 2017, 14). The reasoning behind the introduction of the principle of proportionality was based on the *argumentum a fortiori* (*a maiori ad minus*) put forward by the Constitutional Court (Rodin 2000, 52; on the argument, see Peczenik 2008, 338–339).

The use of the principle of proportionality, ever since it was introduced into the Croatian legal system 20 years ago, is a researched topic, as it could have been expected due to its importance. What follows and what is the aim of the chapter is to analyse the case law[1] of the Court regarding Art. 16(2) of the Constitution, and to connect it with the general theoretical framework regarding the principle of proportionality and balancing presented previously in the chapter. Due to the number of the published decisions related to the Art. 16, I decided to analyse the two most recent ones, each in its aspect.

The decision U-I-1162/2008[2] from June 2011, Official Gazette 77/2011, the most recent one available regarding constitutional review (where the proceedings were instituted and provisions repealed), dealt with provisions of the criminal code prescribing sanctions and their maximum duration. The Court stated that:

> The prescription of criminal law sanctions and their duration, including the security measure of "Prohibition to operate a motor vehicle" must follow a particular goal laid down by the Constitution and the law, and must be proportionate to it. This means that restricting legal rules must be appropriate to achieving a legitimately set goal, and that a balance must be struck between the rights of criminal perpetrators guaranteed by the Constitution and the law on the one hand, and the protection of the objective legal order in the area of imposing criminal sanctions on the other hand. (...)
>
> The Constitutional Court found that the security measure of prohibition to operate a motor vehicle, like any other security measure, means a restriction of the perpetrator's right to operate a motor vehicle, and thus its prescription and imposition is subject to the general constitutional provision related to the principle of proportionality. This principle lays down that when prescribing and imposing a security measure, it must be assessed whether this measure is applied to achieve the legal purpose and the 'nature of the necessity in each individual case'.

1 The case law of the Constitutional Court of Republic of Croatia in English, sorted by the articles of the Constitution can be found on the following link: https://sljeme.usud.hr/usud/prakswen.nsf (accessed 16.9.2019.).

2 https://sljeme.usud.hr/usud/prakswen.nsf/fOdluka.xsp?action=openDocument&documentId=0D014AF843828D20C1257D4000509267, (accessed 16.9.2019.).

In a more recent decision of the Court, in which the proposal to review the conformity with the Constitution of the Act on Amendments of the Consumer Loans Act was not granted (U-I-3685/2017[3], Official Gazette 39/2017), the Court stated, under the section "the principle of proportionality", that:

> In order to examine whether the objections of the proponents concerning the disproportionality of the impugned measure, i.e. its non-conformity with Article 16 of the Constitution, were justified, the Constitutional Court had to answer the following questions: what was the aim of the legislator in adopting the impugned acts and is that aim legitimate; is the measure (conversion) prescribed in the impugned laws proportionate to the aim that needed to be achieved, or does the impugned measure place an excessive burden on the credit institutions?
>
> The Constitutional Court held that the impugned acts have a legitimate aim: to improve social protection, prevent unfair business practices of the credit institutions, and prevent the deepening of the debt crisis.
>
> In relation to the second question, the Constitutional Court held that the impugned measure, i.e. conversion, was appropriate to achieve the legitimate aim because it clearly follows from the data submitted by the Ministry of Finance and the Croatian National Bank, which were not brought into question by the proponents in their proposals, that the conversion did not cause any distortive effects either in the operation of banks or in the monetary policy of the Republic of Croatia, and that the negative effects of the conversion were considerably smaller than assessed. (…)
>
> In the remaining part of the Constitutional Court proceedings, the Constitutional Court had to establish whether the impugned measure imposes, despite its appropriateness and necessity, an excessive burden on the credit institutions. The Constitutional Court examined the legal and economic position of the beneficiaries of the loans in CHF before the passing of the impugned acts, on the one hand, and the potential benefit of the credit institutions from the effects of the conversion, on the other.

Returning to the proportionality scheme presented in the first part of the chapter, these two recent decisions (excluding the two that introduced and elaborated the principle of proportionality into Croatian legal system) can be analysed through that framework to determine the degree to which the reasoning of the Court and the framework are aligned.

---

3 https://sljeme.usud.hr/usud/prakswen.nsf/fOdluka.xsp?action=openDocument&documentId=E2FDAE001D835F1EC125833D0052ECD4 (accessed 16.9.2019.).

For reasons of clarity, I will present the reconstruction of the two cases in the following table, highlighting in italics the relevant parts:

Principle of proportionality	**U-I-1162/2008 (Prohibitions to operate motor vehicles)**	**U-I-3685/2017 (Loans in CHF)**
1) the sub-principle of suitability ("legitimacy of the end" + "factual appropriateness of the limitation to achieve the end")	"...restricting legal rules must be *appropriate* to achieving a *legitimately set goal...*"	"...the Constitutional Court held that the impugned measure, i.e., conversion, was *appropriate* to achieve the *legitimate aim...*"
2) the sub-principle of necessity	"...it must be assessed whether this measure is applied to achieve the legal purpose and the '*nature of the necessity* in each individual case' ".	"...or does the impugned measure place and *excessive burden* on the credit institutions?"
3) the sub-principle of proportionality in the narrow sense (balancing)	"...a *balance* must be struck between the rights of criminal perpetrators guaranteed by the Constitution and the law *on the one hand*, and the protection of the objective legal order in the area of imposing criminal sanctions *on the other hand*".	"The Constitutional Court examined the legal and economic position of the beneficiaries of the loans in CHF before the passing of the impugned acts, *on the one hand*, and the potential benefit of the credit institutions from the effects of the conversion, *on the other*".

5. Conclusions

Two remarks can be made from the previously exposed subject matter. First, the introduction of the principle of proportionality, as a general principle of law, into Croatian legal system by the Constitutional Court in 1999 (U-I-673-1996) and its further elaboration in 2000 (U-I-1156/2000) was, from an argumentative perspective, supported by the argumentum *a fortiori* (*a maiori ad minus*). The Court stated, in the decision U-I-1156/2000, that "in a situation where the Constitution expressly compels the implementation of the principle of proportionality (the proportionality test) under extraordinary circumstances", the principle "should be even more valid under 'ordinary circumstances' in the country". The second remark, which refers to the main question posed at the beginning of the chapter – can the reasoning of the Croatian Constitutional Court be reconstructed through Alexy's scheme of the principle of proportionality and its three sub-principles (suitability, necessity and proportionality in the narrow sense), can be answered positively regarding the two decisions it was applied upon (U-I-1162/2008 and U-I-3685/2017). This comes as a no surprise, since Alexy's work on the principle of proportionality through the reconstruction of the case law of the German Federal Constitutional Court had a worldwide influence, as was previously mentioned. What seems to be the main take from the previously presented seems to be that it provides a valuable analytical tool to analyse judicial decisions and judicial argumentation. Valuable, since conflicts between constitutional provisions are usually followed by tensions, since they can be understood as conflicts between two values (if one goes more *in abstracto*) and any tool that can contribute to the rationality of the judicial decisions (even only formally, if not substantially) helps to settle such conflicts in society. Regardless of the criticisms put forward against the proportionality analysis and balancing, the spread of the idea originating from the idea of *Rechtstaat*, which *limits the limitations* of the constitutional rights into legal systems which only relatively recently became democratic, contributes to the rationality of the judicial decisions and solving conflicts between constitutional rights.

References

Alchourrón, Carlos Eduardo. 1991. Conflicts of Norms and the Revision of Normative Systems. *Law and Philosophy* 10: 413–425.

Aleinikoff, Thomas Alexander. 1987. Constitutional Law in the Age of Balancing. *Yale Law Journal* 96(5): 943–1005.

Alexy, Robert. 2000. On the Structure of Legal Principles. *Ratio Juris* 13(3): 294–304.

Alexy, Robert. 2002. *A Theory of Constitutional Rights*. Oxford: Oxford University Press.

Alexy, Robert. 2003a. Constitutional Rights, Balancing and Rationality. *Ratio Juris* 16(2): 131–140.

Alexy, Robert. 2003b. On Balancing and Subsumption. A Structural Comparison. *Ratio Juris* 16(4): 433–449.

Alexy, Robert. 2005. Balancing, Constitutional Review and Representation. *International Journal of Constitutional Law* 3(4): 572–581.

Alexy, Robert. 2014. Constitutional Rights and Proportionality. *Revus – Journal for Constitutional Theory and Philosophy of Law* 22: 51–65.

Bačić, Petar. 2010. *Konstitucionalizam i sudski aktivizam*. Split: Pravni fakultet u Splitu.

Barić, Sanja. 2016. The Transformative Role of the Constitutional Court of the Republic of Croatia: From the Ex-Yu to the EU. *Analitika – Center for Social Research*, Working Paper 6/2016.

Bernal Pulido, Carlos. 2013. The Migration of Proportionality across Europe. *New Zealand Journal of Public and International Law* 11(3): 483–515.

Borowski, Martin. 2011. Discourse, Principles, and the Problem of Law and Morality: Robert Alexy's Three Main Works. *Jurisprudence* 2(2): 575–595.

Brożek, Bartosz. 2012. Legal Rules and Principles: A Theory Revisited. *I-lex. Scienze Giuridiche, Scienze Cognitive e Intelligenza Artificiale* 17: 205–226.

Cianciardo, Juan. 2010. The Principle of Proportionality: The Challenge of Human Rights. *Journal of Civil Law Studies* 3(1): 177–186.

Cohen-Eliya, Moshe, Porat, Iddo. 2010. American Balancing and German Proportionality: The Historical Origins. *International Journal of Constitutional Law* 8(2): 263–286.

Duarte, David. 2010. Drawing Up the Boundaries of Normative Conflicts that Lead to Balances. In *Legal Reasoning: The Methods of Balancing*, edited by Jan-Reinard Sieckmann, 51–62. Stuttgart: Franz Steiner Verlag.

Dworkin, Ronald. 1967. The Model of Rules. *University of Chicago Law Review* 35(1): 14–46.

Goldner Lang, Iris, Đurđević, Zlata, Mataija, Mislav. 2019. The Constitution of Croatia in the Perspective of European and Global Governance. In *National Constitutions in European and Global Governance: Democracy, Rights, the Rule of Law: National*

Reports, edited by Anneli Albi and Samo Bardutzky, 1139–1177. Dordrecht: Springer.

Guastini, Riccardo. 2011. *Interpretare e argomentare*. Milano: Giuffrè editore.

Kelsen, Hans. 1991. *General Theory of Norms*. Oxford: Clarendon Press.

Klatt, Matthias, Meister, Moritz. 2012. *The Constitutional Structure of Proportionality*. Oxford: Oxford University Press.

Kumm, Matthias. 2007. Political Liberalism and the Structure of Rights: On the Place and Limits of the Proportionality Requirement. In *Law, Rights and Discourse: The Legal Philosophy of Robert Alexy*, edited by George Pavlakos, 131–166. Oxford: Hart Publishing.

Martínez-Zorilla, David. 2011. The Structure of Conflicts of Fundamental Legal Rights. *Law and Philosophy* 30: 729–749.

Möller, Kai. 2007. Balancing and the Structure of Constitutional Rights. *International Journal of Constitutional Law*, 5(3): 453–468.

Peczenik, Aleksander. 2008. *On Law and Reason*, second edition. Dordrecht: Springer.

Pino, Giorgio. 2011. I principi tra teoria della norma e teoria dell'argomentazione giuridica. *Diritto e questioni pubbliche* 11: 75–110.

Pirker, Benedikt. 2013. *Proportionality Analysis and Models of Judicial Review*. Groningen: Europa Law Publishing.

Poscher, Ralf. 2009. Insights, Errors and Self-Misconceptions of the Theory of Principles. *Ratio Juris*, 22(4): 425–454.

Rodin, Siniša. 2000. Načelo proporcionalnosti – porijeklo, ustavno utemeljenje i primjena. *Zbornik Pravnog fakulteta u Zagrebu* 50(1–2): 31–53.

Rodin, Siniša. 2008. Načelo proporcionalnosti u novijoj praksi Ustavnog suda Republike Hrvatske. *Novi Informator* 5623: 1–2.

Ross, Alf. 1958. *On Law and Justice*. London: Stevens & Sons Limited.

Sampaio, Jorge Silva. 2018. Proportionality in Its Narrow Sense and Measuring the Intensity of Restrictions on Fundamental Rights. In *Proportionality in Law: An Analytical Perspective*, edited by David Duarte and Jorge Silva Sampaio, 71–110. Dordrecht: Springer.

Sardo, Alessio. 2012. Three Theories of Judicial Balancing: A Comparison. *Dignitas – The Slovenian Journal of Human Rights* 53: 60–95.

Sieckmann, Jan-Reinard. 2019. The Principle of Proportionality: A German Perspective. *European Commission for Democracy Through Law (Venice Commission)*, CDL-JU(2019)002: 1–11.

Stone Sweet, Alec, Matthews, Jud. 2008. Proportionality Balancing and Global Constitutionalism. *Columbia Journal of Transnational Law* 47(1): 72–164.

von Krauss, Rupprecht. 1955. *Der Grundsatz der Verhältnismäßigkeit. In seiner Bedeutung für die Notwendigkeit des Mittels im Verwaltungsrecht*. Hamburg: Appel.

Webber, Grégoire. 2010. Proportionality, Balancing and the Cult of Constitutional Rights Scholarship. *Canadian Journal of Law & Jurisprudence* 23(1): 179–202.

Zucca, Lorenzo. 2008. Conflicts of Fundamental Rights as Constitutional Dilemmas. In: *Conflicts between Fundamental Rights*, edited by Eva Brems, 19–37. Antwerp: Intersentia.

III. Freedom, respect and reason in Central and Eastern Europe

Enrico Arona

University of Genoa (Italy), Faculty of Law

Towards deliberative democracy: Bivalence and trivalence in a new paradigm of Republicanism

Abstract: The concept of political and republican freedom (Skinner and Pettit) can be interpreted either in a bivalent or in a trivalent way. When we conceive freedom in a bivalent way, we refer to the idea that an agent A can be described as either free or unfree with respect to an action x, and *tertium non datur*: if A is not free to x, she is therefore necessarily unfree, and vice versa. On the other hand, for trivalent interpretations of freedom predicates 'free' and 'unfree' are contraries rather than contradictories (Carter, Steiner or Kramer). I will show that trivalent views are, therefore, qualified by the area of not-freedoms, an "unexcluded middle" between ascriptions of freedom and ascriptions of unfreedom. Finally, I challenge this view by demonstrating how the dichotomy bivalence/trivalence can be written as a relationship of constraints of freedom (y) and the dominion of the actions (z) of the "formula by Mac Callum".

Keywords: Deliberative democracy, bivalence, trivalence, freedom, not-freedom

1. Introduction

The concept of political freedom can be interpreted either in a bivalent or in a trivalent way. When we conceive freedom in a bivalent way, we refer to the idea that an agent A can be described as either free or unfree with respect to an action x, and *tertium non datur*: If A is not free to x, she is therefore necessarily unfree, and *vice versa*. On the other hand, for trivalent interpretations of freedom "predicates 'free' and 'unfree' are contraries rather than contradictories. They are not bivalent or jointly exhaustive" (Kramer 2003, 41): According to these views A can be described as either free or unfree *or not-free* to x. Trivalent views are therefore qualified by the area of not-freedoms, an "unexcluded middle" (Kramer 2003, 41) between ascriptions of freedom and ascriptions of unfreedom.

As Hillel Steiner writes, exemplifying the point of view of bivalence, "any conceivable action is one which" an agent "is *either free or unfree* to do" (Steiner 1994, 41, emphasis added). On the other hand, authors like Matthew Kramer (2003) and Philip Pettit (1997; 2001) explicitly endorse a trivalent interpretation of freedom. Consider, for instance, how Pettit's interpretation of the republican ideal of freedom as non-domination conceives the relations between freedom and legitimate ("non-arbitrary") laws:

> Not only do I not have to say that I am made free by the act whereby I obey a nonarbitrary law or have such a law imposed on me. I do not even have to say that I am unambiguously free when I act under the limitations of the law. What I suggest […] is that where I am dominated by another agency, I should be said to be *unfree* and that where I am restricted but not dominated – as by a conditioning factor such as an unintended obstacle or a nonarbitrary law – then I should be said to be *nonfree*. And so I comment that while the tax levy or even the term of imprisonment might not take away a person's freedom in an ideal world – they might not have the effect of a dominating agency – still they would leave the person nonfree (2002, 347).

The analysis of bivalence/trivalence applied to freedom has emerged quite recently in the literature (Steiner 2001 for a defence of bivalence; Kramer 2003 for a defence of a TTF), and has surprisingly received very little critical attention up to now. This chapter is divided in two parts: in the first part (Section 1) I will suggest an analysis of the bivalence/trivalence distinction, which, I argue, should be interpreted in terms of a complex relation between how theories define the types of constraints on freedom and the range of options to which ascriptions of freedom/unfreedom can be said to pertain. The analysis of bivalence/trivalence has implications for a number of issues concerning the concept of freedom: In the second part of the chapter, I will in particular focus on the implications of such analysis for better understanding of one of the arguments that Pettit has levelled against the negative freedom ideal. In a recent article (2011), Pettit has drawn an analogy between the "anti-adaptation" objection to desire-based conceptions of freedom, and the "anti-ingratiation" objection that republicans level against the pure negative conception of freedom endorsed by Carter, Kramer and Steiner. I will attempt to challenge the validity of such analogy, by arguing that, while the anti-adaptation objection, and other arguments which share a parallel structure, are designed to target trivalent interpretations of freedom, the anti-ingratiation objection, if interpreted as having the same structure as the anti-adaptation objection, does not succeed in the critique to the pure negative conception of freedom, given that pure negative freedom is not *per se* committed neither to a bivalent nor to a trivalent interpretation of the concept. My analysis of bivalence/trivalence will moreover be helpful for understanding at a more fundamental level Cohen's critique of Nozick's *moralized* conception of freedom (Cohen 1979; 1981; 1995; Nozick 1974).

2. Bivalence and trivalence

2.1 The analysis of the bivalence/trivalence distinction

What distinguishes bivalent theories of freedom (BTFs, henceforth) from trivalence theories of freedom (TTFs)? According to MacCallum, every statement about freedom needs to refer, at least implicitly, to an agent x being free/unfree from obstacles y to do/become z (MacCallum 1969). Following Tim Gray we can apply the concept/conception of Rawlsian distinction (Rawls 1971, 8) to MacCallum's analysis: While MacCallum's formula *per se*, without specifying the content of each variable, can be said to represent the concept, the "maximally abstract definition" (Carter 2011b, 15) of freedom, different conceptions of freedom diverge on the interpretation of the extension and specification of each variable (2005). Following Carter, we can express the same idea by referring to the notions of *open* and *closed concepts*: While the (fully) open concept of freedom is represented by MacCallum's formula, which abstracts from any determination of the extension of each variable, variations in the definition of the content of each variable give rise to different closed concepts, to different conceptions, of freedom. Moreover, different conceptions of freedom can leave the interpretation of each MacCallum's variable more or less open, by not stipulating or by stipulating conditions that intervene in specifying the content of each variable (Carter 2011, 15–17).

I argue that the meaning of the bivalence/trivalence distinction should be understood in terms of a complex relation between MacCallum's y variable (the constraints on freedom) and z variable (which encompasses the actions/becomings the subject in question is free/unfree to do/become). Let's start with considering the z variable. I argue that BTFs are characterized by the maximally open interpretation of the dominion of the z variable: This entails, therefore, that ascriptions of freedom/unfreedom can be said to pertain to every possible instance of the z variable, namely to every possible action/becoming. For BTFs there are no possible types of actions/becomings with respect to which attributions of freedom/unfreedom cannot be said to pertain. On the other hand, TTFs are characterized by a more restricted domain of the z variable: They stipulate a condition on such variable, in order to distinguish within the space of the z variable between the types of actions/becomings with respect to which attributions of freedom/unfreedom can be plausibly said to pertain, and the types of actions/becomings with respect to which attributions of freedom/unfreedom cannot be said to pertain.

Indeed, to the latter set of actions/becomings pertain attributions of not-freedom (neither freedom nor unfreedom). Stipulating a condition which restricts the dominion of the actions/becomings to which attributions of freedom can be plausibly ascribed, TTFs isolate, therefore, a subset of actions/becomings, the not-freedom set, with respect to which attributions of freedom/unfreedom cannot be plausibly ascribed. Therefore, the bivalence/trivalence dichotomy is itself a bivalent distinction: Theories of freedom can interpret the concept either in a bivalent or in a trivalent way, and *tertium non datur*.

Take, for instance, negative theories of freedom, and in particular Steiner's pure negative theory of freedom and Kramer's trivalent theory of freedom-as-ableness. Both Steiner and Kramer, remaining faithful to a liberal tenet in the theorizing about liberty, conceive freedom as a social relation, assuming that only other human beings' interventions can be considered constraints on freedom. Moreover, following Steiner (1974/75; 1994), also Kramer (2003) believes that only preventions (interpreted as interventions which render physically impossible the doing of an action) render the agents unfree to do the actions in question[1]. But, whereas for Steiner, if you are not unfree, namely if you are not prevented to x, you

1 Physical impossibility caused (either intentionally or not) by other human beings is therefore assumed as the unique necessary and sufficient condition for attributions of unfreedom. This negative freedom approach is also followed by Carter (1999; 2005).

are necessarily free to x, thus interpreting freedom in a bivalent way; for Kramer, from the sole fact that you are not unfree, that others do not render your acting physically impossible, we cannot infer your freedom to do/become x: For Kramer, physical impossibility is a necessary condition but not also a sufficient condition for attributions of unfreedom. Kramer's theory indeed stipulates that the subjects must be able to do/become x as a further necessary condition for attributions of both freedom or unfreedom to x: Attributions of freedom depend on A being unprevented *and* able to x, while for attributions of unfreedom A must be prevented and, counterfactually, she would have been able to x, if she had not been prevented (2003).

From the ability-condition posed by Kramer it follows that his theory stipulates a set of actions/becomings, those which the agent is unable to do/become, with respect to which do not pertain attributions of freedom/unfreedom, but attributions of *not-freedom*. And this in my view is the reason why the bivalence/trivalence of a theory depends on the interpretation of the z variable, and is determined by how the theory conceives the set of actions/becomings with respect to which attributions of freedom/unfreedom can be said to pertain: If such set coincides with the entire range of all conceivable actions, this will lead to the endorsement of bivalence. This emerges, for instance, from how Steiner expresses his own bivalent view: "any *conceivable* action", he writes, "is one which" an agent "is either free or unfree to do" (1994, 41, emphasis added). On the other hand, trivalence reflects the fact that the theory assumes a restricted set of actions/becomings with respect to which attributions of freedom/unfreedom can be said to pertain. By narrowing down this set of actions through the imposition of a condition (the ability-condition for Kramer), the theory stipulates that the actions/becomings that, not respecting the condition, remain outside such set form the set of not-freedoms (to which neither ascriptions of freedom nor of unfreedom pertain)[2].

2 I'm confident that the analysis of bivalence/trivalence will be helpful for the analysis of the relations between freedom and ability. While the classic liberal understanding of liberty interprets freedom as simply the absence of constraints (Berlin [1958] 2002; Hayek 1960; Steiner 1974; 1994; Carter 1999), other theorists define freedom in terms of the capacity/opportunity to act. It would

Let us now introduce the analysis of the y variable. Much of the contemporary debate on freedom has focused on the analysis of this variable. "Which types of constraints can be said to restrict freedom?" has often been the central question of discussion about freedom. Indeed, theories of freedom tend to qualify the extension of such variable, by imposing one or more conditions on it. The y variable, defining which types of obstacles can be considered constraints on freedom, can be said to define the area of unfreedom. For Steiner, for example, ascriptions of unfreedom are determined by 1) the presence of prevention (obstacles which render physically impossible the doing of the action in question) and by 2) the fact that the obstacles are posed by other human beings (natural obstructions do not infringe social freedom). Steiner's pure negative freedom imposes, therefore, two conditions on the y variable for the definition of unfreedom. Consider Oppenheim (1981), who argued that 1) freedom is limited only by interventions by other human beings (first condition), which render the doing of an action *either* physically impossible *or* punishable (second condition). Also Oppenheim's unfreedom is determined by two conditions, but in this case the second condition presents a *disjunctive* structure.

I will now investigate how the y variable intervenes in determining the bivalence/trivalence of a theory. Take, for instance, Pettit's view: Pettit distinguishes between "factors that compromise liberty and factors that condition it" (1997, 75; see also 2001, 142). For Pettit's republican ideal of freedom the only constraint that "compromises" liberty, that renders you unfree, is domination, namely certain types of forms of subjugation to the arbitrary, or alien,[3] power of other people, and therefore freedom coincides with non-domination (the absence of domination). But there are then other types of constraints that can be said not to compromise freedom, namely to render you unfree, but to condition it in some sense. Pettit here has in mind 1) the absence of the physical capacity to do the actions in question, or 2) obstacles posed not by other human beings, but rather having natural causes, or, finally, 3) cases of interference without

indeed possible to distinguish between bivalent (Sen 1993; 1999; Van Parijs 1995) and trivalent (Kramer 2003) ability-based theories of freedom.

3 While in early formulations Pettits talks of "arbitrary power", he now tends to appeal to the idea of "alien power" (2008; 2011; 2012).

domination (such as an interfering law) (1997, 74–77; see also 2001, 141–144; 2002). In all these cases you are not strictly rendered unfree, but your freedom is nonetheless conditioned, you can be described as not-free:[4] as Pettit writes, "someone is unfree so far as their freedom is compromised by domination, so we may say that they are *not free* in this or that respect – *they are non-free, though not strictly unfree* (Pettit 1989b) – insofar as their freedom is subject to certain conditioning factors" (1997, 76, emphasis added).

Clearly, Pettit here is basing his assumption of trivalence on a distinction between types of obstacles, therefore on a distinction which refers to the y variable: while certain types of obstacles, namely instances of domination, render you unfree, there are different types of obstacles that, though not rendering you unfree, render you not-free. Notice that the fact that the assumption of trivalence originates in virtue of a distinction within the y variable is paralleled by a consequent distinction within the z variable: Pettit argues that we can increase people's freedom not just by contrasting and eliminating domination, namely unfreedom, but also by acting on the area of not-freedom, on the area of the conditioning factors, by "expanding the range or ease of the undominated choices that they enjoy" (1997, 76). Therefore, by turning people's not-freedoms into freedoms: even if people are not unfree, namely do not suffer domination, the freedom they enjoy (the area of "undominated choice") can still be enlarged, to the detriment of the area of not-freedom (this concretely means enabling people).

Therefore, Pettit's assumption of trivalence depends on the interpretation of the y variable, on the stipulation of certain types of constraints which define the area of not-freedom, and which ultimately results in a distinction within the *z* variable between the area to which freedom/unfreedom judgements pertain, and that to which pertain not-freedom judgements.

---

4 And, indeed, Pettit classifies these types of obstacles "as a secondary evil from the point of view of the ideal" (2001, 142).

2.2 Different types of trivalence

Trivalence so conceived is, therefore, analysed in terms of an analytically interconnected combination of:[5]

1) the stipulation of the not-freedom defining obstacles (*y* variable);
2) the resulting distinction within the z variable between the set of actions/ becomings to which pertain ascriptions of freedom/unfreedom and that to which pertain ascriptions of not-freedom. However, I am inclined to think that in some cases the trivalence of a theory is determined by the particular interpretation of the *z* variable only, without making reference to the *y* variable. In the remainder of this section, I will attempt to explore this possibility.

Authors like MacCallum (1969) and Sen (1999, 75)[6] seem to suggest that ascriptions of freedom can be made not only with respect to actions, but also with respect to "becomings", and, according to Kramer, who has given a detailed analysis of the issue, also to "undergoings" (2003, 156–169). On the other hand, Carter explicitly argues that the liberal understanding of freedom entails that ascriptions of freedom/unfreedom can only concern actions (1999, 16). So, we could interpret Carter's position as implying that, given that freedom/unfreedom can be attributed only to actions, you cannot be considered neither free nor unfree with respect to becomings and undergoings, namely that you are not-free with respect to them. But, if so, Carter's position can be interpreted as implying a trivalent understanding of freedom, at least with respect to the analysis of the pertinence of becomings and undergoings to freedom. Such alleged assumption of trivalence does not make reference to the interpretation of the y variable, of the constraints on freedom, as happens in Pettit's case, but

5 In this section I expand the analysis of bivalence/trivalence outlined in the previous section; you may wish to skip this rather technical part and to read directly my discussion of Pettit's objection to freedom as non-interference in the following section.

6 According to Sen, functionings are "various things a person may value doing or *being*" (1999, 75, emphasis added). And Isaiah Berlin defines negative freedom as "the area within which the subject – a person or a group – is or should be left *to do or be* what he is able *to do or be*, without interference by other persons" (2002, 169, emphasis added).

only to the *z* variable. Indeed, if my argument is sound, Carter's exclusion of becomings and undergoings from his theory should be interpreted as a restriction of the *z* variable: for Carter becomings and undergoings do not pertain to the dominion of the instances to which ascriptions of freedom/unfreedom can be said to pertain. And this aspect makes of his theory a trivalent interpretation of freedom. But, if theories, like Carter's, that restrict the dominion of the *z* variable to only actions should be correctly interpreted as TTFs, this means that the restriction of the dominion of the *z* variable is what fundamentally defines TTFs, and not the interpretation of the *y* variable. Indeed, the fact that TTFs narrow down the *z* variable seems to be a necessary feature of TTFs: While both in Pettit's and Carter's case the assumption of trivalence depends on the theories narrowing down the dominion of the *z* variable, only in Pettit's case this aspect is combined with a parallel interpretation of the *y* variable.

However, Carter and Pettit's cases differ in one important respect, they seem to point to two different *types* of trivalence. Pettit's trivalence reflects a normative view concerning the interpretation of the constraints on freedom: Pettit argues that while certain obstacles compromise liberty, rendering us unfree, other obstacles do not render us unfree, but still have an effect on our freedom, conditioning it, rendering us not-free. Following Pettit, therefore, not-freedom is a category that lies in the middle between freedom and unfreedom, and which is normatively laden: people who are not-free have reason to complain for their predicament, because ascriptions of not-freedom imply the presence of certain types of obstacles, which deprive them of the freedom to do particular actions.

Ascriptions of not-freedom imply for Pettit the denial of the freedom of the agents to do certain particular actions which, in principle, the agents could be free to do, if the obstacles were removed. And Pettit indeed can endorse a presumption of redress with respect to instances of not-freedom. The same cannot be said for Carter's theory. While Pettit's trivalence stems from a distinction within the camp of the constraints on freedom, arguing for a sort of ordering among different types of obstacles on the basis of their different compromising effects on freedom (there's a presumption of getting rid of unfreedom generating obstacles which is more urgent than that against not-freedom), the exclusion of becomings and undergoings in Carter's theory only depends on how he defines the *z* variable; and the meaning of such exclusion does not consist in an attempt to define a less compromising form of absence of freedom than that represented by ascriptions of unfreedom, it does not result in a straightforward normative claim, as Pettit's lax lexical priority of relieving from unfreedom generating obstacles does.

Indeed, Carter's exclusion of becomings and undergoings from the dominion of the z variable has the function of excluding them entirely from the discourse about liberty: For Carter, there is no sense in which we can plausibly talk of becomings and undergoings in relation to freedom.[7] In Carter's case, the stipulation of the area of not-freedom, which focuses on the *z* variable, coincides with the definition of those instances (undergoings and becomings) for which it would be meaningless to consider as instances to which ascriptions of freedom/unfreedom can be said to pertain. Pettit's trivalence is different: It consists in a distinction within the camp of the constraints, in an ordering of different types of obstacles, which does not result in the exclusion of not-freedom generating obstacles from the discourse about liberty. Not-freedom remains a type of curtailment, conditioning, of our freedom for Pettit, though not as serious as that represented by unfreedom.

It seems, therefore, that we can identify two different types of trivalence: one which depends on a distinction between different types of obstacles (the y variable), which ultimately results in a distinction within the *z* variable (Pettit), and the other which is defined by a distinction within the z variable only (Carter): We could call *y variable trivalence* the former and *z variable trivalence* the latter. The focus of *y* variable type of trivalence is the definition of unfreedom (the y variable settles the condition for ascriptions of unfreedom). This type of trivalence distinguishes between obstacles that generate unfreedom and obstacles that generate not-freedom, giving priority to the former. The sense of the idea of not-freedom in this case is that of stipulating a range of obstacles which curtail freedom in a less serious way than unfreedom generating obstacles do: not-freedom here means a curtailment of freedom (though less invasive than

7 Or, better, there is no sense in which becomings and undergoings cannot be reduced to actions, namely to a combination of bodily movements (Carter 1999, 145).

unfreedom). Such distinction within the y variable consequently generates a distinction within the *z* variable between actions with respect to which ascriptions of freedom/unfreedom can be said to pertain, and actions with respect to which pertain ascriptions of not-freedom. *Z* variable type of trivalence, on the other hand, distinguishes within the z variable the actions with respect to which ascriptions of freedom/unfreedom can be said to pertain, and the actions with respect to which pertain ascriptions of not-freedom. But this distinction does not stem from a parallel distinction within the y variable, as in the previous case. It follows that the distinction within the *z* variable, which is present in both types of trivalence, characterizes more fundamentally trivalent theories, and that is a necessary condition for attributions of trivalence. Moreover, the sense of the stipulation of a distinction within the *z* variable for *z* variable type of trivalence is that of drawing the boundaries within which the discussion about liberty has sense, by excluding certain sets of instances from the dominion of the instances with respect to which ascriptions of freedom/unfreedom can be said to pertain. Here not-freedom assumes the meaning of isolating all those instances which would be meaningless, or unreasonable, to associate with the discussion about ascriptions of freedom/unfreedom, namely with the discourse about liberty in general.

3. A critique of Pettit's anti-ingratiation objection

Drawing on my preceding analysis, I will now attempt to refuse an objection that Pettit has levelled in a recent article (2011) against the negative freedom ideal endorsed by Steiner, Carter and Kramer (freedom as non-interference, FNI, henceforth). Here is a summarized reconstruction of Pettit's argument.

In his 1958 seminal lecture "Two Concepts of Freedom" Isaiah Berlin seems to appeal in some passages to an ideal of (negative) freedom as the absence of obstacles on what we *wish* to do (Berlin [1958] 2002, e.g. p. 123). Such ideal makes freedom dependent on desires (for a discussion, Arneson 1985); it is a desire-based conception of freedom or, as Pettit aptly calls it (2011), an ideal of freedom as non-frustration (FNF, henceforth). Berlin later recognized such formulation as a slip in his earlier version of the essay: If freedom is the absence of obstacles on actions we desire to do, it suffices to avoid desiring the impeded options and we would be relieved from the unfreedom; the prisoner can liberate herself from the unfreedom she suffers by simply avoiding to desire the actions she is unfree to do (Berlin [1969] 2002: "Introduction"). But it seems absurd that liberation can come not through the removal of the obstacles, but through the adaptation of the prisoner's preferences to the unfreedom situation. FNF, Berlin concludes, should be rejected. Let us call this, following Pettit (2011), the "anti-adaptation" objection to FNF. Berlin's consequently amended and more consistent version of the negative freedom ideal (FNI) conceives freedom as the absence of constraints on whatever action, independently of whether the action is actually desired or not (Steiner, Carter and Kramer are on this point in agreement with Berlin).

After having reconstructed Berlin's objection to FNF, Pettit then proceeds to the presentation of the core of his argument (2011, 704–707). He argues that as the "antiadaptation" objection led Berlin to abandon FNF for FNI, so an analogous argument, the "anti-ingratiation" objection, should lead us to abandon FNI for freedom as nondomination (FND). Here is a brief summary of the anti-ingratiation critique to FNI:

1) FNI entails that B is free to X, even if A has power to interfere but is not disposed to do so; and that B is unfree to X, if A has the power to interfere and is disposed to do so.
2) But then, it seems that "you can make yourself free, without reducing my power of interference, just by ingratiating yourself with me and getting me to let your way" (Pettit 2011, 704).
3) As FNF counterintuitively implies that we can liberate ourselves simply by adapting our preferences, so analogously we should reject FNI on the basis that it counterintuitively implies that we could turn our unfreedoms into freedoms simply by ingratiating the will of the person who has power over us, and is rendering us unfree.

I argue that Pettit's attempt to draw an analogy between the anti-adaptation objection to FNF and the anti-ingratiation objection to FNI (Pettit 2011, 705) fails, because the structure of the anti-adaptation objection problematizes the stipulation of the area of notfreedom which characterizes TTFs, namely that it can be applied only to TTFs. But FNI is not per se committed to either bivalence or trivalence. Therefore, the anti-ingratiation objection misses the point, if applied to FNI. And the fact that the analogy does not hold formally, because the structure of the objections is designed to target TTFs, is only the flip side of the fact that the analogy does not hold substantially: the anti-ingratiation objection is not problematic for FNI.

In the first place it is crucial to notice that TTFs seem all to share the same problem: The stipulation of the not-freedom domain can be in conflict with our intuitions about ascriptions of freedom/unfreedom, because cases of interferences on actions/becomings in the area of not-freedoms are considered instances of not-freedoms by TTFs, but the presence of the imposition of an obstacle – which represents the determining factor for attributions of unfreedom – in the not-freedom domain is in conflict with such a description of the situation as a case of not-freedom. The conflict between TTFs and our intuitions about freedom concerns exactly the area of not-freedoms of TTFs. TTFs seem unable to capture all the range of our intuitions about freedom/unfreedom: Situations that are considered cases of *unfreedom* by our common-shared intuitions are, by contrast, considered *not-freedoms* by TTFs.

Consider, for instance, Nozick's interpretation of freedom (1974). G.A. Cohen has argued that Nozick endorses a "moralized" definition of freedom (1979; 1981; 1995, Ch. 2; Carter 1999, 68–74). Nozick's understanding of freedom is indeed grounded on rights: Cohen interprets Nozick as defining freedom in terms of the opportunity to exercise one's moral rights (see also Olsaretti 2004). It follows that, if an obstacle intervenes in *unjustifiably* impeding the exercise of one's moral (and particularly property) rights, it should be considered a constraint on freedom; if, on the other hand, the obstacle *justifiably* prevents the exercise of one's rights, it should not be considered a constraint on freedom. As Cohen puts it, "on that definition, which I shall call the *moralised* definition, I am unfree only when someone does or would *unjustifiably* interfere with me" (1981, 228). I argue that Nozick's moralized view should be interpreted as a TTF because in Nozick's account moral rights define the condition that specifies the restricted dominion of the z variable to which attributions of freedom/unfreedom can be said to pertain: You cannot be considered free/unfree to do an action which lies beyond the borders of your moral rights. But, if so, from Nozick's theory counterintuitively follows that "a properly convicted murderer is not rendered unfree when he is justifiably imprisoned" (Cohen 1981, 228). In my view, Nozick's alleged implicit assumption of trivalence is indeed the reason that underpins Cohen's critique. Nozick cannot recognize as interferences on freedom those obstacles that prevent us from doing actions which lie beyond the borders of our moral rights. Cohen's critique, therefore, highlights a tension between Nozick's ideal and our intuitions about freedom: Nozick's theory cannot recognize as curtailments on freedom those cases of preventions on actions which lie beyond the borders of our moral rights, that, on the contrary, we would intuitively describe as limitations of our freedom.

It is crucial to notice at this point that this tension between intuitions and the area of not-freedom which qualifies TTFs can be said to characterize most of the trivalent interpretations of freedom: Cases of preventions on actions which lie in the different not-freedom dominions may be recognized as sources of unfreedom by common-shared intuitions, but are interpreted as not-freedoms by TTFs. Kramer, for instance, does not recognize as instances of unfreedom cases of preventions of actions/becomings we would anyway be unable to do/become. TTFs seem all to have, in virtue of their trivalence, analogous counterintuitive implications: If those preventions on actions which lie in the various not-freedom dominions are considered sources of unfreedom by our intuitions, how can TTFs justify the labelling of such cases as instances of not-freedom?[8]

After having clarified this aspect that seems to characterize trivalent approaches, I can now move to the discussion of Pettit's objection to FNI. The first step of my argument consists in noting that Berlin's FNF should be interpreted as a TTF, because it entails that ascriptions of freedom/unfreedom do not pertain to the set of actions which we do not actually desire: you can be described as free/unfree to do an action you actually desire, but, if you do not actually wish to do that action, neither ascriptions of freedom nor of unfreedom pertain to your status. This seems the reason why for FNF the prisoner cannot be considered unfree, if she does not wish to do the actions she is prevented to do: to that set of actions pertain ascriptions of not-freedom. If we adopt FNF, we can change our situation

8 The central point here is which kinds of trivalence defining conditions can be said to fit our intuitions in reflective equilibrium.

in terms of freedom/unfreedom by adapting our preferences, by ceasing to wish to do a particular action, that is by turning an instance of unfreedom into an instance of not-freedom. But, given that it seems hard to deny the counterintuitiveness of such move, the anti-adaptation argument succeeds in its critique of FNF. The anti-adaptation objection, like Cohen's critique of Nozick's theory of freedom, implicitly questions the not-freedom aspect of TTFs: the sense of the anti-adaptation argument is that of highlighting the counterintuitiveness of the possibility of turning unfreedom into not-freedom simply by changing your own preferences, without removing the obstacle.

But the analogy with the anti-ingratiation argument against FNI fails, because FNI is anyway per se committed to a trivalent view: contemporary defenders of the theory either commit themselves to a BTF (Steiner 1994; 2001; and less explicitly Carter 1999) or the characterization of the area of not-freedom in their TTFs has no relevance for the analysis of the anti-ingratiation example (Kramer 2003). Steiner's *bivalent* view implies that, if the obstacle prevents your doing x, you are consequently unfree, while you are free if the obstacle is removed. As Carter and Kramer have argued at length, freedom measurements need to be sensitive to probability judgements and the use of time indexes (1999; 2003): If we assume that B's exercise of ingratiating A renders B free to *x*, this entails that there is a high probability that the obstacle is removed, that in virtue of B's act of ingratiation, it is highly unlikely that A will be disposed to exercise his power over B, while, if we assume that, even if B attempts to ingratiate A, she still remains unfree, this means that the obstacle is not removed, that the probability that A will interfere with B remains high. This latter possibility simply entails that B's acts of ingratiation do not succeed in their intent. Therefore, the anti-ingratiation argument fails to reject FNI, because, if the ingratiation renders you free to x, this entails that, by definition, the obstacle is removed, namely that there is a very low probability that A will interfere (for this line of argument, see Carter 1999, 237–245).

Notice that the appealing of my argumentation to the bivalence/trivalence formal distinction parallels a substantive claim: While the anti-adaptation argument, entailing that you can liberate yourself by modifying your own dispositions, shows the counterintuitiveness of FNF, the anti-ingratiation argument fails to show the counterintuitiveness of FNI, because by attempting to ingratiate A, B does not attempt to liberate herself through a modification of *her own* dispositions, but by attempting to change *the power holder's* dispositions, namely by attempting to remove the relevant obstacle.

References

Arneson, Richard J. 1985. Freedom and Desire. *Canadian Journal of Philosophy*, 3: 425–448.

Berlin, Isaiah. 2002. *Liberty*, Ed. by Henry Hardy. New York: Oxford University Press.

Berlin, Isaiah. 1958. Two Concepts of Liberty, Inaugural Lecture as Chichele Professor of Social and Political Theory, Oxford University, delivered on 31 October 1958. In Berlin, Isaiah. 2002. *Liberty*, Ed. by Henry Hardy. New York: Oxford University Press: 166–217.

Carter, Ian. 2020a. Liberty. In *Issues in Political Theory*, Ed. by C. McKinnon, P. Tomlin and R. Jubb, 4th edition. Oxford: Oxford University Press, forthcoming.

Carter, Ian. 2020b. Self-Ownership and the Importance of the Human Body. *Social Philosophy and Policy*, 36(2): 94–115.

Carter, Ian. 2019. Opacity Respect, Bureaucracy, and Philanthropy. A Response to Nathan. *European Journal of Political Theory*, 28: 541–52.

Carter, Ian, Shnayderman, Ronen. 2018. The Impossibility of 'Freedom as Independence'. *Political Studies Review*, 17: 136–46.

Carter, Ian. 2013a. Basic Equality and the Site of Egalitarian Justice. *Economics and Philosophy*, 29: 21–41.

Carter, Ian. 2013b. Liberty. In *Oxford Bibliographies, "Philosophy"* Ed. D. Pritchard. New York: Oxford University Press.

Carter, Ian. 2013c. Introduction. *Toleration and Respect. Special Issue of Journal of Applied Philosophy*, 30: 191–94.

Carter, Ian. 2012. Equality. In *Philosophy and Politics. Methods, Tools, Topics*, Ed. by A. Besussi. Farnham: Ashgate.

Carter, Ian. 2011a. Entries on "Brute luck", "Throffers" and "Freedom". In *Encyclopedia of Power*, Ed. by K. Dowding. London: Sage.

Carter, Ian. 2011b. *Value-Freeness and Value-Neutrality*. Paper presented at the Workshop "Power and Freedom", Pavia 13/14 June 2011.

Carter, Ian. 2007. General and Sectional Introductions. In *Freedom: A Philosophical Anthology*, Ed. by I. Carter, M.H. Kramer and H. Steiner. Oxford: Blackwell.

Carter, Ian. 2005. *La Libertà Eguale*. Milan: Feltrinelli.

Carter, Ian. 2004. Choice, Freedom and Freedom of Choice. *Social Choice and Welfare*, 22: 61–81.

Carter, Ian. 2003. Positive and Negative Freedom. In *The Stanford Encyclopaedia of Philosophy*. [http://plato.stanford.edu, accessed on 04.02.2020].

Carter, Ian. 2001. A Critique of Freedom as Non-domination. *The Good Society*, 9(3): 43–46.

Carter, Ian, Ricciardi, Mario (eds.). 2001. *Freedom, Power and Political Morality*. London: Palgrave.

Carter, Ian. 1999. *A Measure of Freedom*. Oxford: Oxford University Press.

Carter, Ian. 1996a. The Concept of Freedom in the Work of Amartya Sen: An Alternative Analysis Consistent with Freedom's Independent Value. *Notizie di Politeia*, 43/44: 7–22.

Carter, Ian. 1996b. The Concept of Freedom. Part I: Background, Methodology, and the 'Positive Negative' Debate. *Humane Studies Review*, 10(3).

Carter, Ian. 1995. The Independent Value of Freedom. *Ethics*, 105(4): 819–45.

Cohen, Gerald A. 1988. *History, Labour, and Freedom*. Oxford: Oxford University Press.

Cohen, Gerald A. 1985. Are Workers Forced to Sell Their Labor Power? *Philosophy and Public Affairs*, 14(1): 99–105.

Cohen, Gerald A. 1983. The Structure of Proletarian Unfreedom. *Philosophy and Public Affairs*, 12(1): 3–33.

Cohen, Gerald A. 1979. Illusions about Private Property and Freedom. In *Issues in Marxist Philosophy*, Ed. by J. Mepham, D. H. Ruben, Vol. 4. Hassocks: Harvester Press.

Goodin, Robert E., Pettit, Philip (eds.). 1993, 2007. *A Companion to Contemporary Political Philosophy,* 2nd ed. Oxford: Blackwell.

Gray, Tim. 1991. *Freedom.* London: Macmillan.

Hayek, Friedrich A. von. 1960. *The Constitution of Liberty.* London: Routledge and Kegan Paul.

Kramer, Matthew. 2010. Freedom and the Rule of Law [Meador Lecture on Freedom], *Alabama Law Review*, 61: 805–23.

Kramer, Matthew. 2003. *The Quality of Freedom.* Oxford: Oxford University Press.

MacCallum, Gerald C. Jr. 1967. Negative and Positive Freedom. *The Philosophical Review*, 76: 312–334.

Miller, David. 2006. *The Liberty Reader*. Edinburgh: Edinburgh University Press.

Nozick, Robert. 1974. *Anarchy, State, and Utopia.* New York: Basic Books.

Olsaretti, Serena. 2004. *Liberty, Desert and the Market.* Cambridge: Cambridge University Press.

Oppenheim, Felix E. 1981. *Political Concepts. A Reconstruction.* Chicago: University of Chicago Press.

Oppenheim, Felix E. 1961. *Dimensions of Freedom*. New York: St Martin's Press.

Pettit, Philip. 2012. *On the People Terms*. Cambridge: Cambridge University Press.

Pettit, Philip. 2011. The Instability of Freedom as Non-interference. The Case of Isaiah Berlin. *Ethics*, 121: 693–716.

Pettit, Philip. 2010a. Civic Republican Theory. In *A Political Philosophy in Public Life: Civic Republicanism in Zapatero's Spain*, Ed. by José Luis Martí and Philip Pettit. Princeton: Princeton University Press.

Pettit, Philip. 2010b. Legitimate International Institutions. In *The Philosophy of International Law*, Ed. by Samantha Besson and John Tasioulas. Oxford: Oxford University Press.

Pettit, Philip. 2008. Republican Freedom: Three Axioms, Four Theorems. In *Republicanism and Political Theory*, Ed. by Cecil Laborde and John Maynor. Oxford: Blackwell Publishing.

Pettit, Philip. 2001. *A Theory of Freedom: From the Psychology to the Politics of Agency*. Oxford: OUP.

Pettit, Philip. 1997. *Republicanism. A Theory of Freedom and Government*. Oxford: OUP.

Rawls, John. 1971, 1999. *A Theory of Justice*. Cambridge, MA: Harvard University Press.

Sen, Amartya. 2009. *The Idea of Justice*. London: Penguin Books.

Sen, Amartya. 1999. *Development as Freedom*. Oxford: Oxford University Press.

Sen, Amartya. 1992. *Inequality Reexamined*. Oxford: Oxford University Press.

Sen, Amartya. 1990. Justice: Means versus Freedoms. *Philosophy & Public Affairs*, 19(2): 111–121.

Skinner, Quentin. 1998. *Liberty Before Liberalism*. Cambridge: CUP.

Steiner, Hillel. 2001. *Freedom and Bivalence*. In *Freedom, Power and Political Morality*, Ed. by Ian Carter and Mario Ricciardi. London: Palgrave: 57–68.

Steiner, Hillel. 1998. Freedom, Rights and Equality: A Reply to Wolff. *International Journal of Philosophical Studies*, 6: 128–137.

Steiner, Hillel. 1994. *An Essay on Rights*. Oxford: Blackwell.

Steiner, Hillel. 1983. *How Free: Computing Personal Liberty*. In *Of Liberty*, Ed. by A. Phillips-Griffiths. Cambridge: Cambridge University Press: 73–89.

Steiner, Hillel. 1974/1975. Individual Liberty. *Proceedings of the Aristotelian Society*, 75: 35–50.

Van Parijs, Philippe. 1995. *Real Freedom for All. What (if anything) Can Justify Capitalism*. Oxford: Clarendon Press.

Josef Šíma

Department of Economics, CEVRO Institute, Prague, Czech Republic

On perception of freedom in post-socialist Central Europe

Ladislav Mrklas

Department of Political Science and International Relations, CEVRO Institute, Prague, Czech Republic

Abstract: The fall of communism three decades ago brought opportunity to change rigidly controlled and centrally planned societies of Central Europe to freer regimes. However, the general shift towards more freedom has proven to be a multifaceted process with numerous obstacles. We will focus on the four Visegrad countries (the Czech Republic, Hungary, Poland and Slovakia) and highlight different key historical moments determining today's differing perceptions of freedom by the people of those four countries. We will then analyse current challenges to freedom based on the differing perceptions among the Visegrad countries.

Keywords: Visegrad countries, Central Europe, socialism, transition, freedom, nationalism

Introduction

The fall of communism three decades ago brought opportunity to change rigidly controlled and centrally planned societies of Central Europe to freer regimes. In this chapter, we will analyse the multifaceted process of understanding freedom by people living in what we today call the "Visegrad countries", the Czech Republic, Hungary, Poland and Slovakia. In his authoritative work "The Price of Freedom", Stefan Wandycz formulates the general lesson on the history of those countries:

> A good part of East Central European history has been filled with the struggle for freedom. Oppression came from outside because of an exposed geographic

> position: peripheral in the case of Hungary…., open to invasions from east and west in Poland's case, or surrounded by Germanic lands as Bohemia. But in each case there was usually also an ideological element: outside absolutism versus local constitutionalism. (2013, 9)

In line with this general understanding, we will attempt to draw lessons from key moments of historical development to show that those four Central European countries and polities indeed often share a general drift toward freedom, yet – in a more subtle sense – they differ substantially in the key aspect of freedom that unifies the population and brings about political and social change.

Our historical, political and economic enterprise will be conducted with one goal in mind. We want to shed some light on the last thirty years since the fall of communism, during which these four countries were lucky enough to utilize a chance to make freedom a key part of their deep and thorough political, economic and social changes. We focused on the transition processes, considering individual national appreciation regarding different aspects of freedom in the hopes of providing a better understanding of the initial dynamics pushing institutional change, the logic of transition and the sustainability of the shift towards freedom in Central Europe.

Our chapter is structured as follows. In the first part, we talk briefly about general historical background of the Central European region and then highlight crucial aspects and events that shaped the understanding of freedom in the four respective countries. Part three covers debates over distinctive features of the communist regimes and driving forces of transition towards freer societies after 1989. Part four evaluates the current situation in the Czech Republic, Slovakia, Hungary and Poland which in numerous aspects not only conflicts with the key ideas of previously experienced transition but seems to be sometimes a direct and deliberate attack on crucial tenets of economic and political liberties. We document that limited robustness of newly reformed systems poses many problems, and hence departures from principles of liberal democracy in the region of Central Europe – especially in the wake of deep economic crises – may take a much more unpredictable form.

1. Central Europe – free and unfree

In past centuries, Central Europe was at times a prosperous and glorious place, peaceful, tolerant, with great religious, scientific, economic and political freedom. Unfortunately, though, often and repeatedly, Central Europe was a place of bloody wars, serfdom, xenophobia, barbarism, violence and oppression under authoritarian and totalitarian regimes. All that has framed the coexistence of Czechs, Hungarians, Poles and Slovaks (and other nationalities living in the region). At some points in history, they fought viciously against each other, on other occasions – such as during and after World War II (WWII) – their freedom was significantly violated by foreign invaders, and they suffered together under regimes imposed by force from outside.

A key factor in understanding the region is to appreciate the ethnic and language diversity as well as the religious pluralism, which, when respected, led to social harmony and freedom for holders of both minority and majority views. However, at the same time, the diversity has always been a source of attempts for forced unification and homogenization both for the sake of "more efficient" state organization or plain political domination.[1] Such attacks on freedom and elimination of that plurality was documented too well in plentiful cases and historical contexts – Jews, protestants, defenders of free political party systems and many others have their sad stories of institutionalized oppression.

In the following section, we will focus on all four respective countries and highlight crucial factors in their development which we believe shaped their national understanding of different key tenets of freedom. Once we understand why there are varieties of nationally specific attributes of freedom that constitute intellectual equipment of people in different countries of the region, we can better grasp differing routes of recapturing and regaining freedom in recent history. We will also gain insight into the source of differing values Czechs, Hungarians, Poles and Slovaks were ready to fight for during the communist era, which preceded the changes.

1 More on dangers to liberty from centralization in multi-ethnic societies in Central Europe by a leading 20th-century advocate of freedom in Mises (2006).

Historically, Central Europe has developed for centuries under the reign of the Habsburg monarchy. Classical liberal ideas of freedom and political liberties started to penetrate the territory after the French Revolution, with British thinkers having a great influence. Among the first centres of early liberalism, one can find the south German states of the post-Napoleonic era from which the liberal thought spread into Austria. Both German and Austrian liberalism had built substantially on the idea of the enlightened state as a guarantor of social progress. Driving forces of those ideas have been intelligentsia from cities, bureaucracy and reform-oriented nobility (Křen 2005). In Hungary, defenders of classical liberalism came often from Hungarian lower nobility, the so-called gentry. Among Czechs and other Austrian-Slavic nations (with the exception of Poles where acceptance of liberalism has been prevented by strong tensions between aristocratic conservatism and radicalism of insurgents), the progress of liberalism was tightly linked to movements of national revivals, political emancipation and nation-building. In those epochs, national histories were often reinterpreted and brought to the fore of the development of European civilization and values of the West.

> ...Poles, Hungarians, and Czechs often looked up to the West...with a mixture of adoration and envy. Everything "European", a synonym for the West, seemed worthy of praise and imitation. ...But this feeling of inferiority needed to be, and often was compensated for by a glorification of national history and national uniqueness. Poles, Czechs, even Slovaks all referred at various times to their homeland as the heart of Europe. Hungarians and Poles regarded themselves as defenders of the West. (Wandycz 2013, 5)

The Revolution of 1848 represented a major setback for spreading freedom in Central Europe. Its failure was understood as a failure of liberal reformism. The classical liberal camp suffered a shock which affected the region for several decades. Bourgeois classes – leading voices of freedom – lost their political influence and were pushed from politics to rapidly developing economic sphere (Urban 2003).

A revival of and a new hope for liberalism was initiated by an attitude change in conservative circles in Vienna in the late 1850s and early 1860s. This political shift was driven by an attempt by conservatives to broaden their political base and reorganize the Habsburg political structure. A compromise with liberals (mostly only Hungarian liberals, though) was concluded. Liberals gave up their separatism in exchange for gaining political autonomy within Austro-Hungarian dualism. Czech liberals were excluded from this deal and Polish (and Croatian) liberals achieved only very marginal benefits.

What followed has been an era of semi-liberal and predominantly liberal governments following in many ways a classical liberal agenda: Basics of modern constitutional order are laid down; new legislation strengthens classical liberal attributes of the rule of law which makes room for economic development; a concept of citizenship is forming even for not-yet-emancipated nations. The idea of freedom penetrating social organization in many ways goes hand in hand with the secularization of society and emancipation of the Jewish community, which will later become one of the central pillars of Central European liberalism (Kontler 2002; Aberbach 2012).

It is important, however, to keep in mind that those policy changes were far from fully representing key tenets of classical liberalism and economic and political freedom. Among sources of these imperfections of Austro-German liberalism, one can clearly identify bureaucratic centralism, a defining feature of the Habsburg reign. Moreover, the Czech understanding of liberalism was deformed by an existing political alliance among liberals and several conservative movements; in Hungary, under the name of liberalism, political repression of minorities – Slovaks among others – often took place, creating hostilities toward the "liberal regime".

Moreover, the economic crisis of 1873 discredited – justifiably or not – to a great extent in the eyes of the general public the notion of capitalism and its classical liberal underpinnings. Since that time, a classical liberal political agenda has been often viewed as supporting narrow "class" interests of the "party of capital". If we accept ideas of freedom, epitomized in political and economic classical liberalism, dominated for a short time the politics and economics of the Visegrad countries, we can see the "freedom" period was much shorter than in Western Europe. As a result, the key features of freedom could not take deep root in those societies.

In decades to come, ideas of freedom had to face several waves of hostile confrontations with new political currents emphasizing vested interests of professional, social-religious or strongly nationalistic groups: agrarianism, socialism, catholic-social movement and a variety of nationalisms.

Over time, the idea of freedom within the rule of law lost its appeal even within a bourgeois cadre (or elite-based) party as well (Duverger 1951 and 1959). Proponents of classical liberalism, who most of all represented an ideal of freedom, hence became marginalized politically and often socially, too. Some found their refuge in academia, some left for countries less hostile to the idea of freedom (Křen 2005). At the beginning of the 20th century, classical liberal political parties de facto disappeared from the political scene, though some of the core values (such as rule of law, civil rights and relatively free market) became an integral – though in a limited scope – part of modern political thinking and, during several moments in the coming decades, managed to influence crucial social and political decisions taken by countries of Central Europe.

2. Constituting features of freedom in individual countries

Let us now briefly look more closely at the individual countries and highlight additional historical moments or situations which imprint a particular flavour on the notion of freedom.

2.1. Poland

In Poland, a country which – as Adam Zamoyski aptly noted – "sometimes existed and sometimes not" (2009), the concept of freedom predominantly refers to national independence. For historical reasons, other meanings enter into discussions only much later. There is, however, a strong liberty tradition in Poland, which in many respects ignited the torch of freedom for the whole of Europe especially during the Polish-Lithuanian Republic (1573–1795). The Polish state, Rzeczpospolita (res publica), allowed an unprecedented spread of individual freedom, religious tolerance and provided limited constitutional government. Those achievements stemmed primarily from application of the unanimity principle in the legislature (the liberum veto), the right to resist (the Confederation) and the constitutional constraints imposed on kings (Henrician Articles and Pacta Conventa) (Roháč 2008).

The Polish Constitution of 1791 is the second oldest written constitution in the world, following only the US Constitution. Sovereignty of the people and division of power were among its founding principles. Though in place only for one year, it exemplified the spirit of freedom among Poles and was a reference point for future generations of Polish defenders of freedom. (Another of Polish constitutions signed in 1815 that established constitutional order in Congress Poland – Kongresówka – in the aftermath of the Congress of Vienna was perhaps the most liberal constitution in Europe of that time, granting even more freedoms than the 1791 Constitution.) (Davies 2001; Janowski 2004) Liberal constitutional and economic moments in Polish history notwithstanding, for understanding modern debates it is crucial to keep in mind that the re-emergence of politically independent Poland as a nation after World War I (WWI) was considered *the* meaning of freedom for most Poles. Sadly enough, from the first day of independence, Poland found itself in the middle of tensions. The new state did not have a single neighbour where territorial or other disputes would not spoil mutual relations. Fighting for its place among European nations and facing all those disputes, interwar Poland did not opt for true liberal democracy. During the so-called 2nd Republic,

> not only substantial constitutional modifications took place... but the whole political system changed from democratic to authoritarian, although the period of authoritarianism was rather diverse. (Kubát 2006)

The past division of Poland left visible traces in terms of huge heterogeneity in social-economic, legal and political spheres. In the political system, one could see inherent fragmentation, instability and political polarization, which over time grew into authoritarian tendencies of several kinds. As in the 19th century, Polish liberal circles after WWI were not able to find relevant political representation. The only unifying element of Polish politics (which indeed in itself is not sufficient for forming a relevant classical liberal agenda) was an attempt to keep national sovereignty and independence. Another basis for consensus in interwar Poland was democracy; democracy was understood, among other things, as a defining affiliation between Poland and the European West. Here, however, political actors diverged. Centrists (Christian Democrats) accepted parliamentary republican democracy; socialist were critical of it due to the strong influence of the bourgeoisie, and national democrats criticized such a democracy for its national neutrality. WWII ended this period of newly gained statehood, and its brutality reminded Poles how fragile their independent existence was.

2.2. Hungary

Hungary has a history as a dominant Central European power but also – later – as a state which had to defend itself against Turkish invasions and Habsburg expansionism. Turkish conquest of major parts of its territory, including the capital Buda in 1541 and its consequent abandonment by a part of the domestic nobility with the help of the Habsburgs, represents an important constitutive element of modern Hungarian history and Hungarian perception of freedom. Freedom is understood essentially in its patriotic-national meaning, which is further reinforced by the existential threat coming from the infidels, that is Muslims. Catholic Habsburgs are seen as defenders of both faith and national sovereignty.

An interesting lesson from modern Hungarian history, which is tightly linked with the question of freedom and the question of democracy (and its ex- and inclusivity), is supplied by a development in the second half of the 19th century. After the bloody defeat of the separatist movement against the Habsburgs in 1848–1849, we see a period when an open separatism is replaced by the program of autonomy. Such a program – a key part of a consensus between Hungarian elites and the Habsburgs – was supported by leading Hungarian classical liberals such as Ferenc Deák and József Eötvös. They believed that the Habsburg Monarchy must be preserved as a natural bulwark against huge blocks of Germans in the West and Slavs in the North, South and East. In order to play that role, Vienna needed an alliance with Hungarians, which was conceivable only when their autonomy within the monarchy would be granted.[2]

The quest for Hungarian autonomy was fulfilled with the Austro-Hungarian Compromise of 1867 which, on one hand, gave Hungarians much desired political freedom in terms of political autonomy vis-a-vis Vienna and, on the other, however, lead to a situation in which same freedoms were denied to other peoples living within Hungarian autonomy. The classical liberal maxim demanding equality before the law remained

2 An idea strongly disputed by post-1948 exiled elite which believed that a dramatic change of political relations in Europe opens the door for emergence of new national states.

unfulfilled and liberal political elites confined their policy reforms to bringing about freer economic relations and building new infrastructure. Many social hierarchies rooted in privileges remained untacked.[3] Political parties looked more like gentlemen's clubs without underlying unifying ideological principles (Kontler 2002). Both main political parties united in 1875 and formed the new "Liberal Party", which, however, was not faithful to its name, and the actual policies often represented the antithesis of what liberalism and freedom means. That was also true for several other political entities labelled "liberal", "free" or "independent". These represented a typically conservative agenda, defending the status quo or even putting forward a radical socialist agenda (Kwan 2013).

The interwar period can be characterized as looking for a new identity when the dream of reestablishment of old national glory in terms of country size and importance proved to be an illusion. The turbulent situation in the wake of WWI was not conducive to the establishment of a liberal order – not only the founding of the Hungarian Soviet Republic and occupation of the country by its neighbours but above all the Treaty of Trianon[4] of June 1920 marks a watershed of Hungarian political development setting the key political agenda for the coming years and in a sense for the rest of the century: It was not protection of political liberties and economic freedom but re-establishment of "justice to Hungary".

Especially in the interwar period, attempts to identify "traitors" among proponents of political liberalism, members of left-wing parties, neighbouring countries or Jews[5] established dangerous anti-liberal and

3 According to Kontler, about 80% of deputies came from the strata of land magnates. Only about 6 % of the population had the right to vote which was not unusual in the mid-1860s, but at the turn of the century such a low number was very much a rarity (2002).

4 The Versailles/Trianon treaties constitute a much debated political event which proved to be fatal for the fate of freedom in the 20th century. Critics point to the unprecedented humiliating nature of it which brought to power nationalists and national socialists in Germany and Hungary (Raico 2010, ch. 1).

5 Anti-semitism became an official policy. The first post WWI European *numerus clausus* limiting representation of Jews among students of high schools and especially universities was adopted in Hungary at that time.

anti-democratic moods, resulting in an advent of an authoritarian regime. Such policy consequently led to international isolation which Hungary manipulated itself into.

2.3. Slovakia

Whereas Czechs, Poles and Hungarians have a long history of national emancipation that resulted in the existence of politically independent states, Slovaks lived for centuries in Upper Hungary and only by the establishment of Czechoslovakia, "Slovakia" got for the first time to the name of the state they lived in. Political and cultural emancipation of Slovaks was heavily dependent on the Czech national revival. The idea of freedom predominantly coincided with the quest for resisting Hungarian political and cultural dominance by resurrection of the Slovak language, promoting Slovak culture and gaining political independence. In a predominantly agrarian country with a very low education level, and tiny number of Slovak schools, development of the idea of Czech-Slovak mutuality and links to Czech liberals was chosen as an effective tool for achieving political liberties. Club Detvan and the monthly journal Hlas based in Prague played an important role in this respect. This link to Czech liberals was strengthened by the fact that prior to WWI, the "Slovak National Party", which most visibly represented Slovak national interest, was often criticized by Slovak intelligentsia for its pro-Russian orientation; and no political party promoting a classical liberal agenda existed in Slovakia (Kováč 1998).

After the establishment of Czechoslovakia in 1918, the most influential political figure with classical liberal orientation was Milan Hodža, successful politician and prime minister. Though nominally representing the political agenda called "agrarian democracy", his emphasis on private property, personal freedom and the rule of law coincided considerably with classical-liberal tradition. His accent on rooting Slovak interest in promoting Czech-Slovak unity as a bulwark against the political danger to Slovak independence coming from Russia, Hungary or Germany symbolized accurately the flavour of where the idea of freedom is rooted in interwar Slovakia (Hloušek and Kopeček 2010).

The Slovak State which existed between 1939 and 1945 as a client state of Nazi Germany was far from fulfilling the Slovak dream national independence, a key ingredient in the Slovak understanding of freedom. For achieving that, Slovaks had to wait for almost half a century.

2.4. The Czech Republic

As a historian of modern Czech politics, Otto Urban reminds us, "in the Czech environment, liberal thinking shows a distinctive leaning toward empirical manifestation [i.e. practical application]" (2003). Civic revival, that is a striving for civil liberties, goes hand in hand with national revival, including the Czech language and political independence which after (enlightened) absolutism of the late 18th century was in ruins. There was no solid basis for classical liberal thinking; independent bourgeoisie did not exist in sufficient numbers, true for both Czech- and German-speaking areas, and hence many representatives of Czech liberalism turned to the countryside; political and social reforms, which opened space for ideas of freedom to start spreading, came from state actions, from the top, rather than as grassroots movement coming from citizens reclaiming their rights.

Two aspects of Czech liberalism are noteworthy: the political, exemplified by František Palacký and František Ladislav Rieger, and their work on constitutional changes within the Habsburg Monarchy in 1848–1849; and influential pro-freedom journalism (Karel Havlíček). These two forms of activities created an intellectual breeding ground to understanding liberalism as political demands for federalization of the monarchy and as a cultural phenomenon demanding free journalism, education and schooling for the masses as well as free development of culture generally. A particular aspect of that debate was the anti-authoritarian element seen in the historical struggle of religious reformation against both the power of the state and the Catholic Church.

Due to nationalistic divisions inside the Habsburg monarchy, the increasing influence of classical liberal ideas never led to the formation of a unified Czech classical liberal party. Czech liberals in the "National Party"– a dominant political force between the 1860s and the 1890s – over time turned more and more conservative and were replaced as a leading political force by "The National Liberal Party", which in the mid-1890s became – thanks to Josef Kaizl and Karel Kramář – one of the most well-defined classical political parties in Cisleithania. With the introduction of universal suffrage in 1907, it became clear that new mass parties with non-liberal agendas (both socialist and vested interest) were gaining influence over mostly elitist classical liberals, signalling the retreat of classical liberal sway on political life.

Scholars studying political culture of pre-independent Czechoslovakia, however, document that the declining of influence of Czech liberals over political reforms of the monarchy was replaced by a growing effort to succeed in the economic realm which previous reforms opened room for (Klicperová-Baker 1999). The result was rather rapid growth of Czech economic prosperity, bringing them to the top in terms of well-being in Central Europe. *Economic liberalism* since then becomes a constitutive element of Czech politics and keeps popping up periodically during the 20th century.

Interwar period was a time of several paradoxes regarding ideas of freedom. The independent state of Czechoslovakia emerged as a consequence of the post-war new world order. It indeed meant fulfilment of a Czech classical liberal agenda of national independence and self-determination. For millions of Germans living in Czechoslovakia though, the feelings were the exact opposite as many of them did not identify themselves with the new state and experienced discrimination. In addition, massive land reform that targeted the aristocracy and church took place, but as a consequence, a substantial class of small landowners emerged and constituted a stabilizing element in Czech society in the years ahead.

Over time, many discriminatory features of the immediate post-war period were removed. The country avoided dramatic revolutionary situations and despite the fact that no political party explicitly called itself "liberal", the resulting regime showed strong classical-liberal features. Especially compared to neighbouring countries, it was in many ways an island of liberal democracy, political stability and economic development (Cabada and Waisová 2011).

Foundations of liberal democratic order were, however, too weak to survive attacks from both inside and outside, and sadly even former proponents of classical liberal ideas contributed to the demolition of the interwar regime. The first years after WWII, though not yet under communist rule, showed no signs of a new regime rooted in individualism and political and economic freedom. Prevailing ideas of socialization, confiscation of private property, restrictions on political competition and expulsion of the German-speaking population were only the most drastic signs of the coming of a new era – one that negated freedom. The communist coup d'état in February 1948 established a symbolic watershed.

3. Communism and transition in Central Europe

Two world wars followed by 40 years of communism was a catastrophe especially for the region of Central Europe. WWI buried forever the *ancien régime* with its classical liberal roots and opened the door for dangerous nationalisms in its many forms: WWII[6] and her aftermath eliminated most of region's national and cultural diversity, and communist central planning and political oppression deprived the four countries of economic prosperity and political pluralism. What used to be flourishing and vibrant societies moving successfully from a holistic order of the past to an extended order of the modern West (Zweynert and Goldschmidt 2005) ended up as an impoverished group of isolated countries with barbed wire around their borders to prevent people from leaving (Kornai 2000).

Thus a common pursuit of the people in the Visegrad countries was a move towards free societies in the late 1980s. After many years, freedom came within reach. People in all four countries set off for a joint, largely similar enterprise. They wanted quickly to reclaim autonomy and empower people to self-govern their societies. In these countries, that quest indeed meant getting rid of Soviet political influence or military presence, opening borders (dismantling the barbed wire fences and ending the artificial "East" economic and political orientation), re-establishing rule of law and re-introducing political and economic competition, that is democracy and economic market-oriented reforms. The Visegrad countries (unlike many other post-socialist countries) opted for extensive regime changes (World Bank 1996) with an attempt to replace old elites from the commanding height of their societies (Walder 2003).

6 The horrors of WWII and atrocities committed by different nations against each other looked at that time so irreconcilable that even long-time fierce opponents of political centralization like Ludwig von Mises saw no future for "liberal order" in Central Europe unless being imposed from above by a liberal "Eastern Democratic Union". More in Šíma (2013).

This common approach in the direction of freedom notwithstanding, social elites in individual countries in Central Europe chose different transition strategies emphasizing different values and aspects of the process. Key *actors* of the transition were different, diverse *strategies* were used and dissimilar *speed* of transition adopted.

Let us analyse now how different national traditions (briefly summarized in Chapter 2) influenced pre- and post-1989 development. We will then – in Chapter 4 – take a look at a link between these national specifics and the current problems in Central Europe.

3.1. Different communisms

It is well-known that despite drastic imposition of "real socialism" in the Visegrad countries and forced homogenization through its means, individual communist regimes still reflected many important differences. Whereas in Czech countries and to a smaller extent in Slovakia, communism can be seen as an important domestic ideological and political movement already since the interwar period (as documented by relatively high popular support in elections, where occasionally the communist party was even considered a pro-regime party), Hungary and Poland stood on the other side of the barricade. In those countries, communists were only a very marginal political force until the outbreak of WWII. While communism in post-WWII Czechoslovakia had substantial political support as demonstrated by the landslide victory of the communists in the semi-competitive elections of 1946, in Poland and Hungary communists seized power only with the help of the Soviet Army (in the case of Hungary through a *de facto* occupation). Domestic support of the communists was very weak.

All four countries differed also substantially in other characteristics when entering the communist bloc. The Czech part of Czechoslovakia was a heavily industrialized country while Poland, Hungary and Slovakia were more rural. Social and economic development corresponded to this discrepancy. Religion played a very different role as well. Poland, Slovakia and Hungary – exactly in this order – rank in modern times among the most catholic countries in Europe, whereas the Czech lands belong to places with the highest degree of secularization.

Another important distinction that proved to be important later during the process of re-acquiring freedom after the fall of communism was a different degree of nationalization and violent collectivization of economies. Whereas Czechoslovakia suffered the most drastic elimination of private ownership, in Poland and Hungary private owners never disappeared from the stage and hence large parts of economic activity remained in private hands. Political coercion notwithstanding, some economic freedom allowed for a degree of entrepreneurial activity in those countries for decades. In Czechoslovakia, such a possibility for small business activity was made legal only in the late 1980s (Brada 1996).

The existence of private entrepreneurship and limited economic freedom in Poland and Hungary, as opposed to Czechoslovakia, signalled the weaker grip of central political authorities over those two countries. Hence, not surprisingly, political changes in Poland and Hungary that ultimately led to establishing democratic systems also preceded those of Czechoslovakia. Only after 10 years of liberalization – with the Solidarity movement as a main actor – free elections took place in Poland; in Hungary it was after half that time with mostly younger representatives of the communist party initiating reform steps; in Czechoslovakia, liberalization came about only half-a-year before free elections with students- and political dissent-led revolt against the ruling communist party.

3.2. Transition

Since the 1990s, transitologists have been investigating the common features of Central European countries' trajectories toward economic, political and social transformation as well as the differences that contributed to dissimilar performances of individual countries. One source of differences in Visegrad countries' development seems to stem from the nature of the socialist regimes during their final stages. Herbert Kitschelt (1999) distinguishes among patrimonial, bureaucratic-authoritarian and national-accommodative regimes. Poland and Hungary belong to the national-accommodative category where one can witness certain competitiveness inside the party elite and higher degree of articulation of societal interest, including self-presentation to the general public as defenders of national autonomy. Czechoslovakia occupies an interesting position in this typology. Whereas Czechs are considered typical bureaucratic-authoritarian, Slovakia, which went through a process of political emancipation (federalization of Czechoslovakia in the 1960s) and massive industrialization, is considered a mixture of all three categories.[7]

In the Czech Republic, one can clearly see political conflicts forming transition debates along a socioeconomic cleavage. Key defining points of the political agenda of the early 1990s was speed and depth of economic reform, aiming at re-establishment of the system of private property, privatization, deregulation and market liberalization. It resulted in the inception of a liberal-conservative, that is the civic, political camp, on the one hand, and restoration of historical left with social-democratic leaning, on the other. The concept of freedom resonated in Czech society mostly in its *economic meaning*, as a category emphasizing free-markets, private property and free-enterprise as opposed to state ownership and central planning. Side by side with the debate over state economic interventionism, newly gained political freedoms and formerly non-existing civil liberties enjoyed attention as well indeed, especially through Vaclav Havel who became a symbol of the victory over communism.

After the fall of communism, however, Hungary and Poland went predominantly through political disputes of a national-historical nature. It gave rise to fundamental importance of *nationalistic* cleavage of transformation (Hloušek and Kopeček 2004). The political scene of both countries got divided into a kind of historical Left, that is "social-democratized" post-communist parties, and a kind of historical Right, characterized by anti-communism and nationalist leaning. This dualism of "Solidarity" (and post-Solidarity) Right drawing from national-catholic heritage and post-communist Left defined the first decade of political battles in Polish democracy.

7 Patrimonial regimes, such as the one in Romania, are defined by hierarchical-personal dependency of the communist elites (Ceaușescu) and their supporters. This dependency results in the establishment of strong clientelic relations. In bureaucratic-authoritative regimes and struggles over power control were not visible. The procedures of control were mostly bureaucratic and elimination of opposition harsher. GDR would be an example of this arrangement (Kitschelt 1999).

The Hungarian analogy of this process is a conflict between social-democratized post-communist Left and national-conservative Right. A dominant question in Polish and Hungarian politics was – as many times before – national independence (in the case of Hungary, flavoured by its language specificity and irredentist implications). Classical liberal arguments with their emphasis on economic freedom and property right underpinnings entered the debate only rarely as a third, independent factor. The conflict over freedom thus took place between arguments and policies of the left-modernist liberalism of post-communists and Christian-conservative defence of national independence as a framework for exercising personal rights and freedoms.

This process resulted in seemingly paradoxical steps in terms of policies adopted by the two camps. The Polish and Hungarian Left often liberalized the economy and undertook privatization more than the conservative Right. Classical liberals levitated in between – in Hungary gravitating for various reasons towards the post-communist Left and in Poland enriching both camps and overtime losing its significance almost entirely (Hloušek and Kopeček 2010).

Slovakia offers an example of still another distinct development. As we argued above, in terms of nation-building, Slovaks reached a point of approaching national self-determination only after the fall of communism, a situation which other Visegrad countries had gone through roughly a century before. A fundamental question for the transition period for Slovaks was, therefore, national autonomy, a long-time political ideal. The hybrid nature of Slovak communism represented itself in this process in several aspects. The first one was that national emancipation faced two problems: a common state with Czechs and presence of a sizable Hungarian minority. Both entities embodied for the vast majority of Slovaks a symbol of unwelcome colonization – a current one in the former and a historical one in the latter.

Whereas both Czechs and Slovaks appreciated newly gained freedom, they saw differently what the key element of such freedom amounted to. Czechs saw it as on opportunity to launch into business activities, trade and generation of wealth to make up for the time lost during central planning, to take on where the economic success of pre-WWII Czechoslovakia left off; Slovaks considered new freedom as a tool towards finishing up their national self-determination journey. Unlike in the Czech Republic, the dominant political cleavage in Slovakia was therefore the *nationalistic* underpinning of transition. Slovak political scene was not divided between political Left and Right, but was populated by a variety of less or more radical defenders of Slovak national sovereignty and less or more tight federation with Czechs.

The former tendency gained a dominant stance and what followed was almost a decade of a strong authoritarian regime embodied by prime minister Mečiar, whose name gave the name to this period of Slovak development, a period characterized by a peculiar mix of anti-Hungarian and anti-Czech nationalism, economic paternalism (which was at the same time accompanied by sizable but nontransparent privatization), national deformed "Catholicism" and post-communist nostalgia. Political and civil rights were under attack and both far Left (Association of Slovak Workers) and Right (Slovak National Party) took on political positions in the government. International isolation was not an unexpected consequence of this process. At exactly this point, for the first time in Slovak history, an authentic fight for freedom and liberal-democracy was launched. Mečiar was removed and the Slovak political scene reshaped into a left-right socioeconomic cleavage (weakened only later on as elsewhere in Europe by "anti-corruption" and "anti-establishment" popular agenda).

4. Challenges for freedom in Central Europe

A sober look back on the results of Central European transition suggests that this region on the whole made a huge step towards market- and liberty-based regimes. Compared to the situation a quarter of a century ago (or half-a-century ago), those countries became open and interconnected, fully integrated into the European West and global economy. Though the way economic, legal and social transition was handled has been often viewed critically (Stiglitz 1999), dramatic positive changes are undeniable. Not only did Central European countries become "normal countries" again, but their radical reforms brought them closer to the Western standard of living compared to slow reformers (Shleifer and Treisman 2014). Indeed, the Visegrad countries still jointly bear consequences of their socialist past: they continue to be poorer than the West, their cultural underpinnings of the rule of law are weaker than in the West, "communist nostalgia" is visible at times, but these phenomena had to be expected.

On top of it though, there seem to be non-trivial systemic problems revealing the existence of serious threats to freedom in Central Europe. Whereas for some time one could witness slow and painful effort to dismantle the consequences of socialism and central planning, to get rid of elements of political and economic oppression, and to encourage re-emergence of vibrant markets and civil society to regain tools for flexible response to new social problems, it is not what drives social change today anymore. Not only the initial pro-liberty ethos got lost, but the general understanding that thorough social changes take time was replaced by impatience. Populism and belief in quick solutions of major economic and social problems, swings of public mood and calling for strong leaders are ingredients capable of reversing successes in transition which the Visegrad countries achieved over the last thirty years.

The Czech Republic became a leading example of these forces exerting major influence. It seems that a well-known historical pattern re-emerges. Overblown expectations in the first years of a new regime with celebrated uniqueness of Czech success elevated to unrealistic heights ("island of stability and democracy in Central Europe" in the interwar period; "best reformer" during transition in 1990s) leads to the whole basic social model being abandoned with the first major crisis, resulting in new alternatives being immediately sought. Both interwar and current regimes seem not to contain enough robustness to cope with crises. Political changes of 2010s seem to document this "fatalism" of Czechs, with unprecedented experimentation on the political scene being the result. Several new political parties with anti-corruption rhetoric and strong business vested interest in the background emerged and dominate the political system. The general public seems to accept the idea that a country can be run as a firm and rather than protesting situations of huge conflict of interest, rewards the main actors with appreciation of their new "style". Clearly, a very unpredictable political agenda of "anti-politics" and belief in quick "technical solutions" was substituted for political discourse prevalent during early years of transition.

Slovakia has been going through a very erratic development typical for states with very short statehood. One could witness initial reforms (under Czechoslovakia) alternated by a decade of nationalistic Mečiarism bringing Slovakia to international isolation, replaced by very extensive market reforms giving Slovaks the label of Central European economic tiger, followed by discrediting of the civic Right and the political comeback of populism and national socialism.

Hungary experienced a unique development among the Visegrad countries when the political scene got dominated by Fidesz to a point where the Constitution was changed in 2012 and the regime lost many of its liberal features. As a model for future social changes China or Russia are often mentioned, and Prime Minister Orban openly renounced classical Western liberal democracy, the first leading European politician to do so, and presented his vision of a new Hungarian social model of national democracy without its "liberal" component (2014).

For a long time, Poland seemed to be successfully avoiding the unwelcome new development of the other three Visegrad countries. Despite its remarkable economic performance, however, at first a retreat of economic liberalism became noticeable (Lipiński 2013) followed by a subsequent series of "reforms", which seem to represent most recent attacks on judicial and media independence, corner stones of the liberal order.

Overall, after thirty years off the path of communist oppression, we see in the Visegrad countries delicate social problems, often typical for the region in the past, which may prevent further advancement of liberty. Externally, countries face the traditional Central European dilemma vis-a-vis foreign neighbours from the West and the East and their influence. This manifests itself in EU/NATO membership, on one hand, and the impact of Russian investments and influence in both key industries and the media, on the other. There seems to be no consensus on what the appropriate weight of those two influences should be to ensure sustainable independent development.

Internally, fast changes in all Visegrad countries brought about problems connected with oligarchization of economic and political life, misuse of political power and media control. Populism is on the rise and when captured by political parties, democracy as such seems to be not questioned, but it is transforming itself into a democracy which often does not uphold liberty.

Conclusion

The modern history of Czechs, Hungarians, Poles and Slovaks can be interpreted as a journey towards freedom with many obstacles on the way. It is a long journey and the goal, which seems to be sometimes within reach, disappears from people's sight a moment later. Foreign invasions, wars, domestic oppression, ideologies of envy and conflict all caused a lot of misery, poverty and death and repeatedly tormented the region of Central Europe. Such historical experience significantly affected the way different peoples primarily understand the concept of freedom. This different understanding of freedom dehomogenizes the region which is often treated as one subject – post-socialist Central Europe or Visegrad countries – and gives us better appreciation of underlying social processes, contemporary problems and their suggested solutions.

Half-a-century of communism gave the four countries an infamous experience of what a regime systematically trampling on people's freedom amounts to. Thirty years after communism's fall, it is clear that the journey towards freedom is a thorny one and that the re-emergent liberty-friendly social systems may not be robust enough to keep the countries on track.

It seems that we are approaching once again a point in which the future of freedom in the region is at stake. There were great hopes and partial successes in the establishment of the rule of law, establishment and protection of civil and economic liberties, guarantees of privacy, division of political power, etc. Many of those key ingredients of a free society are under attack again and the old enemies of freedom – be it xenophobia and nationalism, nationalization and socialism or vested interest and corporativism – gain visibility in public debates and are entering the political agenda to an extent unimaginable during the last thirty years.

References

Aberbach, David. 2012. *The European Jews, Patriotism and the Liberal State 1789–1939: A Study of Literature and Social Psychology*. London: Routledge.

Brada, Josef C. 1996. Privatization Is Transition–Or Is It? *Journal of Economic Perspectives* 10(2): 67–86.

Cabada, Ladislav and Waisová, Šárka. 2011. *Czechoslovakia and the Czech Republic in World Politics*. Lanham: Lexington Books.

Davies, Norman. 2001. *Heart of Europe: The Past in Poland's Present*. Oxford: Oxford University Press.

Duverger, Maurice. 1951. *Les partis politique*. Paris: Colin.

Duverger, Maurice. 1959. *Political Parties: Their Organization and Activity in the Modern State*. London: Methuen & Co.

Hloušek, Vít and Kopeček, Lubomír. 2004. *Konfliktní demokracie Moderní masová politika ve střední Evropě*. Brno: Masarykova univerzita.

Hloušek, Vít and Kopeček, Lubomír. 2010. *Origin, Ideology and Transformation of Political Parties: East-Central and Western Europe Compared*. Surrey: Ashgate.

Janowski, Maciej. 2004. *Polish Liberal Thought Before 1918*. Budapest: Central European University Press.

Kitschelt, Herbert, Mansfeldova, Zdenka, and Markowski, Radoslaw. 1999. *Post-communist Party Systems: Competition, Representation and Inter-party Competition*. Cambridge: Cambridge University Press.

Klicperová-Baker, Martina et al. 1999. *Ready for Democracy?: Vivic Culture and Civility with a Focus on Czech Societ*. Praha: Psychologický ústav Akademie věd ČR.

Kontler, László. 2002. *A History of Hungary: Millennium in Central Europe*. London: Palgrave Macmillan.

Kornai, János. 2000. What the Change of System From Socialism to Capitalism Does and Does Not Mean. *Journal of Economic Perspectives* 14(1): 27–42.

Kováč, Dušan. 1998. *Dějiny Slovenska*. Praha: Lidové noviny.

Křen, Jan. 2005. *Dvě století střední Evropy*. Praha: Argo.

Kubát, Michal. 2004. Politický systém Druhé polské republiky (1918–1939). *Politologický časopis* 4: 331–353.

Kubát, Michal. 2006. *Vývoj a proměny státního zřízení Polska ve 20. století*. Praha: Dokořán.

Kwan, Jonathan. 2013. *Liberalism and the Habsburg Monarchy, 1861–1895*. London: Palgrave MacMillan.

Lipiński, Łukasz. 2013. Poland leaning left: Tusk signals an end to his economic liberalism. *V4Revue*, 10. 10. 2013 [on-line http://

visegradrevue.eu/poland-leaning-left-tusk-signals-an-end-to-his-economic-liberalism/, accessed on 4.2.2020].

Mises Ludwig. 2006. *Nation, State, and Economy.* Indianapolis: Liberty Fund.

Orban, Viktor. 2014. Speech at Băile Tuşnad (Tusnádfürdő) of 26 July 2014.

Raico, Ralph. 2010. *Great Wars and Great Leaders*. Auburn, AL: Mises Institute.

Roháč, Dalibor. 2008. It Is by Unrule that Poland Stands. Institutions and Political Thought in the Polish-Lithuanian Republic. *The Independent Review* 13(2): 209–224.

Shleifer, Andrei and Treisman, Daniel. 2014. Normal Countries: The East 25 Years After Communism. *Foreign Affairs*. November-December.

Šíma, Josef. 2013. A Note on Mises's Vision of Social Harmony in (Central) Europe. *New Perspectives on Political Economy* 8(1): 41–48.

Šíma, Josef and Šťastný, Daniel. 2000. A Laissez-Faire Fable of the Czech Republic. *Journal of Libertarian Studies* 14(2): 155–178.

Stiglitz, Joseph E. 1999. Whither Reform? Ten Years of the Transition. *Transition Economics* 3(12): 127–171.

Urban, Otto. 2003. *Kapitalismus a česká společnost: k otázkám formování české společnosti v 19. století.* Praha: Lidové noviny.

Walder Andrew G. 2003. Elite Opportunity in Transitional Economies. *American Sociological Review* 68: 899–916.

Wandycz, Piotr S. 2013. *The Price of Freedom: A History of East Central Europe from the Middle Ages to the Present.* 2nd ed. London, UK: Routledge.

World Bank. 1996. *World Development Report: From Plan to Market.* World Bank Publications.

Zamoyski, Adam. 2015. *Poland: A History*. London: William Collins.

Zweynert, Joachim and Goldschmidt, Nils. 2005. The Two Transitions in Central and Eastern Europe and the Relation between Path Dependent and Politically Implemented Institutional Change. *HWWA Discussion Paper No. 314.*

Enrico Arona

University of Genoa (Italy), Faculty of Law

'Free Church in a free State'? When the public knowledge limits the practice of the faith

Abstract: Here, I will offer a critique of the familiar argument that respect for persons, in a paradigm of political liberalism (PL), generates restraint on the public use of religious reasons. Firstly, after arguing that exercise of political authority begs for appropriate justification, as a matter of respect for persons, I will point out the fact of disagreement conjoined with evidence that points to systematic problems in human reasoning and our general susceptibility to cognitive biases. As I will describe, these tools give individuals reasons to reduce the credence with which they hold their comprehensive doctrines. Finally, public reasons are both capable of capturing widespread intuitions about matters of justice and are widely shared across the constituencies of liberal democracies. Since the aforementioned epistemic component mandates risk-aversion in the exercise of political power, I provide the solution according to which the 'retreat' to public reasons and exercise of restraint appears the most suitable outcome.

Keywords: Religious freedom, reasoning, discourse, argumentation

1. Project of political liberalism

While the dominant narrative[1] traces origins of liberalism[2] to European wars of religion[3] and a principled defence of freedom of conscience (Rawls 1996, xxiv), it is a more robust instantiation of the idea of moral equality,[4] commitment to a range of political and individual rights and liberties and focus on one's reflective capacities that we tend to associate with present-day liberalism (Waldron 1993, 37). The way that these substantive commitments 'fit' into an overarching and systematic theoretical picture is, of course, a matter of intense controversy within the liberal scholarship[5].

---

1 The argument comes with two important caveats: while my main concern is the structure of the *respect argument* as it applies to all political actors, I recognize (a) that breach of respect by public officials might be more onerous, and (b) that there might be some subsidiary considerations that would impose the restraint on public officials, even if the argument for respect does not succeed. For discussion of these points, see: Greenawalt (1995), Boettcher (2009) and Kis (2012). Second, I also assume that a variant of the respect argument can resist paternalistic (as well as perfectionist) state action more generally, rendering a number of religious rationales for public action (i.e. policies aiming at curtailing 'sinful' behaviour that does not harm others) illegitimate. For a variant of this argument see Quong (2011, chapter 3).

2 For more familiar statements of Political Liberalism (PL), see: Rawls (1993), Audi (2000), Larmore (1996) or Estlund (2007).

3 Robert Audi draws a distinction between religious and secular reasons in reference to their different epistemic grounds. Religious reason for action (or belief) is a reason whose status as a justifier of an action (or belief) evidentially depends on the existence of God, or on the pronouncements of person or institution as a religious authority. Secular reason would then simply be a reason whose epistemic status is independent of the existence of God (2000, 67).

4 The most familiar statement of this principle, also called the Principle of Liberal Legitimacy, is given by Rawls: 'Our exercise of political power is proper only when we sincerely believe that the reasons we offer for our political action may reasonably be accepted by other citizens as justifications of those actions' (1996, xlvi).

5 Scholars strongly disagree on the exact content and scope of those rights and liberties, as well as on the kinds of considerations that should be employed in justifying rights and their restrictions. Political liberals suggest a reasonable consensus on the content of appropriate public reasons, but they allow for significant disagreements on what policies these might support. Still, any political

One particularly influential strand of liberal theory, comprehensive anti-perfectionism,[6] ties liberalism closely to the ideal of personal autonomy.[7] An obvious problem with this brand of liberalism is that many citizens[8] might regard the underlying ideal of autonomously conducted life as unduly controversial.[9]

The failure of comprehensive anti-perfectionism merely points to an inseparable aspect of liberal democratic societies – intransigent disagreements on what is a good and successful life, on the nature and content of moral prescripts,[10] on the existence of God and other metaphysical questions, nature of truth, etc. These considerations that determine one's stance on most aspects of life add up to what John Rawls calls a comprehensive doctrine (CD) (1993, 58). What accounts for such diversity of

---

project that licenses forced religious conversion, radical restriction of free speech in peacetime and/or criminalizes consensual sexual behaviour in the privacy of one's home is certainly illiberal. For a taxonomy of contemporary conceptions of liberalism, see Quong (2011, Chapter 1).

6 This conception is comprehensive insofar as it claims that referring to particular ideal of what constitutes a valuable and worthwhile human life (here, ideal of personal autonomy) is the only way to adequately justify liberal principles or institutions. It is anti-perfectionist since it asserts that it is impermissible for a liberal state to promote or discourage activities on the grounds that they are worthwhile or worthless. For more familiar statements of comprehensive anti-perfectionism see Rawls (1971), Dworkin (2000) or Kymlicka (1989).

7 It is precisely because we value and/or pay due respect to the fact that "human beings ... are capable of forming and acting on intelligent conceptions of how their lives should be lived" that we think that both (a) individuals should enjoy wide discretion in their life choices (constrained only by considerations of justice) and (b) that government should not ground its activity on controversial judgments about comparative value of these life choices. See Dworkin (1991, 272).

8 Including most religious adherents.

9 What matters, they might argue, is that one lives in accordance with the divine law – that he or she conducts a life of contemplation and glorification of God. Whether this life has been achieved via self-reflection, or not, is of no interest. Furthermore, some might think that induced critical-reflection might even effectively compromise one's religious devotion by inducing doubt and confusion.

10 We can safely say that genuinely religious considerations regarding issues of abortion, contraception, same-sex marriage and embryonic stem cell research hardly admit of an adequate secular analogy.

agonistic comprehensive doctrines is the existence of the so-called, burdens of judgment[11] (BOJ), six obstacles to human reasoning which frustrate the possibility of consensus on any of the aforementioned issues.

In circumstances of such deep disagreement, liberalism '...entails focusing on what reasonable people can still share, despite their differences....This commitment forms the moral core of liberal thought, and it embodies a principle of *respect* for persons' (Larmore 1999, 602).[12] Theorists of PL find this 'sharable' justificatory currency in the *political culture*[13] of liberal democracies, where ongoing disagreements *seem* often couched in terms of (secular) reasons that adherents of all sides to the debate can appreciate.[14] Political culture provides a conception of *citizens* as being free and equal. Citizens are free and equal in virtue of their possession of two moral powers: capacity to have an effective sense of justice and capacity to form,

---

11 These are: (a) Empirical and scientific evidence is conflicting and complex, (b) Even when we agree about the kinds of considerations that are relevant, we may disagree about their relative weight, (c) All concepts are to some extent vague and subject to hard cases, (d) The way we assess evidence and weigh values is shaped by our total life experience, (e) There are different kinds of normative considerations on both sides of any issue, (f) Any system of social institutions is limited in the values it can admit, so that some selection must be made. Many hard decisions may seem to have no clear answer (Rawls 1993, 56–57).

12 The concept of respect for persons does not seem to commit one to the truth of any particular worldview. Of course, (as I argue below) it does not matter whether all comprehensive doctrines recognize it as a central norm, only whether all reasonable comprehensive doctrines do. A variety of religious and non-religious doctrines seem to recognize it to be a central norm.

13 For more familiar statements of the argument, see Larmore (1999), Cohen (1993), and Boettcher (2007).

14 While one might say that many citizens with religious affiliation might have strategic reasons for voicing their concerns in a manner that even those who do not subscribe to a religious worldview can appreciate, it would not be far-fetched to argue that the constant framing of public debates on matters of common concern in mutually acceptable terminology indicates that this type of public discourse is (a) already sufficiently internalized even by religious participants and that (b) it offers viable avenue for voicing their genuine moral concerns. For a particular example of how the Muslim community in the UK has advocated its appeal for censorship in the so-called 'Rushdie affair' almost exclusively on genuinely public reasons see Horton (2003, 17–18).

revise and rationally pursue a conception of the good.[15] Political culture also nurtures a relatively robust set of over-determined secular values – political values, which do not prejudge the truth of any comprehensive account.[16]

Needles to stay, not all disagreements are normatively relevant;[17] it is disagreements among reasonable people that matter.[18] Reasonable persons are those that recognize others as free and equal, regard society as a fair system of cooperation and accept the existence of BOJ.[19] Of course, a

---

15 That citizens are capable of exercising these powers above a certain threshold is what renders them free and equal. Cf. Rawls (1993, 19).

16 Imagine A and B discussing whether to support a ban on the sale of alcohol in shops after 10 pm. Imagine A defending the ban by claiming that sale of alcohol in late hours heavily contributes to the sinful activity of the constituency. Imagine B defending the ban as well, but by claiming that statistics show that imposing this ban is not only bolstering the local economy (more people will be inclined to visit pubs and nightclubs), but also reduces alcohol consumption among underage population. There is a sense in which A can not only asses the validity of B's reasons, but also accept them as valid, while B's acceptance of A's reasons seems conditional on his or her religious affiliation.

17 Those who advocate racist or other extremist worldviews, that either reject the presumption of moral equality of citizens or actively oppose liberal-democratic institutions, have no claim on theoretical accommodation. Likewise, due to the fact that disagreements among people populating current liberal democracies often reflect no more than selfishness, laziness or misinformation on their part, PL does not develop its conception of public justification and public reasons from the value-belief sets of actual citizens – it idealizes them. While there is some disagreement on the exact level of the prescribed idealization, we can safely say that PL idealizes the value-belief sets of actual citizens across several dimensions: (1) moral dimension – it assumes that they are reasonable, (2) it holds that they are rational and capable of addressing manifest inconsistencies and (3) that they have much of the information relevant for the matters of policy making.

18 On the concept of reasonableness see Boettcher (2004). For an argument on why BOJ should be included in the commitments of reasonableness see Quong (2011, 294–298).

19 Now, to be sure, the content of reasonable disagreement is orthogonal to a secular/religious divide, meaning that one can reasonably dispute many claims that chime with a secularist outlook. The claim can (and does) have some relevance for assessing the distribution of justificatory burden across the society but is not directly relevant to the points brought up in this chapter.

proper justificatory endeavour also involves converging on a set of epistemic practices – that is what counts as appropriate mode of reasoning, what counts as an adequate way to acquire and assess evidence, etc.[20]

2. Argument from respect for persons

While the idea of respect for persons might not seem too controversial when pitched at a fairly abstract level, the attempt to interpret and operationalize it are fraught with difficulties.[21]

We might start with the distinction between two kinds of respect introduced by Stephen Darwall (1977). Appraisal respect is the kind of respect we show to particular individuals in virtue of their exhibited degree of excellence. Recognition respect, on the other hand, is respect we show to people in general, out of recognition of their equal status as persons.

'If we attempt to make others to conform to our directives solely by the threat of force we shall be treating persons merely as means, …, and not also as ends, engaging directly their capacity as persons' (Larmore 1999, 602). Therefore, it is one's capacity for reflective endorsement[22] which we treat as a distinctive capacity of personhood, grounding the duty of respect.

---

20 Still, Rawls (and those supportive of his brand of PL) has been reluctant to offer any stringent criteria for judging the epistemic viability of either relevant modes of reasoning or findings of science. What they argued for – namely, that the appropriate epistemic practices are those that (morally) reasonable people will converge on – seems like a standard that can hardly be satisfactorily operationalized. For Rawls, it seems that comprehensive doctrines can count as reasonable even if they exhibit nothing but moderate coherence among their beliefs and values (1997). This criterion, however, seems compatible with anti-scientific comprehensive doctrines. If this is so, then most scientific claims, even those that command consensus among scientific community, will be claims that not everyone can reasonably accept. In conclusion, the prospective list of epistemic practices on which all reasonable citizens converge might be empty, or fairly minimal. I treat this implication as a *reductio*, and as a strong support for what I later call strict reading of the 'burdens of judgment'.

21 These difficulties concern (1) what morally relevant feature grounds respect, (2) how stringent is the duty of respect and (3) does discharging the duty of respect come in *a* particular currency (a specific course of action) or can it be discharged via different means.

22 Implicit in the 2nd moral power – power to form, revise and pursue a conception of the good.

There seem to be (at least) two renditions (Wall 2014) of the respect argument that we can elicit from the existing literature on PL. We can understand respect for persons either as (1) a respect for their reflective capacity in abstract or (2) respect for contingent normative and theoretical commitments that people 'actually' uphold. I will argue that both readings either end up being too weak to restrict religious reasons from public debate or too controversial to support a plausible PL account.[23]

We might say that, as an interpretation of a blanket commitment to others' capacity, first interpretation of the respect argument carries considerable plausibility.[24] But how is it that the first reading accounts for the restraint on the religious reasons? Some theorists regard the idea that respect requires restraint[25] of this kind, deeply counterintuitive. On what

---

23 The argument comes with a strong caveat. Due to space constraints, I will assume that a variant of the argument from respect for the 2nd moral power offers a strong injunction against enacting paternalistic (and by extension, perfectionist) policies more generally (Quong 2011, chapter 3). Focusing on the nature of the paternalistic state acts, Quong argues that they all seem to be motivated either by a negative judgment about citizens' ability to make effective choices about the good or to rationally pursue their conception of the good, or both. Therefore, paternalistic policies seem to treat citizens as if they (at least temporarily) lack the 2nd moral power, effectively undermining their moral status. If this is so, all religious reasons that aim to further religious devotion or to deter citizens from engaging in 'sinful' activities (i.e. consumption of drug and alcohol, prostitution, etc.) might be deemed *prima facie* objectionable. Still, a number of distinctively religious arguments are not covered by this restriction – think about the religious arguments against abortion, stem-cell research or gay marriage. For a criticism of Quong's argument see Birks (2014).

24 Also, bear in mind that while some conception of autonomy seems implicit in the 2nd moral power, PL tries to stay as non-committal as possible about ascribing value to its exercise, at least in non-political circumstances. This means (roughly) that there is no special concern for how individuals came to endorse their CD's, or whether they reflectively endorsed them at all. Since PL does not ascribe (much) value to one's actual exercise of the 2nd moral power, it gives no special (autonomy based) reason for respecting people's actually held moral commitments. This seems to further support the 1st reading of the respect argument. After all, it would be odd to say that we should respect products of one's reflective capacity even if one never reflectively endorsed his or her choices.

25 That one ought to abstain from using what he or she thinks are the best arguments.

we can call *correctness* account of reasons, showing respect to others requires offering them, what we take to be our best reasons for acting as we do (Galston 1991, 109). The rationale behind this argument is this: If what we are concerned with is one's capacity to reflect and possibly revise his or her comprehensive commitments, then we honour this capacity by offering the reasons that we think merit such revision. There is no talk of circumventing one's reflective capacities as in the case of sheer threat of force. However, this argument makes a strong assumption that we might (plausibly) think it does not hold in the case of religious reasons – namely, it assumes that epistemic status of what we take to be best reasons is readily available to others.[26] But, many have argued, the validity of religious reasons seems conditional on a kind of 'private experiences' that many non-religious citizens cannot be expected to have.[27] Is this fact sufficient to motivate the restraint in question?

Not necessarily. One might argue that religious reasons can be accorded public status through an indirect route – through 'Natural Theology'. Natural theology purports to prove God's existence by using secular reasons alone, without recourse to divine revelation.[28] Provided a plausible secular claim along these lines can be conjured, and provided we add auxiliary premises pertaining more closely to the connection between God's existence and validity of the moral prescripts found in revered religious

26 That there are common evaluative standards according to which members of the public might be able to assess their epistemic pedigree.

27 'It must be possible to present to others the basis of your own beliefs, so that once you have done so, they have what you have, and can arrive at the judgment on the same basis. That is not possible if part of the source of your conviction is personal faith of revelation – because to report your faith or revelation to someone else is not to give him what you have, as you do when you show him your evidence or give him your arguments' (Nagel 1987, 232).

28 Of course, in order to make a distinctively religious argument one cannot merely draw from secular sources. Seemingly, all substantive claims of religious morality are acquired via divine revelation. Still, in so far as natural theology is capable of providing an argument for why (a) God exists and (b) one of his attributes is Omni-benevolence, one can conjure up an argument in which, supposedly, such good would be inclined to communicate with human beings and reveal his moral prescripts to them. Vallier pursues this strategy in Vallier (2011).

texts[29] – the aforementioned accessibility constraint might be suitably addressed.

Still, one might argue that this strategy fails to pay proper heed to the main source of disagreement – the existence of BOJ. Even if I am able to grasp the epistemic character of a religious reason, in so far I adhere to a reasonable secular doctrine, the prospect of regarding it as anything but a particularly bad reason seems unlikely.[30] However, we should be very clear about the role BOJ play in this reading of the respect argument. According to the influential reading of the BOJ, or what I will call 'loose' reading, accepting their existence merely *explains* how different citizens will end up disagreeing with each other, even if they do not reason in bad faith or exhibit manifest inconsistencies (Quong 2011, 294–298). Naturally, what explains one's judgement might not in any way contribute to its justification.[31]

But, now imagine people whose CD's include a commitment to astrology as a reliable source of prediction of future events, or homeopathic medicine as a reliable procedure for treating a variety of illnesses. Would we say that a policy whose content explicitly rebuts the validity of these claims in any way disrespects the *reflective capacities* of persons holding these beliefs? It seems not.[32] Now, while the 'loose' reading seems

29 At least in those instances where their moral prescripts unequivocally converge.

30 As we saw, this is explained by a variety of considerations starting from how our personal history shapes our existing worldview to the fact that proper assessment of all considerations might be too difficult.

31 Think how A's poor eyesight might explain why he thought she saw her friend B, but does not in any way justify her perceptual judgment that she saw her friend B.

32 What we might say is that they are simply epistemically faultless in holding these beliefs. But in so far as (a) we think that there are no cognitive impediments which might prevent them from realizing the validity of the policy in question, (b) the policy is clearly justified by evaluative standards that enjoy wide intersubjective recognition in the community, promotion of this policy could actually be deemed as an instance of genuine respect for the reflective capacities of these citizens. The alternative course of action (exercise of restriction) would seemingly be motivated by a negative judgment about others' cognitive capacities – about their inability to grasp the validity of the claim. That would be an instance of disrespect.

to be dominant in the literature, we can also read BOJ in a more committal manner. Let us propose a 'strict' reading of BOJ according to which acceptance[33] of BOJ confers positive epistemic status on the CD in question, making the resulting reasonable disagreement, a disagreement between epistemically justified worldviews. We can argue that justifying a policy proposal by anything but 'good reasons' fails to accord proper respect to one's reflective capacity.[34] However, provided some religious doctrines do enjoy the epistemic support of this kind, why should the respect argument restrict their use in the political context? (cf. Laborde 2017; 2008; 2000). An intriguing suggestion might be found in Larmore's claim that in cases of disagreement citizens 'should respond to the point of disagreement, by retreating to neutral ground, to the beliefs they still share' (Larmore 1990). There might be several ways to understand the rationale for such departure, but they all seem to point away from the respect argument. We are either inclined to 'retreat' due to considerations of prudence[35] or because we are both equally likely to be right about the matter in question. The former option is certainly not what PL theorists have in mind, while the latter option is a theme familiar from the literature on epistemology of peer disagreement. Notwithstanding controversial[36] character of this latter position, it is clear that the reason for pursuing neutral ground it prescribes is of epistemic, rather than moral, nature.

So, it seems that we are left with the second reading of the respect argument – where respecting others' reflective capacities means respecting

33 And their accommodation in one's comprehensive doctrine.

34 Commitment to a certain account of epistemic justifiability might still maintain comprehensive robustness and need not involve controversial truth claims (that might compromise the project of PL): see Gaus (1996, introductory chapter).

35 That is the cooperation is only possible if we meet halfway.

36 Many people will be inclined to reject the idea that they are equally as likely 'to be in the right' regarding the truth of their CD as others. Furthermore, many people will have good grounds to claim that their CD is better justified than those of others. While I do think that a plausible argument along these lines can be pursued, I think that grounding it on 'equal epistemic status' is misguided. To be clear, what I provided is merely a possible interpretation of Larmore's argument. There is no further evidence that he intended for this claim to be interpreted in this manner.

products of their reason, that is comprehensive commitments.[37] There are several problems with this reading. For a start, it seems to provide a rather inadequate account of the reflective power, as the ability to form, *revise* and pursue one's commitments.[38] Furthermore, the second reading of the respect argument seems to chime better with the 'loose reading of BOJ'. If what grants respect is the fact that one's comprehensive commitments figure prominently in their evaluative sets, then the motivation to pursue an epistemically inflated conception of BOJ seems unwarranted. This is, however, unwelcome result. Since the loose reading of BOJ says nothing about the epistemic pedigree of reasonable beliefs, the account might end up hosting a variety of idiosyncratic beliefs. But now, since political justification cannot make reference to considerations other citizens' cannot endorse,[39] we seemingly end up with an account of policy making that caters an infinite variety of prospective fringe beliefs.

In criticizing this reading of the respect argument, Thomas Christiano points towards its inability to resolve what he calls *deliberative impasse* (Christiano 2008, 219–223). We assume that respect for others should be understood as respect for their comprehensive commitments, their complete account of desirable social circumstances. Respect for others' comprehensive commitments requires restraint, the argument says, since the lack of it would mean others living in the state of affairs they cannot accept. But, requiring of one *not to pursue* the state of affairs that he or she finds most desirable seems similarly burdensome. So, 'either one must impose on one person terms that she doesn't accept or one must

37 Accepting the second reading does not necessitate that we treat *all* of one's commitments as of equal importance. As Steven Wall observes, people might treat some of their evaluative commitments as identity constituting – closely tied to their sense of who they are. So, while they might be able (or willing) to reflect and revise their peripheral commitments, but not those that figure prominently in their worldviews (2014, 484).

38 Needless to say, many religious citizens (and many communitarian theorists) regard their identity-constituting commitments as non-revisable on the pain of identity loss. But the notion that we might (at least) step and reflect on our evaluative commitments (even if not on all simultaneously) seems to be a bedrock of any distinctively liberal account.

39 Or, in this case, cannot make reference to any scientific claims or modes of reasoning that compromise these epistemically unsound beliefs.

require another to live under terms that he regards as fundamentally inadequate' (Ibid., 220). If we assume that the deliberative impasse always tips in favour of the restraint requirement, Christiano concludes, then we seem to fall back to comprehensive liberalism.[40]

3. Conclusions

In this chapter I have criticized the familiar argument that respect for persons generates restraint on the public use of religious reasons. The restraint, however, might be reinforced by adding auxiliary premises to the respect argument. Due to space constraints, I will only gesture toward such strategy. First, I argue, exercise of political authority begs for appropriate justification, as a matter of respect for persons. This justification ought to be indexed to those points of view that are deemed reasonable. Naturally, we should opt for the 'strict' reading of BOJ – maintaining that reasonable disagreement is a disagreement between epistemically justified views.

Second, we should pay sufficient heed to the fact of disagreement conjoined with evidence that points to systematic problems in human reasoning and our general susceptibility to cognitive biases.[41] These, I argue, give individuals reasons to reduce the credence with which they hold their CD's. These reasons become especially pertinent in the circumstances in which one's actions might expose others to great harm. Exercise of political power threatens to do just that.

40 We are respecting others' autonomous choices.

41 By paying 'sufficient heed' I mean that the fact of somewhat idealized disagreement (and our general proneness to systematic errors in reasoning) gives those who disagree a 2nd order reason (as a matter of epistemic normativity) to be less certain about the view they hold. This is a controversial point in the epistemology of disagreement, which mostly focuses on disagreements between cognitive and informational peers. I have doubts about whether the concept of disagreement among 'full' peers is of any practical significance at all. There are insurmountable difficulties in tracking the nuances of one's epistemic situation, so the best we can do is assume 'roughly' equal peers. In this situation, however, the disagreement does not mandate that we suspend judgement, nor does it allow that we completely disregard it – what it does is give some reason to reduce the credence. As to an argument that defends this position see Lackey (2008). For an extensive treatment of common reasoning errors and cognitive biases, see Kahneman and Tversky (2000).

Public reasons[42] are both capable of capturing widespread intuitions about matters of justice[43] and are widely shared across the constituencies of liberal democracies.[44] Since the aforementioned epistemic component mandates risk-aversion in the exercise of political power, the 'retreat' to public reasons and exercise of restraint appears the most suitable outcome.

References

Audi, Robert. 2000. *Religious Commitment and Secular Reason*. Cambridge: Cambridge University Press.

Birks, David. 2014. Moral Status and the Wrongness of Paternalism. *Social Theory and Practice*, 40: 483–498.

Boettcher, James. 2004. What Is Reasonableness. *Philosophy and Social Criticism*, 30: 597–621.

Boettcher, James. 2007. Respect. Recognition and Public Reason. *Social Theory and Practice*, 33: 223–249.

Christiano, Thomas. 2008. *Constitution of Equality: Democratic Authority and Its Limits*. Oxford: Oxford University Press.

Cohen, Joshua. 1993. Moral Pluralism and Political Consensus. In *The Idea of Democracy*, edited by David Copp, Jean Hampton, and John E. Roemer. Cambridge: Cambridge University Press: 270–291.

Darwall, Stephen. 1977. Two Kinds of Respect. *Ethics*, 88: 36–49.

Dworkin, Ronald. 1991. *Taking Rights Seriously*. London: Duckworth.

Dworkin, Ronald. 2000. *Sovereign Virtue: The Theory and Practice of Equality*. Cambridge: Harvard University Press.

Estlund, David. 2007. *Democratic Authority: A Philosophical Framework*. Princeton, NJ: Princeton University Press.

Galston, William. 1991. *Liberal Purposes: Goods, Virtues, and Diversity in the Liberal State*. Cambridge: Cambridge University Press.

42 Political values, conjoined with a more robust epistemic criteria.
43 And responsible policy making.
44 This claim is an empirical one. For empirical evidence that supports it, see Haidt (2012).

Gaus, Gerald. 1996. *Justificatory Liberalism: An Essay on Epistemology and Political Theory*. New York: Oxford University Press.

Greenawalt, Kent. 1995. *Private Consciences and Public Reasons*. Oxford: Oxford University Press.

Haidt, Jonathan. 2012. *The Righteous Mind: Why Good People Are Divided by Politics and Religion*. New York: Pantheon.

Horton, John. 2003. Rawls, Public Reason and the Limits of Liberal Justification. *Contemporary Political Theory*, 2: 5–23.

Kahneman, Daniel, Tversky, Amos. 2000. *Choices, Values, and Frames*. New York: Russell Sage Foundation, Cambridge University Press.

Kis, Janos. 2012. State Neutrality. In *The Oxford Handbook of Comparative Constitutional Law*, edited by Michel Rosenfeld and András Sajó. Oxford: Oxford University Press: 318–335.

Kymlicka, Will. 1989. *Liberalism, Community and Culture*. Oxford: Clarendon Press.

Laborde, Cécile. 2000. *Pluralist thought and the State in Britain and France, 1900–25*. London: Palgrave Macmillan: 191–226.

Laborde, Cécile. 2008. *Critical Republicanism. The Hijab Controversy and Political Philosophy*. Oxford: Oxford Political Theory.

Laborde, Cécile. 2017. *Liberalism's Religion*. Cambridge, MA: Harvard University Press.

Lackey, Jennifer. 2008. What Should We Do When We Disagree? In *Oxford Studies in Epistemology, Volume III*, edited by Tamar Szabó Gendler and John Hawthorne. Oxford: Oxford University Press: 274–93.

Larmore, Charles. 1990. Political Liberalism. *Political Theory*, 18(3): 339–360.

Larmore, Charles. 1996. *The Morals of Modernity*. Cambridge: Cambridge University Press.

Larmore, Charles. 1999. The Moral Basis of Political Liberalism. *The Journal of Philosophy*, 12: 599–625.

Nagel, Thomas. 1987. Moral Conflict and Political Legitimacy. *Philosophy and Public Affairs*, 16: 215–240.

Quong, Jonathan. 2011. *Liberalism without Perfection*. Oxford: Oxford University Press.

Rawls, John. 1971. *A Theory of Justice*. Oxford: Oxford University Press.

Rawls, John. 1993. *Political Liberalism*. New York: Columbia University Press.

Rawls, John. 1997. The Idea of Public Reason Revisited. *The University of Chicago Law Review*, 64: 765–807.

Vallier, Kevin. 2011. Against Public Reason Liberalism's Accessibility Requirement. *Journal of Moral Philosophy*, 8: 366–389.

Wall, Steven. 2014. Perfectionism, Reasonableness and Respect. *Political Theory*, 42: 468–489.

Waldron, Jeremy. 1993. *Liberal Rights: Collected Papers, 1981–1991*. Cambridge: Cambridge University Press.

IV. Social policy: The showcase of the CEE region?

Miriam Laclavíková
Trnava University in Trnava (Slovakia), Faculty of Law

Public care for children in need of help and protection in Slovakia since the end of the 19th century until the mid-20th century

Adriana Švecová
Trnava University in Trnava (Slovakia), Faculty of Law

Abstract: The study focuses on the introduction of the Hungarian and Czechoslovak legal framework of the public care for "children worth of care", that is socially excluded children living in foster care, public children's homes or in substitute child care carried out by their relatives. The core of the study is the legal status of a child. The authors introduce a part of their research on childcare, especially the general preventive and educational activity, as well as the legal and social aid and protection carried out by various social care providers such as the partially official Regional Youth Care or the public children's homes whose foundation dated back to times of the Hungarian Kingdom. This all is introduced on the background of the social and legal peculiarities of the Slovak society.

Keywords: Out-of-wedlock child, social policy, public guardianship, youth care, Czechoslovakia

Introduction

Childcare issue[1] was a very important and especially sensitive topic vividly discussed already in the Hungarian Kingdom since the end of the 19th century and subsequently in the interwar and post-war Czechoslovakia. Children and youth, especially threatened due to the unsettled war-related situation and economic crises, became socially and economically vulnerable, disadvantaged and excluded.

---

1 The study is the result of working on VEGA Project No. 1/0018/19 entitled "The Renaissance of the Forgotten and Re-discovered Institutes of the Hereditary Law in Slovakia".

1 Legal status of the child

Various sciences such as medicine, psychology or sociology have been focusing on a child as a subject. Law and legal science have nonetheless been an exception and provided a definition of the child especially for the purposes of the law of persons and limitation of liability. The legal status of the child in the researched time period was primarily determined by its status in its biological family. Primary was the child's relation towards its parents and substitute child care relations were secondary. Child as a person of minor age was a subject of various legal relations according to the Hungarian and Czechoslovak law:

1) biological family/parenthood relations
2) legal parenthood relations (equal with the biological parenthood)
3) guardianship or curatorship relations
4) foster relations (rather factual than legal relations created for the purpose of substitute childcare).

The main aim of the substitute child care relations was to ensure adequate education and alimentation of a child if the biological family, including distant relatives, failed. Public, private and partially official childcare was necessary besides legal relations such as curatorship and guardianship and besides factual relation such as foster care.

The Hungarian customary law, court practice and Law no. XX of 1877 on Guardianship and Curatorship, which were effective in the Slovak territory,[2] differentiated legitimate and illegitimate children[3] on the ground of their origin and differentiated children on the ground of their age[4] as follows:

---

2 After the establishment of Czechoslovakia, they were taken over into the Czechoslovak legal order and were effective in the Slovak part.

3 The equalisation of rights between legitimate and illegitimate children became a priority after 1948. According to Art. 11, Sec. 2 of the Ninth-of-May Constitution of 1948, children could not be disadvantaged for their origin.

4 It is a simplified explanation as there were various exemptions and rules established by court practice and legal norms of different branches of law (e.g. the legal capacity according to the Marriage Law was different) (Fajnor and Záturecký 1998, 45–47).

1) A child under twelve that did not reach the legal age and hence had no legal capacity;
2) Twelve-year-old child that reached the age of criminal liability[5] and was entitled to draft a testament;
3) A child that reached the age of fourteen had the power to dispose of his or her wage and enter into contracts against payment without the approval of their legal representative;
4) A child that reached the age of sixteen could be a witness at marriage (Law no. XXXI of 1894, Art. 40) and could choose his or her occupation with the consent of guardianship court;
5) A child that reached the age of eighteen could claim at the guardianship court to be declared full aged;
6) The age of majority (Šošková 2013, 94) was according to Law no. 447 of 1919 Coll. twenty-one years of age. Girls could reach the age of majority in the age of sixteen if they entered into marriage. According to the previous Law, the majority age was reached in twenty-four years of age.

The term "youth" was not legally defined. It was rather a medical and sociological term, vaguely defined by a minimum age of fourteen and a maximum age of twenty-one. For the purposes of this study, we focus on children and young adults who were not independent due to their age, that is were of minor age (younger than twenty-one years).

Even after the establishment of Czechoslovakia, a distinction was made between *children born in marriage* (legitimate children) and *children born out of marriage* (illegitimate children), what was an unfortunate heritage from the Hungarian Kingdom, deeply rooted in the Slovak and European society of those times.[6] The child born out of marriage was the most

---

5 The court practice recognised an exemption, that is when the child under twelve was so mature that he or she was able to recognise the effects of own acts and be held responsible for them pursuant to Law no. XXXI of 1894, Art. 127 and Law no. V of 1878, Art. 83 (Hungarian Criminal Code).

6 Legitimate child was the one who was conceived during the so-called decisive period (recognised in European legal orders) of the valid marriage (i.e. the child was born six or more months after valid marriage was concluded or until the tenth month or three-hundredth day since the end of the marriage, or if it was proved

typical social care recipient and therefore is in the centre of our attention. Illegitimate child was born either to a single mother or was born to a mother three hundred days after the day when her marriage ended or was born to a married mother whose marriage was void since the beginning (except of so-called putative marriage) or finally who was born in a valid marriage but the illegitimacy was proved. In the last case, the legal presumption could be applied according to which the husband of the woman who delivered the child was recognised as a father. Nonetheless, it is necessary to emphasise that even during the end of the 19th century, one important positive shift in the status of the illegitimate child happened. The illegitimate child became a part of the mother's family where the child acquired status comparable to that of a child of legitimate origin. If the father voluntarily admitted the illegitimate child, it enhanced the child's status and relation towards the father and the father's family. There was no family relation (*familienrechtliche Gegenseitigkeit*) between this child and the father who hence had no *patria potestas*. It meant that the general family law regulations could only be used optionally and not obligatorily as in case of legitimate children. Since the end of the 19th century, the status of the illegitimate child was subject to change in the court practice. Some rights and duties (such as the alimentation duty) were the same for both those parents who admitted the children and for those who did not admit them. Some were reduced for the father, though.

1. "Child worth of care" and social care providers

There was one common feature of the aforementioned legal relations and that was *the protection of a child*. This protection was safeguarded by the parents or the subjects alternating them while the *patria potestas* was kept. The Hungarian society since the 19th century institutionalised and regulated providing of public and private care for the so-called children worth of care.

---

that the husband had conceived the child before he entered into marriage. This was the legal presumption according to which the husband of the woman who gave birth was recognised as a father ("*Pater est, quem nuptiae demonstrant*") and he could deny his fatherhood opposing this presumption. For more general information on legal status of an illegitimate child see: Luby (2002, 326–327).

There were different groups of threatened children, deemed by state and society as problematic and socially excluded. This social exclusion was based on their subjective feeling of being abandoned and neglected and on objective facts such as low morals and poverty.[7] Among such were especially:

1) illegitimate children;
2) orphans or abandoned children;
3) children living in pathological conditions or socially improper conditions such as children from large workers' families, children from incomplete families, children of alcoholics, children of immoral parents or criminals, children of severely ill parents or children of roamers;
4) children of the roaming Gypsies;
5) children of war invalids.

In a special group there were children physically or mentally handicapped and both young and adult persons who were named often disparagingly such as *abnormal, crazy, perverse, defective* or *bastardised.*

The state bodies were fully aware of the necessity to protect children and youth and of the fact that institutionalisation was multilevel and demanding. Social-care providers had no clear boundaries for the care they provided and so they often interfered into each other's competences. Moreover, it was necessary to solve the issue of interference of the state bodies to the "private zone" of the family.

Providing care for children and youth was theoretically and practically based on the thesis that primary providers were parents, single mother or other family relatives. Only if these could not provide it, did not want to provide it or did not know how to provide it, *secondary providers provided the public care* pursuant to Law no. XXII of 1886 as amended by

---

7 The Annual Report of the Regional Youth Care (Liptovský Sv. Mikuláš, 1932) concisely named the care recipients such as the children abandoned, out-of-wedlock children, orphans, cripples, mentally ill or perverse children. According to this Report, the Regional Youth Care focused on providing help to these children. SNA (Slovak National Archive in Bratislava), f. IMSS, box 21, no. 106.

Law no. 329 of 1921 Coll. Regarding the care for the poor,[8] it can be simply said that the main provider was the home town where the child or the parents had their residency. Except for the home town itself, it was also the town charitable organisations which provided care. These were often based on adherence to faith, ethnicity or class origin.

There was one peculiarity in the Hungarian Kingdom with continuous duration in Slovakia and Subcarpathian Rus as parts of the First Czechoslovak Republic and that was the primacy of the state care (public children's homes) over the private care. The most effective was the activity of the Czechoslovak Red Cross (especially in the 1920s), Czech Care for the Youth in Slovakia (Česká péče o mládež na Slovensku) and Association Živena. Associations which were active in the whole Slovakia were, for example: Bratislava Association for Building Hospitals in Slovakia (Spolok pre stavbu nemocníc na Slovensku v Bratislave), Kremnica Association for the Deaf-Mutes Care (Spolok starostlivosti o hluchonemých v Kremnici), Bratislava association called Salvation of Women of Loose Morals (Spolok Záchrana pre mravne pokleslé ženy v Bratislave), Czechoslovak Youth Department – Country Headquarters for Slovakia (Československý dorastový odbor, zemská pobočka pre Slovensko), Levoča Asylum for the Blind (Ústav pre slepých v Levoči), Country Association for the Blind in Slovakia (Zemský spolok pre slepcov na Slovensku), Centre of the Holiday Care in Slovakia (Ústredie prázdninovej starostlivosti na Slovensku), YMCA and IWCA[9] in Bratislava.[10] In the 1930s, the half-official care providers were institutionalised, such as the Slovak *Country Headquarters of the Youth Care* (Krajinské ústredie starostlivosti o mládež, KÚSoM) which coordinated the activity of the *Regional Youth Cares* (okresné starostlivosti o deti a mládež, OSM). These were the key providers and controllers of the public care for "the children worth of care" in the subsequent decades.

8 For more general information and information about the care for the poor, see Švecová (2014).

9 Both associations specialised in providing social and health-social care for the male youth (YMCA) and female youth (YWCA). In SNA, f. KÚ Bratislava, box 919, no. 601.

10 IMSS Report on County Budget in 1925. In SNA, f. IMSS, box 11, no. 44.

2. Care for "the children worth of care" – Legal framework

Providing care for these children was regulated by Hungarian laws which were taken over into the Czechoslovak legal order, such as Law no. XX of 1877 on Guardianship and Curatorship (partially substituted and amended by Law no. 246 of 1922 Coll.) and Law no. VIII of 1901 on Public Children's Homes – Asylums (amended by Law no. XXI of 1901 (cf. Malinský 1920, 550; Kazda 1921; Román 1933, 53) and amended and executed through Regulation of the Hungarian Ministry of Interior no. I-V/c of 1903, June 23). Law no. VIII of 1901 on Public Children's Homes – Asylums was based on the following principles:

a) foundation of public children's homes for children under the age of seven who were found and officially declared for "abandoned" (Art. 1);[11]
b) placement of vital and healthy children into foster families (Art. 2);
c) placement of ill children and children with special health requirements into institutional care (Art. 2);[12]
d) duration of the institutional care until the 15th year of age; if the child aged three (Art. 2) or seven, the child could not be placed into foster families or other public or private institutions (so-called orphanages).

Care for the children under the age of seven was, pursuant to the Law, funded by the State. Care for the children between seven and fifteen years was funded by the home town. A child who reached the age of fifteen was deemed independent (if such a child was not able to take care of himself or herself, placement in the public or private institution was possible) (Jáger and Janigová 2013, 109).

Pursuant to Law no. XV of 1891 on Care for Children Aged Three to Six Years (Art. 1) and Executive Regulation no. 44000 of 1892 (Valent

11 Law no. VIII of 1901, Art. 1: "Public children´s homes will be established in the capital city of Budapest and in various places throughout the Kingdom, in order to provide protection for children under the age of seven who were found and officially declared for abandoned."

12 Law no. VIII of 1901, Art. 2: "Placement into institutional care is necessary for ill, weak, backward children and children with special needs and health requirements. Other children should be placed elsewhere."

1928, 164–166), children's homes were supposed to be institutionalised for preventive measures, for ensuring proper education and supervision of children. Foundation of these children's homes was a necessity for those villages which collected a certain amount of direct taxes and where the number of children in need was higher than forty (Art. 15 and 16). The state had to establish the children's homes anywhere it was deemed necessary (Art. 14–19) or could fund the existing ones.[13] Care for the children older than seven years old who were in need of public help was regulated by Law no. XXI of 1901 on Care for Children above the Age of Seven in Need of Help from the Village.[14] Confirmed was the principle of Law no. VIII of 1901 according to which the children between the age of seven and fifteen were placed "according to circumstances in children's homes, in reliable foster families – especially in farmer and craftsmen families".[15] Older talented children were supposed to be granted the possibility to study.

Law no. VIII and XXI of 1901 were executed by Executive Regulation of the Ministry of Interior no. 1/1903 B.M. on Protection of Abandoned Children. This Regulation contained the definition of an abandoned child which was as follows: "Abandoned child is an insolvent child under fifteen years of age who has no relatives bound and able to aliment and educate the child (Law no. XX of 1877, Art. 11), if the child's relatives, benefactors, charitable institutions, and organisations do not properly care for the child's alimentation and education" (Law no. XX of 1877, Art. 112 and Law no. XXI of 1901, Art. 1). A child, who was according to the Law abandoned, had a right to be admitted to a children's home. Villages and towns were obliged to take care of children under the age of fifteen who seemed to be abandoned, until the moment when they were admitted to the public children's home, and fund the expenses if the children were under the age of seven.

This legal framework of the public child and youth care continued to exist in Slovakia as a part of the First, Second and post-war Czechoslovak

13 Order of the Ministry of Education no. 48773 of 1921, October 7 abolished all the public nurseries established by the Hungarian Ministry of Education.
14 Law no. XXI of 1901 amended Law no. VIII of 1901.
15 Lecture of the doctor Janovský for the social workers, held from 17th to 27th of August, 1922. In SNA, f. IMSS, box 8, no. 25.

Republic as well as in the war Slovak State.[16] However, the unification process was initialised during the existence of Czechoslovakia, in order to synchronise the systems in the Czech and Slovak part. In Slovakia, it was the private and half-official sector which had to be strengthened what led to the establishment of Regional Youth Cares and Local Youth Cares[17] with certain competency taken over from the State. Due to the situation in Slovakia and Subcarpathian Rus, the public children's homes continued to exist. Namely, it was the Slovak public children's homes and their adjoint foster colonies in Košice and Rimavská Sobota which were kept.

The first Czechoslovak Law (*Law no. 256 of 1921 Coll. on Protection of Children in Substitute Care and Out-of-Wedlock Children*) was adopted in 1921. Executive Government Regulation no. 29/1930 Coll. was adopted in 1930, followed by other orders of the Ministry of Social Care.[18] Law no. 256 of 1921 Coll. was subsequently amended by *Government Regulation no. 40 of 1932 Coll.* which regulated the relationship between public care providers and guardianship courts in Slovakia and Subcarpathian Rus.

Supervision over children in substitute care and out-of-wedlock children was regulated by Law no. 256 of 1921 Coll., Art. 2. The supervisory bodies had "the right of search and domiciliary visit of the homes of foster families or parents, of children's rooms, as well as the right to search the children themselves and ask the foster families, parents and other members of the household to give true information on all circumstances related to children, to their placement, alimentation, nursing, and education and to regularly show the children to them or to the appointed physician in the

---

16 Law no. 213 of 1941 Coll. on Public Care, Public Guardianship and on Regulation of Prophylactic Supervision.

17 Regional Youth Care was a voluntary public provider established following the Czech example (Okresná péče o mládež, OPM). The Regional Youth Cares network was intensively evolving since the 1920s; however, it was only at the beginning of the 1930s when it was completely established and started to be effectively active throughout Slovakia. This apparently happened under the influence of the superior Country Headquarters of the Youth Care. The Local Youth Cares were actually the local branches of the Regional Youth Cares.

18 These acts were abolished in the 1950s when Law no. 69 of 1952 Coll. on Social and Legal Protection of Youth was adopted.

appointed place". The Law regulated also the cooperation of the local self-governmental and administrative bodies with voluntary institutions and organisations (Art. 4).

The Law was executed through Governmental Regulation no. 29 of 1930 Coll. which named more precisely the children enjoying the protection[19] and the particular providers of the substitute care. Pursuant to Art. 1, "the children in substitute care worth of protection" were the children under the age of fourteen, regardless of their legitimate or illegitimate origins, which were placed in substitute care different from the care provided by their mother or father, carried out for payment or without it. The Law did not relate to:

a) the children under public supervision regulated by special Law, such as the children in public children's houses in Slovakia and Subcarpathian Ruthenia;
b) the children in temporary substitute care due to a particular reason, such as commuting to school in the town other than the town of permanent residency of their parents, stay in a holiday village, stay in the hospital, stay in a medical or similar institution, etc.

Law no. 256 of 1921 Coll. and Governmental Regulation no. 29 of 1930 Coll. appointed a *supervisory body* to carry out supervision over children in substitute care. In Slovakia and Subcarpathian Rus, it was the Guardianship (Orphan) Authority of the First Degree (i.e. the relevant county court with a guardianship department[20]/later on solely the guardianship court) that had the respective territorial jurisdiction, that is it was the court of the child's residence, inferior to higher courts and to Ministry of Justice. Supervision over children in public institutional care was carried out by the Country Department and superior Ministry of Social Care which cooperated with the Country Headquarter of the Youth Care.[21]

---

19 The term "substitute care" used in Governmental Regulation no. 29 (Art. 1, Sec. 3) was understood as the care provided by the natural person (fosterer) or by the (private) institution.

20 In this issue it was controlled by superior guardianship departments/courts.

21 The Country Headquarter was supervised by the superior Country Department. In Slovakia, during the existence of the First Czechoslovak Republic, the activity

This supervision carried out by the guardianship department or guardianship court could be transferred to other authorities according to Governmental Regulation no. 29 of 1930 Coll., Art. 3. These authorities were the newly established Regional Youth Cares (Bokesová-Uherová 1989, 257–258) (inferior to the Country Headquarters of the Youth Care) "if the Regional Youth Care consented and could successfully perform this task".[22] Supervision over the children worth of care was performed by the fellows of the Regional Youth Care who were appointed for *the public guardian or fiduciary*. In this case, the supervisory bodies (in Slovakia the guardianship departments/guardianship courts and the Country Department) carried out only the general supervision,[23] decided about the complaints against the measures of the Regional Youth Cares and approved the fiduciaries. If there was no Regional Youth Care in the county or if the Regional Youth Care refused to carry out these tasks, the supervisory body of the first instance, with the consent of the Country Headquarters of the Youth Care, established an advisory committee whose members were the local social workers, assistants of the members of the Country Headquarters of the Youth Care, of the County Committee and of the Public County Board for Educational Administration.

Direct supervision over the children worth of care, usually placed in the foster families, was carried out by the public guardians or fiduciaries appointed by the Regional Youth Care or other supervisory bodies. These had to be "of full legal capacity, of moral character, unimpeachable, both physically and mentally healthy, with enough knowledge, ability, education and sympathy necessary for this function". The local inhabitants who

---

of the Country Headquarters of the Youth Care was only developing and so this function helped them with their establishment.

22 This happened only after establishment and enrooting of the Regional Youth Cares in Slovakia in the 1930s.

23 This general supervision was "the right of search and domiciliary visit of the homes of foster families or parents, of children's rooms, as well as the right to search the children themselves and ask the foster families, parents and other members of the household to give true information on all circumstances related to children, to their placement, alimentation, nursing, education, and to regularly show the children to them or to the appointed physician in the appointed place". Self-governmental local bodies were assisting them too (Law no. 256 of 1921 Coll., Art. 2 and 4).

knew well the local conditions and circumstances were appointed for the public guardians and fiduciaries. They were of the same ethnicity and of the same religion as supervised children. The Regional Youth Cares had to submit reports on supervision to the guardianship department or guardianship court and after their summarisation carried out on guardianship departments or guardianship courts of the third instance they were sent to the Ministry of Social Care.

Public guardians/fiduciaries had to be in frequent contact with the respective persons caring for the children and also with the children themselves. Hence, they were supposed to frequently visit them (as often as necessary but at least once a month) in the foster families and were entitled to carry out the interrogation. They even supervised children with no permanent residency (roaming children) in the place of their actual stay. If the care for children was not carried out properly, the fiduciaries in the first place gave advice to the fosterers; and if it was not possible or satisfactory, they submitted a report to superior supervisory bodies or to the superior Regional Youth Care as well as to the legal representatives of the child.

3. Social care activities

The fundamental social care activities, their aims and supervisory activities of the Slovak division of the Czechoslovak Red Cross and later of the Regional Youth Care (in cooperation with other superior or inferior public or private subjects) can be summed up as follows:[24]

1) educational activity performed in order to "awaken the understanding, teach it, deepen it and spread it together with the interest for children's social care, through written and oral communication addressed to competent public agents and especially to the broad lay public";
2) coordination of all the voluntarily provided care "within a uniform programme and on the basis of an effective division of work";
3) evidence of all the subjects and institutions, namely of the extent, execution and status of their activities and providing these records to other competent public care providers or private persons;

24 Articles of the Regional Youth Care. For more information, visit the State Archive in Trnava (f. OSM Trnava).

4) evidence of the persons worth of care and submission of relevant "*claims, reports and suggestions in order to provide them* (children and youth – note of the authors) *proper alimentation and education, primarily by those who are legally bound to do so*";
5) evidence of the families or persons competent for providing foster care, for spreading educational activities and for carrying out supervision over fosterers;
6) establishment or providing help with the establishment of social care institutions which provided care for children and youth, such as advisory boards, asylums, nurseries, kindergartens, orphanages, children's homes, family colonies, crèches, etc.;
7) consulting service for youth regarding their studies, apprenticeship, job selection; selection of convenient employers and masters; cooperation with job agents; further care for adolescent youth;
8) establishment of the network of fiduciaries;
9) assistance and cooperation with public bodies (especially with the regional political administration bodies, guardianship departments/courts and municipal authorities); "performance of public social care tasks transferred upon them through administrative or legal means;"
10) execution of preventive family measures if the child or youth was physically, mentally or morally threatened;
11) establishment and support of children recovery homes where few hundred orphans, half-orphans and malnourished and weak children were placed during school holidays or recovery events in order to recover;
12) transfer of children into hospitals, expert institutions, orphanages and foster families and cooperation with the Ministry of Transport in order to grant discounts on travel expenses for children and their companions.[25]

---

25 Memorandum on Social and Health Care for Children and Youth of the 26th of January 1940, prepared by Country Headquarters of the Youth Care in Slovakia, signed by the chairman of the Country Headquarters Prof. A. J. Chur. For more information, visit the State Archive in Trnava (see the f. OSM Trnava, box 2, no. 5 c). See also the Articles of the Regional Youth Care, available in State Archive in Trenčín (f. OMS Trenčín, box 2) or in State Archive in Trnava (f. OSM Hlohovec, box 1, no. 1).

Conclusion

In Slovakia, the end of the 19th century and beginning of the 20th century was marked by essential social problems such as bad health of the population, high neonatal mortality, low hygiene standards, poverty, unemployment, congestion of countryside, violation of traditional social bonds and emigration. Children and youth were, together with seniors, the most threatened subjects. This threat related to their health, social and economic situation. The authors aimed to outline the shift in child protection which had only been a private matter before and to introduce the institutional system, that is the network of voluntary religious and charitable organisations, half-official institutions (Regional Youth Care) and public social care providers (children's homes).

Legal regulation of care for the so-called children worth of care recognised and supported multiple care providers and emphasised the duty of general control carried out by the guardianship department/court over fosterers and the possibility of direct interference of the state bodies in cooperation with the Country Headquarters of the Youth Care into the institutional care system. Regulation no. 29 of 1930 Coll. imposed information and record-keeping duty on villages (Art. 22). Hence, the villages were bound to provide relevant information on children in their district to the Regional Youth Cares (e.g. information about children in substitute care or out-of-wedlock children), to submit reports on the administration of childcare and to notify the supervisory bodies about the necessary measures in favour of these children. If requested, the schools attended by these children had the same duty.

The above-mentioned summary of the fundamental activities and functions of the dominant social care providers such as the Czechoslovak Red Cross and Regional Youth Cares gives an original and complex insight into the social and legal care for children and youth in the researched period. These secured the minimum standards of the child and youth care or cooperated with other bodies in order to secure them. The standards were named on an international conference held in 1922. Among others, these standards related to the family life, education, preparation for the future work, healthy mental development, home care, institutional care, rights of the out-of-wedlock children to parental care, to father's liability, to healthcare for single mother and newborn, care in the countryside, recovery possibilities, care for the young criminals, care for mental health and mentally ill children and adults and adoption of legal acts regulating the providing of social care (Driml 1922, 218–220).

References

Bokesová–Uherová, Mária. 1989. *Dejiny zdravotníctva na Slovensku.* [History of Healthcare in Slovakia]. Bratislava: Osveta.

Driml, Karel 1922. Minimální požadavky ochrany dětí, vyžadujících zvláštní péče. [The Minimum Social Care Standards for the Children in Need]. *Péče o mládež*, I: 218–220.

Fajnor, Vladimír, Záturecký, Adolf. 1998. *Nástin súkromného práva platného na Slovensku a v Podkarpatskej Rusi so zreteľom aj na banské právo a na právne predpisy o pozemkovej reforme (s príslušnými časťami návrhu čsl. všeobecného zákoníka občianskeho, zhotovného superrevíznou komisiou).* [Outline of the Private Law Applicable in Slovakia and Subcarpathian Ruthenia…]. 3d. ed. Šamorín: Heuréka.

Jáger, Róbert, Janigová, Emília. 2013. *Vývoj právnej úpravy poskytovania sociálnej pomoci na území Slovenska (od najstarších čias do roku 1939).* [Providing Social Care in Slovakia since the Ancient Times until 1939 – Legal Framework]. Banská Bystrica: Právnická fakulta Univerzity Mateja Bela v Banskej Bystrici.

Kazda, V. 1921. Státní péče o opustěnou mládež na Slovensku a v Podkarpatské Rusi. [Public Care for the Abandoned Youth in Slovakia and Subcarpathian Rus]. *Sociální revue,* II: 158–162.

Luby, Štefan. 2002. *Dejiny súkromného práva na Slovensku.* [History of Private Law in Slovakia]. Reprint. Bratislava: Iura edition.

Malinský, J. 1920. O organisaci a úkolech sirotčích stolic. [On Organisation and Tasks of Orphanage Care System]. *Sociální revue*, I.

Román, J. 1933. *Obecná samospráva na Slovensku a jej dnešné položenie. II. Ako odstrániť krízu obec. samosprávy a obecného hospodárenia verejného.* [Village Self-Governance in Slovakia Today. II. On Elimination of Crises in the Village Self Government and Economy]. Prešov: Tlačou kníhtlačiarne Pallas.

Šošková, Ivana. 2013. Plnoletosť ako predpoklad svojprávnosti v podmienkach 1. ČSR. [Full Age and the Legal Capacity in Czechoslovakia]. *Historia et theoria iuris - teoretický časopis pre otázky štátu a práva*, 5.

Švecová, Adriana. 2014. Starostlivosť o sociálne minority na Slovensku v období I. ČSR. [Care for the Social Minorities in Slovakia during the First Czechoslovak Republic]. In Mosný, Peter et al. *Právnohistorická realita sociálnej doktríny 20. storočia*. Kraków: Spolok Slovákov v Poľsku – Towarzystwo Słowakow w Polsce: 171 – 218.

Valent, V. 1928. Správa osvety. [Administration of Education]. *Administratívny vestník,* VII: 164–166.

Andrea Kluknavská

Matej Bel University in Banská Bystrica (Slovakia), Faculty of Law

Sovietization of Czechoslovakia illustrated by the example of social security[1]

Abstract: The author focuses on the welfare state and its sovietization after February 1948. The concept of the communist welfare state was based on Marxist perception of the state as a supreme organization seeking unification of interests of all classes and strata of the population and on the strong influence of the Soviet Union. Despite the proclamation of the Czechoslovak Communists to build a strong welfare state, which was supposed to be the showcase of the socialist regime, their interests were directed to other areas, which did not respond to the social needs of the population, and which subsequently led to unrest of the population.

Keywords: Czechoslovakia, social security, sovietization, social insurance, national insurance

Introduction

In terms of development, we consider the welfare state to be younger than the modern state and the rule of law.[2] The rise of the welfare state in Europe can be dated back to the end of the 19th century in connection with laying the foundations of the insurance system in Germany by the chancellor Otto von Bismarck. By contrast, in the United States and the United Kingdom, we can only trace back the beginnings of the welfare state in connection with the Great Depression in the 1940s. The concept of the German "*Wohlfahrtstaat*" and the Anglo-Saxon concept of "welfare state" is marked by differences (see Blaha).

---

1 The contribution is the outcome of the VEGA 1/0138/18 grant project "Marxism Still Alive? To reconsider K. Marx's teachings in contemporary legal and economic thinking".

2 The modern state is conceptually the oldest example of the present-day's state being conceptually different from the state of Antiquity and of the Middle Ages. Without the establishment of the modern state, there could be no rule of law.

Only in the 1950s did the welfare state begin to be seen as an integral part of the rule of law. This connection stems from the fact that human dignity as a fundamental right is conditional on the existence of not only the rule of law but also the welfare state (see Věčeřa at al. 2013, 114).

As we know from the historical development, the existence of the rule of law in the absence of the welfare state, for example at an early stage of the rule of law, is possible, as well as is the existence of the welfare state in the absence of the rule of law. The latter statement is to be discussed in more detail in the next part of the contribution, as it is where the totalitarian socialist states may be classified, while the focus of our attention will be Czechoslovakia in the 1950s and the attempt to find an answer to the question of what status social rights had in Czechoslovakia after February 1948, or how important this matter was for the Communists, and what influence did the Soviet Union have on the concept of the welfare state in Czechoslovakia. For this reason, we do not address the individual social rights in detail nor analyse the relevant legislation in detail, but rather try to create an overall picture of the society at that time through changes in social security between the years 1948 and 1956.[3]

Post-war Czechoslovakia as a welfare state

If we want to study the period in question, it is necessary at the beginning to deal with the question of whether the term "welfare state" may apply to the period of socialist dictatorship. At this point, however, we encounter the first problem, which is the term "welfare state" itself, which is not defined in a uniform way in the scholarly literature and, at the same time, since individual definitions are based on different perspectives, their comparison is more or less impossible.[4] This plurality of definitions then

3 The concept of social safeness in the present-day perception of social security is an archaism, which has not been used in terminology since the 1960s.

4 M. Potůček defines the welfare state as "a state which assumes responsibility for ensuring the basic standard of living of its citizens". For more detail see Potůček (1999, 56). Matlák considers a state to be a welfare state if such state takes care of ensuring a human dignified life (subsistence minimum) for everyone (Matlák 1996, 10).

inherently entails the fact that each of these definitions has its pros, but also contras.

There are two contradictory opinions in the current scientific literature, the first reducing the existence of the welfare state only to market economy societies, and the second view regarding the welfare state as a common feature of modern industrial societies, irrespective of their economic and political system (for more details see Rákosník, J. – Tomeš, I. et al. 2015, 22 ff.). However, if we understand the concept of a welfare state as the idea of comprehensive protection of citizens, it makes sense to talk about the welfare state both in post-war liberal democracies and in dictatorships of communist type as well (ibid., 22ff.). We are in favour of this perception of the welfare state, and during the period in question, we consider Czechoslovakia a welfare state.

The period preceding February 1948 already outlined a new concept and direction of social policy, even after taking into account the initial efforts to ensure the functioning of the existing (inter-war) system, which was "fatally" disrupted as a result of the dissolution of the state and the war. The egalitarian structure came to the fore, for example regarding family allowances, despite the fact that the allowance was still labelled and considered a prenatal allowance, but this was no longer the case.[5] In this case, the state provided a guarantee for any possible lack of funds, whereas this scenario was unlikely due to high levies (see Rákosník, J. – Tomeš, I. et al. 2015, 135–136).

---

5 Pursuant to the last sentence of Section 1 "family allowances are provided if they care for dependent children (Section 2)", whereas Section 2 defined a dependent child in par. 1 as follows "Married, illegitimate, step and adopted children up to 18 years of age are considered as dependent" and in paragraph 2 "Children (paragraph 1) above 18 years of age are also considered dependent (a) if the child is being prepared educationally or professionally for his/her future occupation (as a full-time vocational school student, apprentice, trainee, etc.), in this case not beyond 24 years of age, (b) if the child due to a mental or physical disability is unfit to any gainful activity, and the child's own income does not exceed Kčs 1800 per calendar quarter". From the above provisions it is possible to deduce unequivocally the principle of egalitarianism and the principle of solidarity of the childless population with the population which took care of minors. See more details in Act No. 154/1945 Coll. on family allowances of certain persons insured against sickness.

Also, unpopular labour market governance regulations, which were not new, were given new façade, new packaging, and their need was presented to the population so as to highlight the benefits – the personal contribution of each worker in "vital" specializations. Therefore, in July 1948, by means of Regulation No. 13/1945 Coll. on the temporary establishment of labour protection authorities the taken-over Labour War Offices were dissolved and replaced by the District Labour Protection Offices. The objective of the new labour protection offices was defined directly in the Regulation.

Pursuant to Article 1 of the Regulation, the duty of the newly established authorities was to integrate "into work, wage policy, trade inspection, occupational medicine and other care for employees".[6] Just like in the previous period, the allocation of employees or their removal from their jobs for other work was envisaged, but with a new goal, which was the personal contribution of each citizen in building a new society on new foundations. The reasons for such arrangements were also highlighted by B. Glos, a social policy expert, as follows: "Under some circumstances, we will not always be able to wait for the necessary number of our citizens to switch to vital labour specializations. If you do not go voluntarily, some pressure will have to be applied" (1945–1946, 114).

Paradoxically, the issue of national insurance was not in the centre of attention of political parties, even though the work on new legislation began after the end of the war, the main driver being the trade unions. The issue of national insurance became interesting also for political parties when they suddenly realized, at the most unfortunate time shortly before February 1948, what serious issues the law addressed – the interests of private medical doctors and the benefits of high-income insurance groups – namely, it was related to the objective of liquidating the remainders of the exploitative stratum (see Rákosník, J. – Tomeš, I. et al. 2015, 136), which sounded very good to the electorate.

The whole period after the end of World War II can be characterized by the fact that works on the reform of social insurance were started. The aim of this reform was to achieve, on the one hand, uniformity, with the

6 See, in particular, Section 1 of Regulation No. 13/1945 Coll. on the temporary establishment of labour protection authorities.

clear objective of improving the social status of workers up to the level of private employees and miners so as to eliminate the differences between insured persons and, on the other hand, universality, with a view to eliminate any differences among insured persons, after taking into account all possible social events from birth to death (see Tomková 2009, 693).

The social system during the period following the assumption of power by the communists and the high Stalinism (1948–1953)

The coup d'état in February 1948 did not mean, in general, any fundamental change in the field of social rights and social policy. The (new) Gottwald government took the position of protector and executor of the post-war government programs. And so, the legislative whirlwind of reform laws began – one of them was the National Insurance Act No. 99/1948 Coll., adopted only a few weeks after the February coup d'état.

The paradox was that even though a new society, other than the bourgeois one, began to be built, the National Insurance Act was more inspired by the British model than the Soviet one, as can be even seen from the title (1911 National Insurance Act). The political leaders, however, resolutely rejected any influence of the Beveridge Plan, and in the parliament also made a proper effort to eliminate any influence of the British plan on the Czechoslovak social reform.[7]

The National Insurance Act had been drafted as outlined above since 1945 and was intended to unify all occupational and other insurance schemes of gainfully employed persons, and the Central National Insurance Company was to be the sole medium and all situations from birth to death were to be covered. However, the text suggested that under the new circumstances the social policy was to have a completely different dimension. "The generations to come after us will bow before the Czechoslovak people of February 1948. However, they will also consider the work of the Gottwald government and of the people it relies on as a

7 Rákosník points out to the influence of the deviations between Beveridge's work of Social Insurance and Allied Services and its six principles and the national insurance in Czechoslovakia.

matter of historical significance. What the nationalization is in the economic policy of the People's Democracy, that is the national insurance in social policy".[8]

The new National Insurance Act repealed all previous laws on sickness insurance. The Act[9] included both sickness and maternity insurance and provided cash benefits and benefits in kind, that is health care as well as pension insurance, where, subject to the statutory conditions of this insurance, cash benefits were provided to citizens who, due to old age, permanent incapacity for work or loss of the breadwinner, were not able to provide for their basic subsistence from their income. These benefits also substituted the income of persons who could not work due to state-recognized reasons. The Act did not include unemployment insurance, except for sickness insurance, due to the mandatory general labour obligation. The financing was ensured both from the insurance premium income and from the state's contribution, and the insurers' assessments could be subjected to review by the insurance court.

At the same time, it should be noted that the National Insurance Act, on the one hand, implanted in the sphere of social insurance elements corresponding to constituting social relations in line with the ruling ideology, while on the other hand, at least improperly interfered with the essence of the insurance system. We can consider this Act as a transitional measure necessary to execute the change of the scheme to the social security scheme, which culminated in the adoption of Act No. 54/1956 Coll. on sickness insurance for employees (see Matlák 1996, 25). At the same time, however, it is also possible to mention the benefits of this regulation, such as the creation of a single national insurance system, a partial increase in allowances, equalization of entitlements of workers and other gainfully employed people and broadening of pension insurance coverage to persons who were never insured, thereby having solved the problem of retirement pensions.

During the year 1949, the contours of the new direction towards the Sovietization of social administration began to become clearer, even

8 Statement made by Minister Erban. Cited pursuant to Tomková (2009, 694).
9 For more details see Horňáček (2011, 141–142), Matlák (1996, 24–25) or Tomková (2009, 694).

though it was not apparent to what extent the "time-proven Soviet experience" would relate to Czechoslovakia. It was during this period when new building efforts were commenced, typical for the first half of the 1950s, when the accomplishment of the economic plan was at the top of the agenda. The second feature of this period is the fact that the Communist Party considered the issue of social security to be resolved and devoted itself fully to other sectors (see Rákosník, J. – Tomeš, I. et al. 2015, 143). This lack of interest was related to other circumstances of that time.

First, it was probably linked to the fact that ideology elevated the economic base over the political, cultural and legal one, which they considered only as a derivative thereof, and, at the same time, there was an important influence of the USSR and its radically perceived investment policy focused only on selected sectors (e.g. heavy industry) (ibid., 143). Here, Stalin's theory of intensifying the class struggle also manifested itself, which resulted in discrimination against class enemies. The enforcement of this newly defined class policy of the "strict direction" consisting of constraints and suppression of capitalist elements was reflected in the measure adopted in 1948, introducing class preferences in supplying the population. Since January 1949 this proceeded to an open class-preferential supply system, which had not been in force until then (ibid., 143). It is also possible to observe that from summer of 1948 until 1953, reduction in sovereignty of social policy took place, which was characterized by suppression of middle classes, subordination of the economy to central planning, assumption of the "steel concept", over-mobilization of human resources with far-reaching social implications, backwardness of the agriculture and consumer industry, while "class perception, nationalization of social insurance, healthcare" came to the fore (see Kalinová 2007, 115).

Second, the Communists were convinced that social policy would not be necessary in the new system because they considered social pathological phenomena to be a consequence of the previous bourgeois system. They even assumed that there would be no poor people and, therefore, no social protection would be needed. Authorities, which had ensured such social protection were gradually dissolved. In 1951, even the Ministry of Labour and Social Welfare was dissolved and replaced by the Ministry of Labour Force, which was established in accordance with the theory of development of production and the constant mobilization of the labour force (paradoxically, dissolved already in 1957).[10]

Shortly after the adoption of the National Insurance Act, however, criticism began to emerge from the ranks of the leaders of the Party. Antonín Zapotocký already in July 1950 proclaimed: "We want and we must, however, as soon as possible according to the Soviet model ensure that our national insurance with its allowances becomes an instrument supporting production and labour productivity, so that in addition to its social function, it also takes over the economic function".

In this context, Tomková (2009, 695) states that the perception of social policy was simplified to such an extent that it almost ceased to be referred to as an individual phenomenon. This claim can be accepted only partially. It should be noted here that in the given period we can truly observe the elimination and simplification of national insurance, but national insurance has not ceased to be talked about; on the contrary, like other sectors of the "superstructure" of the society, national insurance and social policy changed in line with the general line of socialism building and it was to assume additional functions.

Still, all this has led to a sense of uncertainty in the society and a loss of trust in the improvement of the situation; therefore, measures leading to the "rebuilding" of the national insurance took place by means of Act No. 102/1951 Coll.[11] The rebuilding of the national insurance resulted in the creation of three relatively independent packages of social protection of citizens, namely, the package of the state-therapeutic and preventive health care, the package of sickness insurance and the package of pension insurance including social care (see Rákosník 2010, 260). The importance of this change is stated very clearly in Section 1 of this Act: "the great work of national insurance is one of the main achievements of the working people achieved by the working class with its famous February victory. Learning from the experience of the Soviet Union, we will rebuild the national insurance so as to support the development of production, to take

10 The Ministry of Labour and Social Affairs was restored at government level in 1968.

11 See more details in Act No. 102/1951 Coll. on the rebuilding of national insurance.

care of any worker on a versatile and ever-developing basis, to ensure that the workers are managers themselves and are directly accountable for it and so that insurance, in line with the development of production, is a tool for continuous improvement of the standard of living of all workers".[12]

And so, since January 1952 the so-called benefits in kind became included in health services and were financed directly from the state budget. At the same time, by means of Act No. 102/1951 Coll. there was a change in sickness insurance, when it was entrusted to the Revolutionary Trade Union Movement and the administration thereof was transferred onto the production plants. The pension insurance was separated from the sickness insurance and its administration was entrusted to the State Pension Agency and the National Committees. The economic independence of both sectors was abolished and the assets of the Central National Insurance Company were transferred onto the state. Health care was unified on the basis of Act No. 103/1951 Coll. on uniform preventive and therapeutic care.

Despite any attempts for change, the situation in society was unsustainable and the Communists themselves responded to the growing need for social policy. Therefore, in the 1950s we can see activities in this area, but these were not sufficient. The events that influenced the next period were especially the monetary reform, which would impoverish the population of Czechoslovakia, but also the problems underestimated by the Communists such as housing construction, mass consumption, elimination of harmonization of social security systems, economic stimulation in the form of allocation of work force, as well as supply problems due to reduced agricultural production coupled with the process of collectivization and the support for the heavy industry. Also the deaths of Stalin and Gottwald started another phase in the development of social policy.

Still, even after 1953, no ground-breaking changes comparable to the rebuilding of national insurance in 1951 were approved. However, one could witness the gradually changing direction of state policy towards the promotion of living standards, which nevertheless did not mean any fundamental change in social care (see Rákosník 2010, 260). The change

12 Section 1 Purpose of the Act, Act no. 102/1951 Coll. on rebuilding of national insurance.

came after 1956 with the completion of the rebuilding of national insurance by Act No. 54/1956 Coll. on sickness insurance for employees. This action put an end to the adoption of the Soviet model of social security, and the features of communist social policy started to be apparent, which prevailed mostly in the 1970s and 1980s.

Conclusion

The political and socioeconomic changes, through which the Czechoslovak society went after the end of World War II, became a decisive moment for reflection on the future conception of social policy, social rights and social security. The work on the concept of a national insurance scheme began immediately after the war, but this area was more in the focus of trade unionists than politicians. Politicians entered this sphere more actively shortly before February 1948, which was more related to the material scope of the concept. The social changes after February 1948 affected this area similarly as other areas of society. The Communists introduced class stratification while, in in their own way, they perceived these changes only as an accomplishment of post-war governmental programs and preferred to focus on other areas, especially on the economy, heavy industry and the implementation of economic plans.

At the same time, they tried to point out that the "lazarettes of capitalism" were over (see Rákosník 2010, 260). However, the socialist state had no plans for any social welfare or any support of the unemployed or the poor, albeit the social system following the Soviet model was supposed to be the showcase of the new regime, and at the same time, it was to put up a fight against all capitalist elements. Thereby, the paradox is that despite the Communists' efforts to point out, for example, the fundamental differences between the new socialist society being built and the bourgeois one, the influence of the bourgeois countries, especially in the form of the Beveridge Report, on the National Insurance Act of 1948 was apparent and clearly visible.

Thus, should we try to answer the question raised at the outset, we can conclude that although the 1948 Act and subsequent laws adopted during the "rebuilding" of the national insurance were based on the postulates of the communist ideology, these can still be regarded (given the period) as modern and progressive. At the same time, however, it should be noted that these regulations did not stand in the very centre of interest of the new regime, focusing rather on the economy – under the influence of the Soviet Union.

Still, it soon turned out that even the Communist elite itself found out that it had to address social problems, and therefore attempted to rebuild the national insurance. However, the dissatisfaction of the population could not have been reversed even by the changes of 1956, since the reform was only partial. The subsequent dissatisfaction of the population and its distrust finally led to the unrest that culminated in reformist Prague Spring of 1968.

References

Blaha, Ľuboš. 2008. *Sociálny Štát V Kocke*. [Www.Akademickyrepozitar.Sk/Sk/Repozitar/Socialny-Stat.Doc; accessed on 20.04.2020].

Glos, Bohuslav. 1945–1946. Plánovitá Distribuce Pracujících. *Naše Doba*, 52.

Horňáček, Vladimír. 2011. Vývoj Sociálneho Zabezpečenia V Tehotenstve A Materstve. In *Sociálne Riziká A Základné Ľudské Práva – Výzvy Pre Pracovné Právo 21. Storočia*. Trnava: Trnavská Univerzita v Trnave, Právnická Fakulta.

Kalinová, Lenka. 2007. *Společenské Proměny V Čase Socialistického Experimentu: K Sociálním Dejinám V Letech 1945–1969*. Praha: Academia.

Matlák, Ján. 1996. *Právo Sociálneho Zabezpečenia V Historickom, Súčasnom A Európskom Kontexte*. Bratislava: Vydavateľské Oddelenie Právnickej Fakulty UK.

Potůček, Martin. 1999. *Križovatky*. Praha: Karolinum.

Rákosník, Jakub. 2010. *Sovětizace Sociálneho Státu. Lidově Demokratický Režim A Sociální Práva Občanů V Československu 1945–1960*. Praha: Filozofická Fakulta Univerzity Karlovy.

Rákosník, Jakub, Tomeš, Igor et al. 2015. *Sociálny Štát V Československu. Právně – Institucionální Vývoj V Letech 1918–1992*. Praha: Auditorium.

Tomková, Milada. 2009. Sociální Zabezpečení. In *Komunistické Právo V Československu, Kapitoly Z Dějin Bezpráví*. Brno: Masarykova Univerzita, Medzinárodní Politologický Ústav.

Act No. 99/1948 Coll. on national insurance

Act No. 154/1945 Coll. on family allowances of certain persons insured against sickness

Act No. 102/1951 Coll. on rebuilding of national insurance

Act No. 103/1951 Coll. on uniform preventive and therapeutic care

Act No. 54/1956 Coll. on sickness insurance for employees

Regulation No. 13/1945 Sb. on the temporary establishment of labour protection authorities

V. Darker legacies of the CEE region

Rado Pezdir

University of Primorska; International School for Social and Business Studies; RE-FORMA, research and development, ltd.

State-managed parallel economy in the socialist economic system: Evidence and conceptualisation from recently disclosed historical records

Janez Šušteršič

RE-FORMA, research and development, ltd.

Abstract: Using recently disclosed documentation from the Archives of the Republic of Slovenia, the chapter analyses the operation and structure of the state-managed parallel economy during the socialist period, and its implications for transition. It begins with the formative period when, in the aftermath of the Second World War, an extensive business network was established outside of the country, operated by the secret service and formalised by official state institutions. It continues with other historical episodes, most notably the parallel banking system, which show how the parallel economy was used as an instrument of economic policy. Finally, it provides important clues about the role that the network and resources of the parallel economy played during the transition. Discovery of a formalised and state-managed parallel economy brings new insights into the structure and transition of socialist economies and challenges the conventional distinction between formal and informal institutions used in institutional economics.

Keywords: Parallel economy, socialism, Slovenia, Yugoslavia, archives

1. Introduction

The Archives of the Republic of Slovenia (ARS)[1] has recently disclosed documents of the Slovenian branch of the Yugoslav State Security Service

---

1 In Slovene: Arhiv Republike Slovenije (ARS).

(SDV) and its predecessor State Security Administration (UDV).[2] Whilst it has long been known that UDV/SDV was the striking power of the repressive apparatus (comparable, for example, to Eastern German Stasi), the newly accessible historical records allow exploration into its widespread economic and financial activities. This chapter is the first attempt at a systematic study of these new materials and their contextualisation.

Our preliminary reconstruction of historical archives clearly showed that economic activities of the UDV/SDV were not sporadic and independent operations, but rather a hierarchically organised, time-consistent activity directed by formal political institutions. What emerged through our analysis of the archives was a picture of a fully developed parallel economy, organised and managed by state institutions. It has complemented the official economic policy and served as a hybrid institutional instrument by which companies from the socialist self-management economy extended their – often illegal – activities into market economies.

The term "parallel economy" is conventionally used to describe self-organised activities of private economic agents in highly regulated economies with unsecure property rights (De Soto 1989). That is also how activities such as "grey markets" or unregistered provision of goods and services were analysed in the context of socialist economies. Kornai (1980) famously described planned economies as "shortage economies", where shortages were an inevitable consequence of central planning and the main reason for widespread informality. State-owned companies also engaged in these informal activities and created economic rents that were distributed through the political hierarchy (Hillman and Schnytzer 1986).

The parallel economy described in this chapter differs from these conventional types in that it came into being through decisions made by the formal political institutions and was controlled and managed through the institutional hierarchy. Rather than a private alternative to inefficient and state-controlled formal economy, it was a direct extension of the official economic policy. Yet, perhaps due to illegality of activities and their incompatibility with socialist economic ideology, it was not only kept secret but also operationally entrusted to the political "secret service" (UDV/SDV).

---

2 In Slovene: Služba državne varnosti (SDV) and Uprava državne varnosti (UDV). Internationally it is better known under the Serbian acronym UDBA.

This chapter provides an account of several historical episodes of parallel economy that we were able to sufficiently reconstruct from available documentation. Section 2 focuses on the formative period of the parallel economy which centred on the Free Territory of Trieste for its business activities but syphoned the surpluses to an offshore financial centre in Lichtenstein. Section 3 describes how the same network was used to set up a parallel banking system that solved an important economic policy problem of financing the national economy. Section 4 briefly looks at some other instructive examples. Finally, Section 5 describes how the parallel economy was transformed into an informal network that persisted until today and had an important influence on economic policy during Slovenia's transition to a market economy. We conclude by underlying the implications of these findings for our understanding of socialist systems, their transition and the theoretical distinction between formal and informal institutions.

2. The free territory of Trieste: Formation of the parallel economy

Immediately following the end of World War II, Trieste and surrounding areas were under the administration of the Federal People's Republic of Yugoslavia (FPRY), delegated to the Regional National Liberation Committee (RNLC) for Slovene Littoral.[3] This ended with the agreement signed in Belgrade on 9 June 1945 between the Yugoslav, British and American governments.[4] The agreement divided the contested territory along the so-called Morgan line into Zone A, administered by the Allied Military Government, and Zone B, which transitioned to the Military Administration of the Yugoslav Army.[5] Within the same month, on June 25, Allied and Yugoslav military administrations signed the Duino Agreement, which regulated the matters of coordination and logistics between the two zones. These two agreements resulted in the withdrawal

3 In Slovene: Pokrajinski narodno-osvobodilni odbor (PNOO) za slovensko Primorje.
4 Agreement for the Provisional Administration of Venezia Giulia.
5 In Slovene: Vojaška uprava Jugoslovanske armade (VUJA).

of FPRY institutions from the territory that was now under the Allied administration. The formation of the Free Territory of Trieste, divided into Zone A and Zone B, was formalised at an international level in the Paris Agreement of 10 February 1946.

These political circumstances had important implications for the operation of the business network that was part of the Yugoslav economic policy. Prior to the Belgrade Agreement, economic reconstruction of the entire Trieste area, including establishment and management of economic enterprises, was coordinated by the Economic Commission of the RNLC office in Trieste.[6] With the withdrawal of Yugoslav institutions, the Economic Commission lost any formal role within the Allied Military Government, and the method of management of companies in Zone A had to adapt to the new institutional framework.

At first, the reconstruction of economic governance in Zone A was attempted through the cooperative "Uivod", established by private persons in Trieste, and Centroprom Trst,[7] a subsidiary of Centroprom Belgrade, a foreign trade company under the authority of the FPRY Ministry of Foreign Trade. But both Uivod and Centroprom Trst, the latter also involved in illegal trade, were extremely unstable with disorderly business operations. Their operational challenges were exacerbated by the fact that Yugoslav companies ignored the directives of the Foreign Trade Ministry and traded with Italian companies directly, without involving either of the two companies. The situation has not improved even after the control of Uivod and Centroprom Trst was taken over by Eksport, a company from Ljubljana under the direct authority of the Slovenian Ministry of Foreign Trade.[8]

The failure of the Yugoslav administration to organise stable economic operations in Zone A through Uivod, Centroprom Trst and Eksport led to a new, more fundamental reconstruction of business infrastructure. Through this, the operation of Slovenian companies in Zone A was

---

6 ARS 1931, 2137, p. 351 (Responses to questions raised by the economic commission). In all citations of archive documentation, the first number identifies the archive fund and the second its technical unit (unless otherwise indicated).

7 Trst is the Slovenian name of Trieste.

8 ARS 1931, 2137, p. 366. Report on accounting balances, 23 June 1949.

increasingly coming under direct control and management of UDV; this was ultimately formalised by a decree of the Interior Ministry of the FPRY from 22 November 1951.[9]

Slovenian UDV had emerged as a key player through the takeover of the Italian financial company SAF (Societa anonima finanziera per traffici internazionali) in the spring of 1948. The takeover of SAF was carried out and paid for by the Slovenian branch of UDV through the use of fictitious owners. The purpose of SAF was to finance the entire set of Slovenian companies in the Trieste area and, in addition, to fund the operation of political organisations of Slovenian minority in Trieste, Gorizia and Venezia. Moreover, an informal general directorate of this group of companies operated within SAF, which managed the companies and their commercial, financial and human resource policies.

The reconstruction and operation of the business network in Zone A following the takeover of SAF is most evident in the annual reports of the economic section of the Slovenian UDV.[10] UDV reports perceived SAF as its financial centre in Trieste. SAF collected deposits from various Yugoslav institutions, for example the Yugoslav trade delegation in Trieste, the Central Committee of the Communist Party in Trieste and the Economic Section of the Istria Bank in Koper. The funds thus collected were allocated to companies with the explicit approval of Franc Karo, an important member of the economic department of the Slovenian UDV. This effectively means that, through Karo, UDV performed the supervisory function in relation to the use of funds that came to SAF.

In parallel with takeover of SAF, a new company, Continental, was established in Ljubljana under full control of UDV to replace Eksport in its role of conducting business with Zone A companies. Furthermore, although the network of companies under the control of the Slovenian UDV in the period reviewed was the densest in Zone A, the reports also refer to individual companies in other countries. In Austria, timber company Harsch and a hotel in Vienna are mentioned. In Germany, operations were organised through Munich-based Globus, which was obliged

9 ARS 1931, 2137, pp. 1–3.
10 ARS 1931, microfilms in the material archive.

to, through a commissions arrangement, transfer 80% of its income to Continental.[11] In Switzerland, companies Adria and Colcommerz were operated by UDV at the time.

Colcommerz in Switzerland had the leading role in management of financial flows within this international network of UDV companies. The basic operational mechanism was that unreported profits of companies in Zone A were transferred to Colcommerz through schemes such as repayment of fictitious loans and deposited in Swiss bank accounts or paid out as dividends to Continental in Ljubljana. Due to high taxes and regulatory problems in Switzerland, it was decided that Colcommerz headquarters should be moved to Liechtenstein. As the head of the economic directorate of the Slovenian UDV, Niko Kavčič, explicitly explained, in Liechtenstein "it is not necessary to disclose the books" and "no one will ask how and in what way Colcommerz Vaduz operates".[12] This makes it clear that the purpose of moving Colcommerz to a tax haven was to conceal its business. Thus, with the consent of Yugoslav authorities, UDV established the first Slovenian financial offshore company already in 1951.[13]

2. Parallel banking: The parallel economy as economic policy

Let us move forward two decades and look at the emergence of a parallel banking system. In economic terms, it was created in response to the failures of the extremely confused Yugoslav economic policy, which most of the time acted as an accidental experimentation. In the second half of the 1960s, the Slovenian economy was in complete disarray. Most companies did not have any equity to invest, and liquidity was poor. The banks acted as savings institutions and non-repayable lenders to the economy but did not have access to genuine financial resources. Financing of banks was left to the mercy of the National Bank of Yugoslavia (NBY), with scattered Slovenian banks only able to get the breadcrumbs left after the NBY had met resource requirements of strongest Serbian and Croatian banks. In

11 ARS 1931, Material archive, A-10-7, p. 84.
12 ARS 1931, Material archive, A-10-7, p. 81.
13 For a more detailed account of the UDV-controlled network of companies and siphoning of profits, see Pezdir and Šušteršič 2018.

addition to low investment, export competitiveness was weakened by the policy of over-appreciated dinar, which made foreign currencies an increasingly scarce commodity. The lack of foreign currencies prevented normal import activity of Slovenian companies, including weak imports of investment goods which put a further crunch on the already modest investment activity (Sirc 2010, 159–160).

In these circumstances, Slovenian politics decided to establish a strong republican bank, which would be more successful in competing for the NBY's scarce resources and which would place the funds in the most important enterprises of the national economy. In 1968, the merger of the two largest Slovenian banks at that time created the Ljubljanska Banka (LB). The proposal for the merger was put forward by Niko Kavčič, former head of the UDV's economic department, who then became the first director of the merged bank. Kavčič solved the problem of acquiring resources for LB in much the same way he had solved the problem of financing parallel economic activity in the Free Territory of Trieste. He established a system of parallel banking, through which the LB obtained sources from abroad and financed selected Slovenian companies.

The first form of parallel banking developed from the combination of corrupt Yugoslav institutions and the particular international trade arrangements with other communist countries of Central and Eastern Europe. The scheme was based on the fact that Yugoslavia had a clearing surplus in trade with this group of countries. In order to reduce the surplus, the NBY provided funds to banks for lending to importers from the clearing arrangement countries. However, a look at the credit documentation of LB gives a much different view of this business. The imports, which were made exclusively through three companies (Sigmacommerce Vienna, Fintramac Zug and ATKO Zug), did not come from the clearing area but from elsewhere. In addition, LB entered into agreements with the borrowers under which they were required to repay part of the loan in foreign currency to an account opened with the Swiss bank Wegelin of St. Gallen.

A look at the ownership structure of the three companies that brokered the imports and chanelled money to the black fund at Wegelin reveals that parallel banking was entirely based on UDV associates. Sigmacommerce and Fintramac were owned by Serbian businessman Slobodan Todorović, and both companies were operated by Djoka Andjelković. Both were UDV collaborators immediately after the war, but soon it turned out that they also had a sense for business. Todorović had set up a series of companies abroad that spread from Bangladesh through Iran and Israel to North Africa and all of Europe, while Andjelković mainly engaged in illegal trade and smuggling.

The third company, ATKO, founded in Zug in 1969, further illuminates the scheme. The founding capital of the company was 100,000 Swiss francs, half of which was paid in by Todorović and Andjelković, while the other half was invested by Kavčič and Miloš Ogrizek, a high-ranking officer and former head of the Slovene UDV. The latter pair obtained the funds from an account held in Switzerland by the LB, which was not documented in the bank's books and was, therefore, part of the parallel economy.[14]

This scheme, however, had quite a few problems. First of all, it depended entirely on the attitude of Yugoslav politics to clearing debt. Moreover, it was necessary to pay bribes at the NBY and Belgrade administration to obtain clearing credits which did not go to finance imports from the socialist bloc. Finally, Slobodan Todorović, due to his collaboration with former federal UDV head Ranković, who had been politically sacked, found himself under the scrutiny of the federal and Serbian UDVs. All this added unnecessary risks to the scheme. In order to mitigate these risks, a completely new form of parallel banking has emerged, most comprehensively demonstrated in the case of the creation of black funds in Switzerland for the purpose of financing armaments and equipment of the Slovenian Territorial Defense.

The Territorial Defense, which was created in response to the Soviet invasion of Czechoslovakia in 1968, faced a lack of funds to buy weapons and equipment. When Miloš Ogrizek moved from the UDV to the post of Territorial Defense Intelligence Officer, he turned to Niko Kavčič for help. LB then agreed on a loan with the Austrian bank Bawag. The holder of the loan, however, was not the LB, but the Austrian company Austrointercommerce. This company was owned by an Austrian citizen of

14 ARS 1931, 1404, Dossier Kavčič, pp. 299–307, and ARS 1931, 1404, Dossier Todorović.

Slovenian descent, Boris Ban, Kavčič's acquaintance and once a source of UDV. Ban then placed the loan as a deposit with LB. With this, the NBY was not able to know that the deposit was in fact a loan, and by obtaining a deposit, LB obtained the funds it could use to lend to selected national companies. In this transaction, the recipients of the loans also undertook to pay additional foreign currency interest, which was collected in a foreign account. This time again, funds were transferred to Switzerland by foreign brokers or suppliers, so that there were no traces in the books of Slovenian companies about the payment of additional interest abroad.

Again, an account was opened with Wegelin Bank. According to the documentation, 640,000 Swiss francs and 200,000 US dollars were collected in total during 1971 and 1972 on the account ODE 1007. Part of the funds was used to service LB loans with foreign banks and companies, part was allocated to finance the needs of the Territorial Defense and the remainder, 223,000 Swiss francs, was deposited into Etablissement Colcommerce's account with Merck, Finck & Co in Munich. This account was controlled by the same persons who, as members of the UDV's economic department, established the offshore company Colcommerz in Vaduz in 1951.[15]

What can be deduced from this account of parallel banking? First, it confirms that parallel schemes emerged as a solution to an important problem of economic policy – the parallel network of companies in the Free Territory of Trieste solved the problem of establishing economic activity in the area, and parallel banking was a solution to chaotic conditions in the Slovenian economy and banks. Second, there is a clear continuity through time, not only in the way the parallel economy operated (withdrawal of financial flows from regulatory control and their use for economic policy purposes), but also in their main actors (the network of UDV associates and the companies under their control). Third, also in this case, the parallel mechanism was not created as an independent UDV action, but in agreement with the political leadership of Slovenia.

---

15 ARS 1931, 1404, Headquarters of the Slovenian Territorial Defense, p. 400, and ARS 1589, 2624/24, Activity of the President of the Central Committee of the Slovenian League of Communists, p. 4.

3. International cooperation: The parallel economy as organised crime

While establishment of the informal business network and the parallel banking served broader economic policy goals, as argued above, many economic activities of UDV simply performed a para-fiscal function, that is they provided extra-budgetary revenues through illegal activities. Here we look at two most widespread activities, that is government smuggling and cooperation with foreign organised crime groups.

UDV archives are abundant with records of smuggling operations that were undertaken regularly from 1945 until 1989, the last year documented in the archives. Niko Kavčič, in his reports on UDV's economic activity in the Free Territory of Trieste, boasted of having extended the illegal trade networks of UDV, primarily for cigarettes, into Austria, West Germany, Switzerland and along the Italian coast to Ancona. But he was not alone in that endeavour – secret service branches from other Yugoslav republics also engaged in smuggling, and they did so in competition with one another. This prompted the Federal Ministry of Interior to call a conference which resulted in an agreement on market sharing and price setting, and a rulebook on organisation and reporting of illegal trade.[16]

Another well-documented episode took place in 1971. The Slovenian Assembly approved purchase of technical equipment for the UDV but failed to provide for the budget. UDV and the state-owned trading company Emona approached the minister of interior with the proposal to secure the funds by illegal sale of cigarettes from Emona's warehouse to clients in Italy. The minister consulted the president of the government and approved the plan. Emona provided the cigarettes, UDV took care of the logistics and conspiration and the customs and police did their best to look away. The total revenue from this operation amounted to 72.3 million Italian liras. But after the operation, the funds for UDV equipment were nevertheless provided in the federal budget, and the revenues from smuggling, which were no longer needed for equipment, were deposited in a special UDV fund at disposal of the Slovenian minister of interior.[17]

16 ARS 1931, MA 213–7, pp. 2–3.
17 ARS 1931, MA, 213–6 A.

More sinister than illegal trade was cooperation with organised crime. The best reconstructed case so far is that of Casino Portorož on the Slovenian coast during the 1980s.[18] The casino primarily attracted customers from neighbouring Italy and the operation of the lending service was entrusted to private foreign companies. As the Italian parliamentary investigation revealed, these companies were an outpost of the organised crime group Mala del Brento, which was organised around the casino in Venetia and engaged in activities such as drug trade, blackmail and abductions.[19] On the Slovenian side, the activity of the lending service was controlled and facilitated by UDV, which also approved its directors. The key operational person was Gino Chiesa, a character who was convicted in Italy for organised crime, but found shelter in Slovenia as an associate of, first, the military intelligence service, and then UDV.

In return for their cooperation, UDV was entitled to a third of profits generated by the casino's lending service. The revenue, which amounted to around 250 million Italian liras per year, was transferred to UDV partly in cash, partly to their Swiss bank accounts via an umbrella Panama company Pleasure Investments ltd., and partly deposited in anonymous saving books at the Association of Cooperative Banks in Klagenfurt, Austria. This savings books were actually held by the Slovenian Socialist Alliance of Working People (SAWP).[20] But that is not all. A criminal investigation, ordered by the first democratic government in early 1990s, indicated that similar schemes were operated in other casinos as well, notably in Gorica on the Italian border.[21]

18 ARS 1931, 2597; ARS 1931, Dossier Gino Chiesa aka Aldo Fanelli.
19 Commissioni parlamentare di inchiesta sul fenomeno della mafia e sulle altre associazioni, annche straniere.
20 SAWP (in Slovene: Socialistična zveza delovnega ljudstva) was a typical socialist mass political organization and as such an extension of the ruling Communist Party.
21 Report on the criminal investigation into UDV activities in casinos, 7 June 1990.

4. The great transformation: Parallel economy as an informal network

UDV archives end in 1990. But that does not mean that the parallel economy ceased to exist. The evidence collected by the recent parliamentary investigative commissions on the political responsibility for the banking crisis in 2008–2011, and on corruption in health procurement, as well as our own research of foreign and Slovenian business registries, allow us to offer a brief sketch of how the socialist parallel economy transformed itself into a clandestine network that has played a significant role in Slovenia's transition to a market economy.

The most telling in this respect is the transformation and merger of the two financial backbones of the parallel economy, that is of Ljubljanska banka and SAF (later Safti). First, in 1989, LB and SAWP developed a scheme of fictitious loans and invoices with the purpose to transfer money to a Slovenian minority's publishing company in Trieste. The funds ultimately ended with Safti, which used them to establish a financial company Proteus in Zurich and Luxembourg. In the second step, in 1990, LB recapitalised Proteus and transformed it into LB Interfinanz Zurich. In the third step, a few years later, when Safti ran into financial and regulatory troubles, LB Interfinanz returned the favour by facilitating a complicated scheme by which most of the parallel economy funds were extracted from Safti and transferred to a newly established company in Trieste, KB1909.

KB1909 entered into three lines of business. First, it took over the influential Ljubljana weekly Mladina and transformed it from a liberal democratic paper, as it was before the transition, into an outlet of socialist and radical left ideology. Second, it took control of the Slovenian publishing house in Trieste and its daily newspaper. But most lucratively it entered into the business of supplying medical equipment to Slovenian health care institutions. According to the parliamentary investigative commission, the value of profits from overpriced public procurement that was going on undisturbed until very recently amounted to several million euros.

Evidence from business registries shows that companies holding secret UDV funds were kept alive long into the transition. The Liechtenstein company Etablissment Colcommerz, which we mentioned above as part of parallel banking, was liquidated only in 1998, and so was Comexim, another offshore outlet of the parallel economy. Another UDV controlled black fund company, Scudo Ag, was liquidated at the end of 2011. Knowing the *modus operandi* of the parallel economy, the remaining funds were probably transferred to some other Swiss bank accounts and offshore funds.

The evidence on the use of these funds is still scattered. It was, for example, documented that they were used to establish Factor banka in Ljubljana in 1993. Another bank established by the same capital was Noricum. There is also evidence that foreign subsidiaries of Ljubljanska banka continued to facilitate operations of members of the parallel economy network, and, in addition, cultivated strong business relationships with UDV networks and even organised crime groups in other former Yugoslav republics.

Obviously, reconstructing a more complete picture of the parallel economy and its role in transition requires more research work, which is painstakingly limited by availability of reliable information and non-disclosure. Nevertheless, even the scattered evidence revealed so far convincingly demonstrated that the parallel economy network persisted until today and played an important role in Slovenia's transition. Surely its role was not only about doing business and making money through their connections, but how exactly it influenced the key political decision makers, including their decisions on privatisation, economic policy and government coalition building, remains a question for further research.

5. Discussion

The well-documented historical episodes presented in the chapter reveal that the clandestine economic operations were not a sporadic and independent activity of the secret service, concealed or receiving a blind eye from formal political leadership. To the contrary, these activities were continuous throughout the socialist period, had a stable structure of key actors (the network of key persons and companies established abroad and in offshore centres) and were not only endorsed, but also institutionally formalised by state institutions. The first archival document proving that the parallel economy was organised and regulated by formal state institutions is a decree of the Interior Ministry of the Socialist Federal

Republic of Yugoslavia from 22 November 1951.[22] The decree formalised the decision to transfer control over a part of the economic activity to the UDV, which was formally a directorate within the ministry. UDV was empowered to establish, close and control companies abroad; engage in legal and illegal trade outside Yugoslavia; execute financial operations and build reserves of foreign currency and gold.

The decree was followed by instructions sent to branches of UDV in all republics of Yugoslavia, which proves that activities similar to those undertaken by the Slovenian UDV were also carried out by other UDV branches. These instructions completed the institutionalisation of the parallel economy. Institutions to be acting as agents in the parallel economy were determined, as well as the rules concerning the mode of operation, internal structures, interrelations between national sections of UDV and relations between individual national sections and the federal UDV. Financial relations and a set of permitted business activities were also defined. With this, the parallel economy had in fact become complementary to the economic policy of Yugoslavia and individual republics.

The thesis that the parallel economy was an institutionalised complement to the official economic policy is further confirmed by evidence from later periods. We mentioned that permission to create para-fiscal revenues by smuggling needed to be granted by the government. The parallel banking system addressed the problems of acquiring foreign exchange resources for the banks and of providing sufficient financing for selected companies of the national economy. Even when Niko Kavčič, who set up the system, had to leave Ljubljanska banka, much the same activities of parallel banking continued through the network of LB subsidiaries in Western Europe and the USA.

In addition to complementing the economic policy, the parallel economy created considerable surpluses which were transferred to various Swiss bank accounts or offshore financial companies. There is now evidence that these hidden financial resources remained active long into the transition period, together with the personal and business network established as part of the parallel economy. During transition, this network remained

22 ARS-1931, 2137, pp. 1–3.

operational and used the accumulated funds to take part in the privatisation process and to found new lucrative business activities, such as banking, publishing and medical supplies. The extent to which the state was captured, and still is, by this informal and corrupt network, is a matter to be clarified within further investigations.

The discovery of the system of institutionalised, state-managed parallel economy brings new insights to our understanding of socialist economies and their transition. While it has been long known that members of the old communist elite actively participated in the privatisation process by asset-stripping, leveraged management buy-out schemes and offshore financial operations (Frydman, Rapaczynski and Earle 1993a, 1993b), the theoretical interpretations have mostly framed this as a transformation of the political elite members into private entrepreneurs. For example, an early theoretical model hypothesised that communist elite members formed rational expectations about the likelihood of regime change and reacted by trading their collective political power for profitable individual business activities (Schnytzer and Šušteršič 1996). The present chapter challenges these interpretations by showing that, when it came to transition, communists were no novices to private business activities and offshore financing. As the newly accessible archives show, the first offshore financial enterprise was established by the Slovenian branch of UDV in Liechtenstein already in 1951.

Existence of this type of a parallel economy also challenges the conventional distinction between formal and informal institutions prevalent in institutional economics (North 1991). Formal institutions are established by legislatures and other legitimate decision makers and codified in laws, bylaws, statutes and codes of conduct. Informal institutions emerge spontaneously through interactions of economic and social agents, which leads to the evolution of widely accepted informal rules that may later become codified in formal legislation. However, the historical evidence of a parallel economy presented in this chapter showcases the exact opposite mechanism, that is that the formal decision makers intentionally created and codified an informal economy, operated by state institutions and serving their economic interests.

Evolution of the parallel economy during socialism and its persistence into the transition period clearly demands and motivates further study of accessible historical sources. We hope that new historical evidence presented and contextualised in this chapter will contribute to the accessibility of archives in other former socialist countries and motivate similar studies that would put the operation of a parallel economy in Slovenia and Yugoslavia in a comparative perspective. Such further research could considerably contribute to a better understanding of the structure of socialist economic systems and their transformation into market economy.

References

ARS 1589 – The Archives of the Republic of Slovenia, Ljubljana (ARS), fund AS 1589: CK ZKS – predsednikova dejavnost [Activity of the President of the Central Committee of the Slovenian League of Communists].

ARS 1818 – The Archives of the Republic of Slovenia, Ljubljana (ARS), fund AS 1818: Pokrajinski narodnoosvobodilni odbor za Slovensko primorje in Trst [Regional National Liberation Committee for Slovene Littoral and Trieste].

ARS 1931 – The Archives of the Republic of Slovenia, Ljubljana (ARS), fund AS 1931: Republiški sekretariat za notranje zadeve [Republican Secretariat of Interior Affairs].

Atti Parlamentari, Resocconti stenografici della sedute della commissione parlamentare d'inchiesta sul fenomeno della maffia e sultre altre associazioni criminali (legge 23 marzo 1988, n. 94 modificata con lege 27 liugio 1991, n. 229, anni 1987 – 1992), Tomo 4.

Commissioni parlamentare di inchiesta sul fenomeno della mafia e sulle altre associazioni, annche straniere (istituita con lege 4 agosto 2008, n. 132), doc. XXIII, n. 16, Tomo I;

De Soto, Hernando, 1989. *The Other Path: The Invisible Revolution in the Third World*. New York: HarperCollins.

Frydman, Roman, Rapaczynski, Andrzej, Earle, John S. (eds.). 1993a. *The Privatization Process in Central Europe*. Budapest: Central European University Press.

Frydman, Roman, Rapaczynski, Andrzej, Earle, John S. (eds.). 1993b. *The Privatization Process in Russia, Ukraine and the Baltic States*. Budapest: Central European University Press.

Hillman, Arye L., Schnytzer, Adi, 1986. Illegal Economic Activities and Purges in a Soviet-Type Economy: A Rent-Seeking Perspective. *International Review of Law and Economics*, 6: 87–99.

Kornai, Janos. 1980. *Economics of Shortage*. Amsterdam: North Holland.

North, Douglass C. 1991. *Institutions, Institutional Change and Economic Performance*. St. Loius: Washington University Press.

Pezdir, Rado, Šušteršič, Janez. 2018. Yugoslav Companies in Zone A of the Free Territory of Trieste: The Formation of an Institutionalized Parallel Economy Controlled by the State Security Service. *Archivio storico italiano*, 176: 313–346.

Reporton the criminal investigation into UDV activities in casinos, June 7, 1990.

Schnytzer, Adi, Šušteršič, Janez. 1996. Transition by Secession: The Case of Slovenia. *Acta Oeconomica*, 48: 375–392.

Sirc, Ljubo. 2010. *Brezpotja socializma* [The futility of socialism]. Ljubljana: Slovenska matica.

Marica Mišić

PhD Student at the Faculty of Law, University of Niš; Scholarship holder of The Ministry of Education, Science and Techonological Development of the Republic of Serbia

Show trials – Law between ideological-political ends and legal values[1]

Abstract: What are mounted court proceedings or judicial farces whose legal, political and ethical aspects are the subject of this chapter? The main topic of this chapter considers show trials as phenomenon which is related to law and politics, but also raises ethical problems. Although in the legal literature, as well as in newspaper articles, we can often find the term 'show trial', yet there is no coherent and consistent meaning attributable to it. However, in addition to the traditional, pejorative meaning we have briefly outlined, which is a specific departure from justice, it should be mentioned that there is a more recent positive sense of the term. In this chapter, we will be interested in the 'show trial' in the traditional meaning of judicial criminal proceedings, which represents the politicisation of judicial proceedings in which justice is eroded.

Keywords: Show trial, legal values, politics, ideology, dissidents

1. Introduction – What is show trial?

Even if we want to think of law as something sublime and divine with the purest purpose, we cannot deny that law (both national and international) is often mere means in the hands of politics and corrupted, selfish politicians. Judith Shklar remarks that from the standpoint of legalism, which she criticises, "politics is regarded not only as something apart from law, but as inferior to law. Law aims at justice, while politics looks only

1 This chapter is the result of work on a project „Zaštita ljudskih i manjinskih prava u evropskom pravnom prostoru" (no. 179046) implemented at the Faculty of Law, University of Niš with the support of the Ministry of Education, Science and Technological Development of the Republic of Serbia.

to expediency. The former is neutral and objective, the latter the uncontrolled child of competing interests and ideologies. Justice is thus not only the policy of legalism, it is treated as a policy superior to and unlike any other" (1964, 111). The criticism is perhaps valid in relation to normal political and legal system, but legalism is right when referring to politics as uncontrolled child of interests, especially when it comes to perverted political and legal orders.

As we will see within the following pages, the cited definitions for the term 'show trial' are basically similar and underline essential characteristics. We will analyse these characteristics within the further text. In order to do that we need to start from the hypothesis that law is not merely realm of values or only realm of norms or just a system of human behaviour, but that law is compound phenomenon consisting of all of these three elements (Visković 1981, 31). In the case of mounted court proceedings, we have a misuse of law present, which is to the greatest extent possible a tool of the political power holders. With the respect of the rules prescribed by law, the desired consequences which are achieved cannot be considered legally and ethically valid. It is important not to look at the mounted court processes from the perspective of the strict normative, positivist theory of law, because it would restrict our deliberation. The definitions of show trials imply a value dimension that law has. This chapter supports integral theory of law and integral concept of law which represents synthesis of those three aspects of legal phenomenon. As a criterion of legality, integral theories of law[2] most commonly invoke value, normative and relational (sociological) criterions (Visković 1981, 35).

---

2 Georges Gurvitch, Giorgio Del Vecchio, Emill Lask, Gustav Radbruch and Carlos Cossio are characteristical representatives of modern integralist movement (Vukadinović and Mitrović 2019, 173) with a note that Radbruch's and Lasks's work has methodologically completed integralist theory with culturalist conception of law (ibid, 175). For those integralist authors law is a special process in which behaviours, value stances and normative conscience are causally, functionally and profoundly interdependent that neither of these elements can be learned if separeted from others (Visković 1981, 33). Some Serbian (Yugoslav) authors pointed out the significance of integral study of law, firstly Toma Živanović, who analysed law as system of norms, substance of law and legal values. Similary, Radomir Lukić and other Yugoslav legal theorists, although

Anyone who is interested in this topic could do some searching on the Internet and can come up with more or less similar definitions. Show trial is a term first used in 1928, according to Merriam-Webster dictionary. The same dictionary defines show trial as trial "in which the verdict is rigged and a public confession is often extracted". Another explanation of the term 'show trial' given by the dictionary Lexico powered by Oxford defines it as "a judicial trial held in public with the intention of influencing or satisfying public opinion, rather than of ensuring justice". Another one which could be found in Cambridge Dictionary says that show trial is "a trial organized by government in order to have an effect on public opinion and reduce political oppression, and not in order to find the truth". Similar to this one is that from Longman Dictionary for Contemporary English: "an unfair trial that is organized by a government for political reasons, not in order to find out whether someone is guilty". The term as most commonly used in British English according to Collins English Dictionary means "a trial conducted primarily to make a particular impression on the public or on other nations, especially one that demonstrates power of the state over the individual", and in American English as given by the Webster's New World College Dictionary it is "a trial widely publicized and seemingly open and fair, of a person regarded as a political subversive or ideological dissident, in which a verdict of guilty is assured by means of false evidence, a forced confession, etc." (Collins n.d.). The term is also used with a meaning of "(especially in a totalitarian state) the public trial of a political offender conducted chiefly for propagandistic purposes, as to suppress further dissent against the government by making an example of the accused".

"I plead guilty to having followed sentimental impulses, and in so doing, to having been led into contradictions with historical necessity [...] to having placed the idea of man above the idea of mankind [...] I admit that these points of view are, in the present situation, objectively harmful and, therefore, counterrevolutionary in character", confessed the man who was – in *Darkness at Noon* by Arthur Koestler – a literary symbol of many Stalin's victims, revolutionary comrades pushed into the opposition

---

they have adopted normativ notion of law, emphasized beside normative, the importance of social and value dimension of law, as well (Trajković 2008, 45).

by Stalin, perished during Stalin's purges and slain in the Great Terror in the 1930s. "The appeals to party loyalty, the requests to render a last service to world communism through confession, came only at the very end of the ordeal, after the process of physical and psychological destruction was complete". After the Second World War and Tito's break with Stalin, Stalin set his Eastern European adherents in satellite countries on trials accusing them for being titoists (e.g. Trajče Kostov and others in Sofia trial, Laszlo Rajk and others in Budapest trial and other trials in Albania, East Germany, Poland, Romania and Czechoslovakia); but this kind of show trials and purges would have occurred even without Tito-Stalin split. "In the factional, ideological, and power struggles of the 1930s, the victims were selected first and the necessary scenario written afterwards. In the Eastern Europe of the 1940s, the scenario was created before the victims were selected" (Hodos 1987, xi-xiii). During the Nazi regime in Germany most of the trials held at the People's Court, the kangaroo type of court, were political and show trials. One of many victims who were sentenced to death for having their own opinion (which was tantamount to high treason) was Helmuth James von Moltke, German jurist, "liberally minded individualist in an authoritarian society – and an authoritarian society suffering from acute paranoia" (Balfour and Frisby 1972, 331). Show trials were held in Yugoslavia against Stalinists and right after the war against monarchists (Draža Mihajlović and others in Belgrade process), and there were also purges and repression against intellectuals such was Mihailo Đurić, esteemed professor at the Faculty of Law at the University of Belgrade (Rajković 2002, 305–309). These mentioned examples are some of the many political and show trails held during the totalitarian and authoritarian regimes in Europe in the 20th century, but similar proceedings occurred also in the People's Republic of China during under Mao Zedong and his Communist Party of China. Political and show trials are not only reserved for fascist, Nazi or communist regime. For Griffith, relative responsiveness of the judiciary to political pressure is not attribute of communist societies only, but also of capitalistic ones (Griffith 1977, 207), which means that "the judiciary in any modern industrial society, however composed, under whatever economic system, is an essential part of the system of the government and that its function may be described as underpinning the stability of that system and as protecting that system from attack by resisting attempts to change it", so that we "live in a highly authoritarian society, fortunate only that we do not live in other societies which are even more authoritarian" (ibid, 213) and "there are innumerable ways [...] in which the judges fulfil their political function and do so in the name of law" (ibid, 216). Although the liberal states are not immune to the show trials, according to some liberal authors such as Mark Osiel, speaking about trials for the atrocity crimes "there is nothing inherently misguided or morally indefensible" about liberal show trials, which cannot be against the interest of justice, since they are "designed to 'show' the merits of liberal morality and the imperatives of the rule of law" (Allo 2010, 46). However, the classical meaning of show trials is the one linked to the mounted court proceedings, judicial farce, great media spectacle for eliminating adversaries of the regime, expressing supremacy of politics over the law, intimidating, giving an example to audience, but at the same time covering pure force in the clothing of law, legality and justice. Show trials give an illusory legitimacy of the power and please the public wish for the triumph of law and justice in the war against evil enemy of the nation, people (in the end of the state, monopartism and the regime). As a tool of terror and indoctrination – "instrument of terror and strategic means of transforming the public consciousness", show trials are in the service of "an oppressive ideological industry that produce their own versions of reality and compel defendants and the audience to adopt the official reality as their own" (Allo 2010, 53–54). The system does not truly care for the legality and legitimacy of its own actions, but the presence of the audience is essential in order to create desired public opinion which will "validate the alternative reality" and educate members of the state, community (ibid, 56).

Hodos defines show trial as "a propaganda arm of political terror. Its aim is to personalize an abstract political enemy, to place it in the dock in flesh and blood and, with the aid of a perverted system of justice, to transform abstract political-ideological differences into easily intelligible common crimes. It both incites the masses against the evil embodied by the defendants and frightens them away from supporting any potential opposition", using the term in narrower sense referring to liquidation of communists by communists, not to real political opponents or critically thinking individuals and intellectuals (ibid, xiii). "The most dangerous enemy became the one who held a party card and occupied a high position. Tito's revolt seemed to Stalin the proof of his pathological nightmare of spies and enemies everywhere; it led directly to the show trials", actually it just has "speeded up the process". "The postwar purges in the USSR, therefore, were restricted to covert liquidations, secret mass murders, unmentioned and unmentionable. In the satellite countries, no such restraints existed. There, the road was open for the show trials" (Hodos 1987, 2–3).

2. Achieving party's ideological and political ends

Political power belongs to sovereign of the state, while its exercise 'informed by a particular form of ideological formation' frequently excludes certain groups from the political process, making their 'voices inaudible', 'images unseeable' and 'words unsayable'. Being 'the most pervasive and totalizing', political power produces resistance against itself, by subjects who are opposed to its domination and oppression (Allo 2010, 42). For Radbruch, ideal state should be oriented towards transpersonal culture of act which means that individual and collective values should serve to values of the act and that morals, law and state are all in the service of culture. However, that kind of state which would band together and coordinate individual and supra-individual elements has never been actualised. Law and state were understood individualistically and supra-individualistically in party's ideologies according to which they were historically incarnated (Radbruch 1980, 79). The most common usage of the term ideology is in pejorative sense. Experience with regimes before, during and after the Second World War has led authors such as Hannah Arendt, Karl Popper and Daniel Bell (The End of Ideology theorist) to use the term restrictively, to denote a 'closed' system of thought, which serves as a form of social control that produces obedience and subordination and also is intolerant to opposing ideas and beliefs. This official state ideology has a totalizing character, and the state in which it is valid has been called a totalitarian state. For them, liberalism is not ideology, since it is an example of open system of thinking, as opposed to fascism, nazism and communism (Hejvud 2005, 6–12).[3] Karl Mannheim distinguishes

3 Although its origin is linked to the French Revolution (1789) and Antoine Destutt de Tracy's conception of ideology as science about ideas, which would

particular and total meaning of ideology, claiming that the first ones represent ideas and beliefs of specific individuals, groups or parties, and the other ones encompass worldview of social class, society or even whole historical epoch (Mannheim 1954, 49). For ideology and politics ideas are merely instrument of power, ideologist and politicians are interested in covering real truth, if it brings them practical benefits (Šušnjić 1971, 97). More than often in the name of the most humane ideology happen the most inhumane deeds. Ideology has a tendency to presents particular interest as common social interest, striving for expansion of its worldview as absolute and solely correct, it becomes totalitarian, helping itself by any means in any possible way, whether rational or irrational (Šušnjić 1971, 110–111). Ideology must not allow open confrontation about its fundamentals; any discussion may be presumed as expression of instability of social order which is maintained by that very ideology. It is always absolutist and does not hesitate to reach out for force in order to prevent any open critique. Whoever doubts and thinks with his own head is suspicious, politically and ideologically. He is also dangerous and brings in feeling of insecurity (ibid, 114–115). Ideological dogma is intolerant to way of thought and behaviour which differs from the one it prescribes as the only right. One of many functions ideology has is being the instrument of domination by destroying the opposing ideologies, by continuous strengthening of ruling ideology and by censorship which allows only ideas which are in accordance with ruling ideology, suppressing and banning unfavourable ones at the same time. The only affirmed ideological practice is based on testing and verifying loyalty to ideological dogma, with suspicion and oppression of any critical theory, while ensuring fidelity to ideological truth,

---

be queen among sciences. Instead due to Marx the term 'ideology' was widely, and even now is used with derogatory meaning. For him its purpose is to form false worldview – false conciousness in class system in which ruling class is not willing to recognize itself as an oppressor and utilitizes ideology as a manifestation of power in order to hide from the proletariat the fact of its own exploitation. This system of class power, class society for Marx and Engels is actually liberal capitalist state and bourgeois society and their values and ideas. Paradoxically, their follower Lenin used the notion in a more nautral sense, labelling a set of proletarian ideas as 'socialist' or Marxist 'ideology' (Hejvud 2005, 6–12).

which is total and supreme (ibid, 121–123). It does not matter if you are a honest, honourable and innocent man if you are ideologically labelled as enemy. And if someday you get murdered, it is murder in self-defence, for the common and greater good. You are not being punished for the crime you have committed, but for the potential offence. First you have to admit publicly that your ideas are harmful and objectively destructive to public order and peace, and then you may die. In such regimes supported by ideology there is a need for ideological police the main goal of which is to discover evil-doer, while approaching everyone as a prospective malefactor. Dogmatic thinking does not hesitate to remove anyone who thinks critically if it is the only way to eliminate critical thinking. Open dialogue with those dissenting does not exist and even when it seems that there is one, it is for the purpose of exposing those who think differently in order to disable them in some efficient manner of silencing (Šušnjić 1971, 125–126). The politically useful, beneficial is what matters for politics and politician, be it lie or secret. Politics requires absolute trust in the political cause, identification with the political group and loyalty to the ideology which is, for a politician, identical to a political program (ibid, 140–141).

Ideology, a unifying set of political ideas and values in a society, can be imposed from above, as a form of social control and the creation of obedience. Through the process of ideological manipulation of the ruling elite, political ideas are put at the service of restraining political dissenters and opposition, limiting political dialogue (Hejvud 2005, 4–5), as well as recruiting new adherents (Radbruch 1980, 80). In political practice, there are examples of states where there was a formal ideology. In Nazi Germany, the official ideology was National Socialism, in Mussolini's Italy fascism, in the Soviet Union and other countries of the Eastern bloc Marxism-Leninism, pejoratively called Stalinism, while in Yugoslavia after the split with Informbiro and therefore with Stalin, officially it was the 'right' path towards socialism, Marxism-Leninism, which is derogatorily called Titoism. The situation was similar in China, where Maoism was 'in effect'. The condition in those countries was according to Alfredo Rocco, who wrote The Political Doctrine of Fascism: "Everything in the state, nothing beyond the state, nothing against the state" (Kovačević 2012, 111–112) or more precisely: the sole, ruling, official party is everything, there is nothing beyond and against it. The holy triad of the French

Revolution: 'Liberté, égalité, fraternité' ('liberty, equality, fraternity') is replaced by Benito Mussolini with: 'Authority, order, justice' ('Il regime fascista è autorità ordine e giustizia'). Although all of these regimes emphasized the significance and will of the demos (people) or nation, it was only a phrase for mobilization of the masses and making an impression of the ruler appointed by the people, when in reality it was quite the opposite. The ruler was placed above the people to govern in the name of the whole, drawing his authority and sanction not from the will of the people, but from above, from history and religion, legitimacy and God's grace or charisma of the leader. On the other hand, individuals are subordinated, instruments for common good, general benefit of collectivity (Radbruch 1980, 90–91). Needless to say that in regimes which used legal procedure (show trials) as its own political tool, general good and other values such as justice and truth were understood in accordance with their will and hunger for power.

Characteristic of the mentioned regimes is that the official state's (party's) ideology dominated political life, social institutions, art, culture, education, media and other spheres of social life, while opposing opinions, values and beliefs were censored, suppressed or forbidden (Hejvud 2005, 5); controversy and critique were stifled and soldier obedience was promoted. Liberal theorists have characterised these regimes as "oppressive systems of government" (Hejvud 2005, 10).

For this kind of regimes, the enemy is permanent and peace is in danger. Combat for peace is represented as a priority in order to draw attention away from economic, political and other problems within the existing system, status quo. The imagined enemy is threat not just during the wartimes, but during peacetime as well (Šušnjić 1971, 208–209), the inner enemy has the function of imaginary outer enemy, the potential traitor to the fatherland (Тадић 2007, 344). It is not surprising that the most often accusations of the innocent people in the show trials are of espionage or high treason. Totalitarian society is one-dimensional society with total control of way of thinking and behaviour (Šušnjić 1971, 218). Show trials are perfect instruments in the hands of political power and ideology. Otto Kirchheimer stated in his *Political Justice: The Use of Legal Procedure for Political Ends* that the judiciary eliminates political enemies and opponents to the regime 'in accordance with some prearranged rules'. The essential characteristics of judicial power, -independence, neutrality and impartiality, trusting that it is a guardian of values of justice and certainty, peace and order – make the judiciary perfect platform for the "powerful, the invisible, the inaudible, the excluded, and the marginalized" (Allo 2010, 42). As history and political experience have shown us, the political power has the capability and potency to use the judiciary as a perfect tool in liquidation of real or imaginary adversaries of the regime. Show trials were not against political opponents only, but against any human who thinks differently and critically. The 'political' in show trial 'excavates tangled issues' for public consideration and "makes the 'show' appealing to the audience" (Allo 2010, 45).

3. The failure of law to achieve its purpose

As we may see by analysing definitions of show trials cited earlier, law is related to values. Show trials are actually a negation of those values and represent failure of law in accomplishing its purpose. Values which should be fulfilled and actualised by law as mentioned by its definitions are justice and truth, but beside these, law should accomplish various social and legal goals. Law as a value – creation of the human spirit – has a tendency of bringing the empirical, experiential realm in accordance with realm of values. This aspiration is lying in the man himself and all of his actions are conducted and motivated by some values. Values define purposes and aims which give meaningfulness and purposefulness to whole reality of human life (Vukadinović and Mitrović 2019, 80).

Radomir Lukić lists peace and order as values which are the best accomplished by law. Justice, fairness, truth, freedom and human dignity are sociolegal values (Лукић 1992, 461–477). On the other hand, purely legal values are legality, expediency, efficiency, clarity and certainty. Justice is value itself, supreme human value, which comes from truth and aspires towards beneficence. As the most important value of justice some emphasise truth, and beside this essential characteristic they add proportionality or harmony. Achieving justice is the supreme aim of normal law in normal state. This is not the case in a situation when the state and law are corrupted and perverted, where they are tyrannical and totalitarian and being such that they cannot be considered as just law and just state; on the contrary, they are opposites (Vukadinović and Mitrović 2019, 106–107). Gustav Radbruch includes as a legal value – besides justice and certainty – also the expediency. Radomir Lukić disagrees with classifying this last one as one of the legal values in a way Radbruch understands it (Лукић 1992, 482). But ideological understanding of expediency is quite understandable in a light of realistic view of law. Related to expediency of law is its purpose, purposefulness. Purpose of law is determined by political and party's ideology, and it can be in conflict with other two values of justice and certainty, which are higher and should be priority. Purpose of law is inseparable from purpose of state because law is in major part the state' will, and state on the other hand in great part represents a legal institution (Radbruch 1980, 70). Substance of law is determined by justice, legal certainty, but mainly by the principle of purposefulness (ibid, 98–99). And answer to the question about purpose and purposefulness of law is relativistic, since determining purpose depends on parties' understanding of law and state, which may differ (ibid, 94).

Closely connected with our topic of 'show trials' is the intersection of law, justice and procedure. It is needed here to emphasise that there is no such thing as procedural justice as some authors have argued (for example: John Rawls, Otfried Höffe). Both iusnaturalists (Lon L. Fuller) and legal positivists (Herbert Hart) advocated similar teaching. With a desire to represent positive law as justly or properly conducted procedure, these theorists pledged that procedural justice is created by intersection of legal procedure with justice. But if we want to analyse deeper the problem of show trials, we have to reject this assertion as an illusion. Law requires form, formalism and proceduralism in law are needed as mechanisms and means for substantiation and achievement of legal values such as legal certainty and predictability, and perhaps ultimately the justice itself (Vukadinović and Mitrović 2019, 126–127). Show trials are presented at first sight as formally in accordance with law and legal procedural norms.

Höffe, for example, asserts that pure justice lies within procedure and relativising justice, he derives it directly from procedural norms which do not have to ensure just outcome in a form of legislative and judicial justice. He distinguishes this pure justice from perfect and imperfect ones, which are accomplished through proceedings. According to him, there is some objective, impartial, self-sufficient criterion for just outcome, realised with approximate certainty by proceeding. Also, there is one impartial, self-sufficient criterion for imperfect justice. Using criminal procedural justice as an example to illustrate imperfect justice, he claims it means that all true culprits are punished properly according to their guilt. Neither such a criterion exists, nor impeccable legal system exists which punishes only true culprits. Höffe himself admits that proceeding which would exclude judicial errors and prevent punishing of the innocent and prevent impunity of the culprits does not exist. Speaking of procedural justice, he does not make a clear difference between the right to a fair trial, which is a part of substantive law, inspired by justice and concerning conduct of investigation, and judicial procedure. Contrary to Höffe's and similar opinions, justice should be derived from nature, that is truth. Procedural rules ensure correctness, lawfulness and rightfulness in the sense of regularity, predictability and certainty, but cannot provide justness (justice) and truthfulness (truth), being a desirable outcome or possible purpose. Rightfulness as correct and proper procedural handling serves truth, that is justice which has its own purpose. If something is truthful it does not mean that it is also procedurally correct and vice versa; procedural correctness does not mean at the same time truthfulness. That explains the possibility of acquittal due to incorrectly implemented procedural rules in spite of determined material truth by court and also otherwise cases of correct implementation of procedural rules with untruthful outcome owing to wrongfully determined material truth (Vukadinović and Mitrović 2019, 130–131, 133–134). For law, truth is only what is determined in precisely specified and defined legal proceeding – consequently, conflict of legal and objective truth is quite a possible occurrence which can be hardly or even impossible to revise. Actually, we have here conflict of two values, legal certainty and truth. Legal finality gives to determined legal truth the inviolability and – more than we want – in spite of all possible legal remedies allows for unjust outcome (Лукић 1992, 471–472). Rightfulness in the sense of correctness, regularity and predictability is primarily a means for impartial application of law and secondarily an instrument for achieving fairness which is 'justice in action'. Positivist jurists more and more often aspire to consider just legal order as based on the correct application of law in accordance to prescribed procedure, leading them to look on legal order in which law is not always correctly applied as legitimate (Vukadinović and Mitrović 2019,

136). In cases of conflict between legal truth and truth, due to legal finality in the service of legal certainty, law becomes instrument of untruth, turning itself into its own antithesis – lawlessness. The lawlessness we may say is the consequence of legal proceedings and of verdicts which are labelled as show trials. Legal finality which we speak about refers to individual and concrete acts and norms. It is meant to be everlasting. On the other hand, when it comes to legal finality of general acts and norms, it is imperfect, because general legal norms and acts are not immutable and infinite, they can be derogated and abrogated, in line with social changes. However, legal finality of individual acts and norms is necessary for normal functioning of law. Purpose of law is to regulate human behaviours, and in order to fulfil this, people need to be familiar with rules which are to be guidance to their actions. Legal finality may produce adverse effects in the conflict of legal and real truth, but its non-existence would cause far more harmful consequences (Лукић 1992, 472–474).

Speaking of negative effects of legal finality and show trials held during the authoritarian regimes, successor transitional regimes and nowadays democracies are trying to compensate these by judicial rehabilitation. In normal state, legal certainty is a value conditioned and qualified by legal finality and ensured by another legal value – legal efficiency which is subordinated to it as to a higher value. Objectively, legal certainty means well-timed and complete application of law, and subjectively it is a reliable belief that law will be applied. Its significance is great, especially because it ensures normal functioning of law when people are not afraid that law will be violated, unapplied. Otherwise, they would be restraining from establishing legal relations and executing their legal duties, firstly because of fear of miscarriage and then due to hope that their non-fulfilment of legal duties would not be sanctioned. Uncertainty erodes legal order and leads to anarchy or anomie. For this reason, law has to be efficient, has to be applied in timely manner. The need for timeliness leads to conflict among legal values, though – legal efficiency and certainty on the one side and truth, justice and legality on the other; but this imperfection of law is the sacrifice which has to be tolerated (Лукић 1992, 478–481).

Freedom is maybe the most important man's good and essential human value and at the same time legal value, giving value to human life. Law has a dual purpose; it is an instrument in protection and achieving as fully as possible man's freedom and at the same time it imposes reasonable restrictions on freedom aimed to avoid injuries to the other man and society in general. Law has the monopoly of coercion which is necessary for ensuring freedom in the situations of its endangering by unlawful coercion. The monopoly and legal authority of the state to restrict freedom was abused in perverted political systems in official state party's dealing with its dissidents.

Other mechanisms which should provide for man's freedom are democracy of the legislature and independence of the judiciary. The traditional view on judiciary is based on assumption of judicial neutrality. "The function of judiciary is to decide disputes in accordance with the law and with impartiality. The law it thought of as an established body of principles which prescribes rights and duties. Impartiality means [...] absence of personal bias or prejudice in the judge but also exclusion of 'irrelevant' considerations such as his political or religious views. Individual litigants expect to be heard fairly and fully and to receive justice [...] the judge [...] must act like a political, economic, and social eunuch, and have no interest in the world outside his court" (Griffith 1977, 187). More sophisticated standpoint on judiciary and judges views them as 'a part of democratic organization', as an arbiter in private and civil matters and with their creative and interpretative function as protector of the individuals against mighty Executive as well, in the matters between Governmental power and individuals, specifically in the criminal proceedings (ibid, 188–189). The failure of pursuing this protective function in criminal proceeding such as show trials is the best test for judiciary, legal system and democracy of the political regimes.

Still, Griffith argues about the myth of neutrality, claiming that: "judges are part of the machinery of the authority within the State and as such cannot avoid the making of political decisions" (ibid, 190). An important element which makes a trial to be deemed as show trial is the absence of even the tiniest degree of risk that the accused may be acquitted (Allo 2010, 45). By removing this 'risk' element and pre-determined outcome of the trial, it ceases to fulfil goals of fairness, and "ultimately taints the legitimacy, and even the legality of that trial" (ibid, 26). With no chance to be freed, show trials are essentially "rituals of vengeance, akin to parading the state's enemies through the streets on their way to the slaughter" (Allo 2010, 45–46).

People are born equal, so in accordance with that they should be enjoying human dignity equally, without discrimination based on their individual differences such as educational, material, racial, ethnical, religious, *political* and *ideological views*. The last-mentioned difference is important to our topic as it had and, daring to say, still has a great role in political and show trials. Human dignity is human value, legal value as well, but at the same time law has been and it still is the greatest mechanism for its violation – for example by support of slavery, feudalism, gross injuries of human dignity in socialist and bourgeois society, as well as when using or threatening to use coercion in the form of legal sanction, particularly criminal legal sanction – especially in its most intimidating forms of capital punishment, imprisonment and hard labour. Outcome of show trials in the form of condemnation of innocent people, only politically and ideologically guilty, being sentenced to imprisonment, death or hard labour is in its core a harsh violation of human dignity (Лукић 1992, 475–478).

4. Final words

Show trials are a product of removed procedural safeguards for the accused, violating rights of the defendant including the standard of the presumption of innocence. The established procedures of law are used against pre-determined defendants to show their guilt which "jeopardize not only the interest of the individual on trial, but also justice itself" (Allo 2010, 58). Show trial is misuse of law for achieving extralegal ends, monopolizing the state power in the hands of one party and its leader, and creating memory and history. History abounds with examples of mounted court proceedings, or politicised court proceedings, in which the judge is well aware of the sealed fate of the defendant. Still, we should exclude some of these practices from this category, given the evolution of law. After everything being said about judicial farces, we should refer as such to those of the 20th century that took place under totalitarian and dictatorial regimes (the People's Court in Nazi Germany, Stalin's purges, the Belgrade process, Tito's purges and the Naked Island), in which many people were killed, being the most intimidating.

Consequences of show trials as well as eliminations of opponents behind the court stage are irreversible. Victims of show trials and purges are as numerous as the victims of war. If the war is deemed to be evil, negation of values, we must conclude that show trials and verdicts are negation of values as well, such as justice (truth), human life and dignity. Even if the applied general legal acts are not unjust (unjust were, e.g. the Nuremberg Laws during the Nazi regime), law which was produced in the form of concrete legal act, verdict, was not just. The harm to individual is done and in majority of cases cannot be undone. Further questions linked to this topic may take directions towards measures of repairing or in most cases measures of satisfaction for damage caused to innocent individuals which were tried as a state's and people's enemies and spies, and to their families. For example, one, daring to say, poor shape of justice is rehabilitation of the tried victims, which opens further problems in cases of victims who perished behind the stage, without the show trial. The way of reckoning with former regimes and treatment of former legal system raised interest for transitional justice in legal and political discourses, first after the Second World War and even nowadays, especially in transitional societies and states after the fall of the Berlin wall (Teitel 2003). "In the transitional justice discourse, revisiting the past is understood as the way to move forward [...] the paradoxical goal in transition is to undo history" (Teitel 2003, 86–87). Teitel claims that there is a "potential for politicization in the use of trials to construct transitional historical understanding" in emerging democracies, labelling them also as 'show trials', which are extreme cases of "sacrificing individual rights to the societal interest in establishing history record" (2003, 75–77). Historical and political experience opens debate among legal and political theorists on the effects and the core of such regimes and their political and legal order. Interesting legal debate, still relevant, is the one between Herbert Hart and Lon L. Fuller. Using an example of Nazi regime the two legal philosophers postulated the problem of treating unjust general and concrete legal acts after the collapse of Nazi regime together with a dilemma whether a man has a moral duty to disobey unjust law and legal order, another problem of retrospective application of law in order to try and punish for denunciation, or whether the former system even deserves the name of law and legality, voicing their thoughts on the problem of two maxims 'an order is an order' and 'a law is a law', motto advocated by positivist jurists. Validity and value of such statutory law was also considered by Radbruch in his essays "Five Minutes of Legal Philosophy" and "Statutory Lawlessness and Supra-Statutory Law" (see: Hart 1983, 72–78, 79–82, Fuller 1958, 644–646, 648–661, Фулер 2011, 189–196, Radbruch 2006a, 13–15, Radbruch 2006b, 6–11). Radbruch considers that validity of unjust and wrongful positive law cannot be affirmed absolutely. Evaluation has to be done not only from the standpoint of legal certainty, but also through criterions of justice and purposefulness. Police state tries and aspires to make the principle of purposefulness its only governing principle, setting aside justice and legal certainty within its cabinet judiciary without any hesitation (Radbruch 1980, 99–100).

References

Allo, Awol K. 2010. The „Show" in the "Show Trial": Contextualizing the Politicization of the Courtroom. *Barry Law Review*, 15 (1): 41–71.

Balfour, Michael, and Julian Frisby. 1972. *Helmuth von Moltke: A Leader Against Hitler.* London: Palgrave Macmillan.

Fuller, Lon L. 1958. Positivism and Fidelity to Law: A Reply to Professor Hart. *Harvard Law Review*, 71 (4): 630–672.

Griffith, John Aneurin Grey. 1977. *The Politics of the Judiciary.* Manchester: Manchester University Press, Fontana Books.

Hart, Hebert L. A. 1983. Positivism and the Separation of Law and Morals (1958). In *Essays in Jurisprudence and Philosophy.* Oxford: Clarendon Press.

Hejvud, Endru. 2005. *Političke ideologije.* Translated by Milanka Radić. Beograd: Zavod za udžbenike i nastavna sredstva.

Hodos, George H. 1987. *SHOW TRIALS: Stalinist Purges in Eastern Europe, 1948–1954.* New York: Praeger Publishers.

Kovačević, Braco. 2012. Totalitarna država i pravo. *Годишњак Правног факултета Универзитета у Бањој Луци* 111–130.

Mannheim, Karl. 1954. *Ideology and Utopia: An Introduction to the Sociology of Knowledge.* New York: Harcourt, Brace & Co., Inc.

Radbruch, Gustav. 1980. *Filozofija prava.* Beograd: Nolit.

Radbruch, Gustav. 2006a. Five Minutes of Legal Philosophy (1945). *Oxford Journal of Legal Studies,* 26 (1): 13–15.

Radbruch, Gustav. 2006b. Statutory Lawlessness and Supra-Statutory Law (1946). *Oxford Journal of Legal Studies,* 26 (1): 1–11.

Rajković, Danilo. 2002. *Upotreba neprijatelja: Politička suđenja u Jugoslaviji 1945–1991.* Beograd: Montena.

Skhlar, Judith N. 1964. *Legalism: An Essay on Law, Morals and Polirics.* Cambridge, Massachusetts: Harvard University Press.

Šušnjić, Đuro. 1971. *Otpori kritičkom mišljenju.* Beograd: Biblioteka Zodijak.

Teitel, Ruti G. 2002. *Transitional justice.* New York: Oxford University Press.

Teitel, Ruti. 2003. Transitional Justice Genealogy. *Harvard Human Rights Journal*, 16: 69–94.

Trajković, Marko. 2008. *Etička dimenzija prava - pravnoteorijski aspekt (doktorska disertacija).* Novi Sad: Pravni fakultet, Univerzitet u Novom Sadu.

Visković, Nikola. 1981. *Pojam prava - prilog integralnoj teoriji prava.* Split: Logos.

Vukadinović, Gordana and Dragan Mitrović. 2019. *Uvod u teoriju i filozofiju prava.* Beograd: Dosije studio.

Лукић, Радомир. 1992. *Систем филозофије права: I Филозофија II Филозофија права.* Београд: Савремена администрација.

Тадић, Љубомир. 2007. *Поредак, ауторитет и слобода.* Београд: Завод за уџбенике - Службени гласник.

Фулер, Лон Л. 2011. "Проблем завидног доушника." In *Моралност права*, by Лон Л Фулер, translated by Силва Митровић, 189–196. Београд: Правни факултет универзитета у Београду.

Online sources:n.d. *Cambridge Dictionary.* [https://dictionary.cambridge.org/us/dictionary/english/show-trial, accessed on 20.02.2020].

n.d. *Collins.* [https://www.collinsdictionary.com/dictionary/english/show-trial, accessed on 20.02.2020].

n.d. *Dictionary.com.* [https://www.dictionary.com/browse/show-trial, accessed on 20.02.2020].

n.d. *Lexico*. [https://www.lexico.com/definition/show_trial, accessed on 20.02.2020].

n.d. *Longman*. [https://www.ldoceonline.com/dictionary/show-trial, accessed on 20.02.2020].

n.d. *Merriam-Webster*. [https://www.merriam-webster.com/dictionary/show%20trial, accessed on 20.02.2020].

Central and Eastern European Forum for Legal, Political, and Social Theory Yearbook

Edited by Jürgen Busch / Péter Cserne / Michael Hein /
Miklós Könczöl / Miodrag Jovanović / Marta Soniewicka

Vol. 1 Péter Cserne / Miklós Könczöl (eds.): Legal and Political Theory in the Post-National Age. Selected papers presented at the Second Central and Eastern European Forum for Legal, Political and Social Theorists (Budapest, 21–22 May 2010). 2011.

Vol. 2 Miodrag A. Jovanović / Bojan Spaić (eds.): Jurisprudence and Political Philosophy in the 21st Century. Reassessing Legacies. 2012.

Vol. 3 Péter Cserne / Miklós Könczöl / Marta Soniewicka (eds.): The Rule of Law and the Challenges to Jurisprudence. Selected papers presented at the Fourth Central and Eastern European Forum for Legal, Political and Social Theorists, Celje, 23–24 March 2012. 2014.

Vol. 4 Antonia Geisler / Michael Hein / Siri Hummel (eds.): Law, Politics, and the Constitution. New Perspectives from Legal and Political Theory. 2014.

Vol. 5 Luka Burazin / Đorđe Gardašević / Alessio Sardo (eds.): Law and State. Classical Paradigms and Novel Proposals. 2015.

Vol. 6 Martin Belov (ed.): Global Governance and Its Effects on State and Law. 2016.

Vol. 7 Fekete, Balázs / Gárdos-Orosz, Fruzsina (eds.): Central and Eastern European Socio-Political and Legal Transition Revisited. 2018.

Vol. 8 Alexandra Mercescu (ed.): Constitutional Identities in Central and Eastern Europe. 2020.

Vol. 9 Tomáš Gábriš / Ján Sombati (eds.): Central and Eastern Europe as a Double Periphery?. Volume of proceedings from the 11th CEE Forum Conference in Bratislava, Slovakia 25-26 April 2019. 2020.

www.peterlang.com

www.ingramcontent.com/pod-product-compliance
Ingram Content Group UK Ltd.
Pitfield, Milton Keynes, MK11 3LW, UK
UKHW011005120926
8556IPUK00027B/70

9 783631 830611